Members of His Body

Members of His Body

Shakespeare, Paul, and a Theology of Nonmonogamy

Will Stockton

FORDHAM UNIVERSITY PRESS

New York 2017

Fordham University Press gratefully acknowledges financial assistance and support provided for the publication of this book by the English Department and the College of Art, Architecture, and Humanities, Clemson University.

Fordham University Press also publishes its books in a variety of electronic formats. Some content that appears in print may not be available in electronic books.

Visit us online at www.fordhampress.com.

Library of Congress Cataloging-in-Publication Data available online at http://catalog.loc.gov.

Printed in the United States of America

19 18 17 5 4 3 2 1
First edition

CONTENTS

NOTE ON TEXTS

Except when citing from modern editions and translations, I have retained medieval and Renaissance spelling and punctuation, but expanded contractions and modernized i/j, u/v, and the long "s."

Unless otherwise noted, quotations from the Bible reference the 1560 Geneva edition. Other editions of the Bible that I cite are freely and easily available to scholars, and are therefore not included in the bibliography.

Unless otherwise noted, quotations from Shakespeare's works refer to the second edition of *The Norton Shakespeare*, edited by Stephen Greenblatt, Walter Cohen, Jean E. Howard, and Katharine Eisaman Maus (New York: W.W. Norton, 2008).

Members of His Body

Introduction: Marriage and the Body of Christ

(22) Wives, submit your selves unto your housbands, as unto the Lord.

(23) For the housband is the wives head, even as Christ is the head of the Church, and the same is the saviour of his bodie.

(24) Therefore as the Church is in subjection to Christ, even so let the wives be to their housbands in everie thing.

(25) Housbands, love your wives, even as Christ loved the Church, and gave him self for it,

(26) That he might sanctifie it, and clense it by the washing of water through the worde,

(27) That he might make it unto him self a glorious Church, not having spot or wrincle, or anie suche thing: that it shulde be holie and without blame.

(28) So oght men to love their wives, as their owne bodies: he that loveth his wife, loveth him self.

(29) For no man ever yet hated his owne flesh, but nourisheth and cherisheth it, even as the Lord doeth the Church.

(30) For we are members of his bodie, of his flesh, and of his bones.

(31) For this cause shal a man leave father and mother, and shal cleave to his wife, and they twaine shalbe one flesh.

(32) This is a great secret, but I speake concerning Christ, and concerning the Church.

(33) Therefore everie one of you, do ye so: let everie one love his wife, even as him self, and let the wife se that she feare her housband.

—EPHESIANS 5:22–33

Forget, for a moment, 1 Corinthians 7:9—the apostle Paul's begrudging endorsement of marriage as preferable to burning. No biblical passage has been more important in the long history of marriage's redefinition than Ephesians 5:22–33. In the context of the New Testament epistle, these verses comprise most of what biblical scholars refer to as its household codes—conduct instructions to husbands, wives, children, and servants. In the context of the European Reformation, these verses, and verse 32 especially, focus theological debates over marriage's status as a sacrament. The author of Ephesians, who purports to be the apostle Paul but is likely not, accounts marriage a *mysterion* (μυστήριον), a term rendered in Jerome's Vulgate and throughout Latin Christianity as *sacramentum*. The Geneva Bible tries to shuffle off this sacramental coil by translating *mysterion* as "secret," while the Book of Common Prayer and the King James Bible do the same with the more literal "mystery." Shakespeare's work emerges against this Reformation backdrop. Accordingly, Shakespeare's work allows us to gauge the persistence of Catholic marriage theology in Renaissance England. The four Shakespeare plays I analyze in this book—*The Comedy of Errors*, *The Merchant of Venice*, *Othello*, and *The Winter's Tale*—demonstrate that the Protestant denial of sacramental status to marriage marked no instance of theological supersession. The history of marriage's Western reformation includes synchronous, often competing explanations of the institution's significance, and this history is ongoing.

One may easily observe the persistence of sacramental marriage theology in the Protestant construction of the institution as a means for the realization of Christian community—or what Ephesians 5:30 describes as membership in the body of Christ. Reformers denied marriage's status as a sacrament, arguing that marriage was not a means by which God extended grace to believers. Leveraging the "mysterious" distance between signifier and signified, reformers recalibrated the institution as a metaphor for Christ's relationship with the church.[1] Yet they hardly banished the logic of Christian communitarianism imbued in marriage alongside its sacramental regard. This logic endures, for example, in the Book of Common Prayer, which lists three reasons for God's establishment of the institution:

> One was, the procreation of children, to be brought up in the fear and nurture of the Lord, and praise of God. Secondly, it was ordained for a remedy against sin, and to avoid fornication, that such persons as have not the gift of continency might marry, and keep themselves undefiled members of Christ's body. Thirdly, for the mutual society, help, and comfort, that the one ought to have of the other, both in prosperity and adversity.[2]

None of these reasons was foreign to medieval and Renaissance Catholic theology. Catholic arguments about marriage routinely held that the good of the state depended on the religious health of the citizenry, while the health of the citizenry depended in turn on marriage's ability to foster Christian children, protect Christians against sexual sin, and provide Christians with spiritual support and companionship.[3] Although medieval and Renaissance Catholicism is generally regarded, and not without reason, as idealizing celibacy (remember 1 Corinthians 7:9), it is also true that Protestants perpetuated and amplified Catholic regard for the family. It is hard indeed to hear any anti-Catholicism in the reformer Thomas Becon's championing of marriage as the means through which "the publique weale is defended, naturall succession remaynethe, good artes are taught, honest order is kepte, Christendome is enlarged, Goddes word promoted, and the glory of God hyghely avaunced and set forth."[4] If no longer a sacrament, marriage remained in most Protestant theologies a way to produce Christian citizens of states both earthly and spiritual. Under Protestant reform, marriage retained, and at times even enhanced, its status as a vehicle of Christian citizenship.

Largely gone from early modern historical and literary scholarship are narratives of the Reformation (or reformations) that assume monolithic conformity in belief and practice to magisterial decree.[5] "Protestant England" was peopled by Protestants of various types and with various degrees of fervency, as well as by recusants and so-called church papists. This diversity partly accounts for the comparatively slow and uneven pace of England's marriage reform.[6] In Germany, Lutherans transferred jurisdiction of marriage from ecclesiastical to civil courts. In Calvin's Geneva, the regulation of marriage came into the hands of a civil body, the Consistory. In England, by contrast, where Mary's brief reign halted marriage reform and the Elizabethan Settlement started it back at a snail's pace, marriage as a matter of law largely remained under ecclesiastical control. The 1571 Thirty-Nine Articles of Religion denied marriage's sacramental status and authorized clerical marriage, but otherwise left marriage laws alone. The next major piece of reform legislation, the 1604 Canons and Constitutions Ecclesiastical, in several ways only doubled down on Catholic marriage tradition, upholding separation over the right to divorce and forbidding remarriage. This brief legal history suggests that any analysis of marriage in Shakespeare needs to wrestle with the imbrication of English Renaissance Christianities.

In a persuasive study of the English Renaissance life of the *corpus mysticum*, Jennifer Rust argues that Shakespeare and his contemporaries demonstrate the continuing vitality of embodied models of English Christian citizenship in the wake of reformed critiques of the sacraments.[7] I suggest that Shakespeare likewise demonstrates the considerable degree to which Protestant campaigns to promote marriage as a social and religious good—a holy institution for members of the body of Christ—obscured the doctrinal point that marriage was irrelevant to salvation.[8] Working within this deep historical construction of marriage as a means of making Christians, this book investigates Shakespeare's representations of marital connections among a Christian citizenry. Guiding my investigations are questions about Christian embodiment that emanate from the collective described in Ephesians 5 as the body of Christ. To what extent does Shakespeare figure Christians as united to one another and to God, in the body, through marriage? Through what discourses does he depict interpersonal connections at the level of a marital body that is also the body of Christ? And how might reading Shakespeare help us reflect on the post-Reformation entrenchment of marriage in Christian, especially evangelical, body politics?[9]

Drilling down to the scriptural bedrock of the promotion of marriage as a religious and social good, I attribute much of this entrenchment to Ephesians 5:30–31: "For we are members of his bodie, of his flesh, and of his bones. For this cause shal a man leave father and mother, and shal cleave to his wife, and they twaine shalbe one flesh." According to both Protestants and Catholics, marriage joins husband and wife in the *flesh*. It does so according to Adam's foundational statement on the institution in Genesis 2:24, the verse repeated in Ephesians 5:31.[10] In the Hebrew of the book of Genesis, this flesh denotes man, mankind, persons, and kinship. It has since come to signify original sin, ongoing sin, temptation, desire, the temporal, the earthly, the secular, the ethnic, the racial, the body, the foreskin, the law, and bare life under sovereign power. The flesh can code a literalist hermeneutic (the "letter of the law") opposed to a figural one ("the spirit"), and the component of the self (often exteriorized) opposed to the spirit (often interiorized). The use of the term *flesh* throughout any of the Pauline epistles almost always resists reduction to just one or two of these meanings.[11] In Ephesians 5, however, the flesh seems most contiguous with the body as a spiritual collective in which individual persons physically participate. The flesh is the fabric of the body of Christ, which the author proposes men and women join through marriage. The Catholic Church has never regarded marriage as a sacrament of Christian initiation such as baptism, confirmation, and the Eucharist. Much of what this book posits about the endurance of sacramental marriage theology in Shakespeare's

England and beyond nevertheless hinges on the *causal* logic of Ephesians 5:30–31. Through marriage, men and women join the body of Christ. Through their union in the flesh, men and women become Christians.

II

Analyzing the Shakespearean consequences of Ephesians 5's conjunction of the body of the married couple to the body of Christ takes this book in several directions that I hope prove surprising. Because this book in many ways differs in aim and conclusion from others concerned with Shakespeare's relationship to the Reformation and the Bible, let me first be clear about the directions this book does not pursue. This book advances no claim about Shakespeare's personal religious or sectarian commitments. It does not taxonomize Shakespeare's representations of marriage as mostly Catholic or mostly Protestant, much less claim his plays for either side of these religious disputes.[12] While noting many of the scriptural allusions in Shakespeare, this book does not catalog those allusions or systematically track Shakespeare's treatment of Ephesians 5. Instead, this book capitalizes on the reformed entrenchment of marriage at the foundation of "Christian society" to advance a series of local claims about individual Shakespeare plays, as well as a larger queer theological claim about the causal logic of Ephesians 5:30–31. These verses, and the household codes of which they are a part, suggest that marriage erodes the distinction between the couple and the group. United in marriage, husband and wife join the many-membered body of Christ. The dyad becomes a plurality.

I characterize this theological claim as queer because it locates the ostensibly anti-Christian institution of plural marriage (usually but not necessarily imagined as polygyny) *within* today's evangelical imagination of monogamous, heterosexual marriage as properly biblical. My reading of Ephesians 5 queers the presumptively straight institution, responding—via a protesting "return to the text"—to centuries of political, cultural, and theological priority afforded the heterosexual couple. In the United States, evangelicals recently rallied round this privileged figural couple as they argued against extending the legal right to marry to homosexuals. This extension, evangelicals frequently maintained, would open the door to legalizing plural marriage—the antithesis of the institution that God fashioned in paradise and, through the apostle Paul, described in Ephesians 5. But my more dialectical claim is that biblical marriage *is* plural marriage—an ancient tradition still practiced by a minority of Jews of the first century, however at odds with Greco-Roman norms of monogamy.[13] (The practice began its decline in the intertestamental period.) Signaling the conflict between these imbricated cultures, Ephesians 5's joining of the couple to the body of Christ translates the two into the one and the many. Letting slip the "secret" about Christ's relationship to the church, these verses short-circuit the gap between monogamy and polygamy.

Early modernists may well consider this queer thesis a restatement of Marc Shell's 1988 anthropological one about the relationship between marriage and incest. Through an extended reading of Shakespeare's *Measure for Measure*, Shell argues that Christian political efforts at sexual regulation, including marriage laws and the criminalization of fornication and adultery, mediate between the taboo against sibling sexual relations and the idealization of all Christians as brothers and sisters in Christ.[14] *Measure for Measure*'s dually metatheatrical and economic rendering of human value—its veritable obsession with substitution, individuation, and the ethics of equivalence—repeatedly collapse licit and illicit relations, figuring the telos of Christian kinship as universalized incest. With Shell, I read for short circuits between the one and the all within Christian theologies of sex and sexuality. I share Shell's belief that Shakespeare's texts offer fine, although by no means exclusive, illustrations of the relationship between taboo and ideal. At the same time, my concentration on marriage as an institution that joins the one to the many extends my conclusions beyond incest's inevitability. Invested in the body's universal telos as much as that telos's hindrance, I examine how, in Shakespeare, differences of sex and race partition the body of Christ, compromising its ostensible promise of incorporation. I also reassess chastity, both premarital abstinence and marital monogamy, as an impossibility for members of the body of Christ, all of whom share flesh. Overall, this book offers less a Shakespeare-based anthropological unfolding of structures of kinship and exchange (à la Shell), than four Shakespearean accounts of how the marriage of husband and wife to the body of Christ cuts against idealizations of monogamy, often to violent and perverse ends.

Early modern scholarship has produced other rubrics beyond the religious and the anthropological for approaching Shakespeare's interest in the individual as both "a single human being" and as "a group or body of people regarded as a single entity."[15] Ready to hand is the classic narrative of the rise of the individual out of medieval communal society, and the roughly coterminous "birth" of individuating selfhood and subjectivity through discourses of interiority and inwardness.[16] Comedies, especially but not exclusively, have cued critics to the rise of the commercial theater and its translation of bodies into exchangeable commodities, as well as to sumptuary culture and the importance of dress in the performance, fixture, and confusion of identity.[17] More recently, scholars have stressed the cultural importance and political centrality of friendship discourse in constructing two (or more) people as versions of the same.[18] Finally, work on the humors has revealed the considerable degree to which early modern bodies were understood as interconnected, porous, liquid, and mutually affecting.[19] My interest in the discourse of marriage is not intended to displace any of these often overlapping rubrics, however skeptical I am about claims regarding the Renaissance origins of the individual or the subject. By considering Shakespeare's marital conjunction of spouses to the body of Christ, I aim rather to supplement and extend these rubrics. My focus on marriage leads me to hypothesize that we may often analyze Renaissance discourses of the single individual as reactions against the Christological pull of the corporate individual. Whether interiorized as subjectivity or inwardness, or exteriorized as sex, status, or ethnicity, discourses of the single individual insist on differences that marital membership in the body of Christ might otherwise mitigate.

My analysis of the marital body in Shakespeare draws still further on recent conversations about Renaissance political theology. In Graham Hammill and Julia Reinhard Lupton's concise formulation, political theology "name[s] a form of questioning that arises precisely when religion is no longer a dominant explanatory or life mode." A study of the political, sometimes secular life of theological concepts, political theology emerges from "a crisis in religion, whether that crisis is understood historically (as the Reformation) or existentially (as doubt, skepticism, or boredom)."[20] Broadly speaking, each chapter of this book takes up the historical crisis of the Reformation as it investigates the complex relationship between marriage and the growth of Christendom in a Shakespearean world often seen as sloping toward secular modernity. Each chapter also addresses existential crises that stem from an insufficiency or, more often, incoherence in religious explanation—crises involving the reasons for love and the criteria of ethnic belonging, definitions of chastity and purity, and determinations of sexual, racial, and species difference.

Much historicist (new or otherwise) and feminist scholarship on marriage has accustomed critics to regard the institution as primarily political, with the relationship between a husband and a wife mirroring the relationship between a state sovereign and his or her subject.[21] This political analogy, by no means wrong, is what we usually hear when *The Taming of the Shrew*'s Kate declares, "Thy husband is thy lord, thy life, thy keeper, / Thy head, thy sovereign" (5.2.150–51). As one engine of the religious turn in early modern studies, however, political theology insists that marriage is inseparably a theological institution—integral throughout Christendom to a life understood as straddling the here and the hereafter.[22] This study attempts to restore God to the shared life of Shakespeare's husbands and wives, to the marital body those husbands are supposed to head (Ephesians 5:22–24), and to the polity united in Christ's flesh through marriage.

III

Today's commonplace Christian citations of the Bible to defend the restriction of marriage to the union of one man and one woman require careful cherry picking and rigorous decontextualization. These citations assume that the Bible speaks with one voice—God's voice. But it is difficult indeed to find anyone in the Bible, God included, arguing for this restriction.[23] The authors of 1 Timothy and Titus come close. Both list being "the housband of one wife" among the qualifications for a church bishop (1 Timothy 3.2; Titus 1.6). This qualification nevertheless attests to the ongoing practice of polygyny among at least some early believers in Christ. It additionally suggests that polygyny is not necessarily a problem for believers without designs on a bishopric.

The apostle Paul, who is likely not the author of the letters to Timothy and Titus, just as he is likely not the author of Ephesians, has no interest in debating the relative virtues of monogamy or polygamy. On the topic of same-sex marriage, he (like every biblical writer) also has nothing to say. Instead, Paul's apocalypticism informs his preference that the unmarried remain unmarried (1 Corinthians 7:7–8). The unmarried have more time, here in the short time that remains, to focus on the Lord. Paul's reasoning may explain why the authors of 1 Timothy and Titus would require bishops to be monogamous. Marital restraint helps assure their attention to the church.

Paul's views on marriage seem quite close to Jesus's own. Usually assumed to be a lifelong bachelor, Jesus preaches that the proximity of the Kingdom militates against what evangelicals now call "traditional family values."[24] "If anie man come to me," he states in Luke, "and hate not his father, and mother, and wife, and children, and brethren, and sisters: yea, and his owne life also, he can not be my disciple" (14:26; see also Matthew 10:37). Luke's Jesus does not appear to be speaking hyperbolically or metaphorically here. Indeed, Mark's Jesus, one of the models for Luke's, teaches that marriage is an earthly institution that will not survive the resurrection: "For when they shal rise againe from the dead, neither men mary, nor wives are married, but are as the Angels which are in heaven" (12:25). For Jesus and Paul, apocalyptic preachers both, divorce is anathema (Matthew 5:31–32, 18:3–9; 1 Corinthians 7:10–16). But marriage, be it to one spouse or many, is otherwise a distraction from the urgencies of spiritual business.

Looking back from the New Testament to the Old, Christian apologists for traditional marriage are often quick to claim that God made his straight, monogamous ideal quite clear in Genesis 2, when he created one woman as the companion for one man. As the saying goes, God created Adam and Eve, not Adam and Steve, or Susan and Eve, or Adam and Eve and Susan, or Susan and Adam and Steve, or Susan and Eve and Adam and Steve. One problem with this claim is that no one in the Bible reads the story of Genesis 2 in this way. Nowhere in the laws of Exodus or Deuteronomy does the union of husband and wife as one flesh restrict the number of wives a man may possess (although a king should not have too many: Deut. 17:17).[25] Nor does this union imply any restriction on same-sex intimacy. The author of 2 Samuel does not condemn David for loving Jonathan with a love "passing the love of women" (2 Samuel 1:26).[26] The author of Ruth does not condemn Ruth her attachment to Naomi—"wither thou goest, I wil go. . . . Where thou dyest, wil I dye" (Ruth 1:16–17)—or pit this attachment against Ruth's marriage to Boaz.[27] As biblical scholars outside of evangelical circles well know, the sexual politics of the Bible are considerably more complicated than most popular citations of the book allow. The Bible speaks with many voices. Not all of these voices agree, and none of them shares the standard evangelical assumption that married, heterosexual coupledom constitutes the godliest form of human sexual relations.

The two biblical voices with which this book is primarily concerned belong to the apostle Paul and to the author of Ephesians. In the four Shakespeare plays I analyze, the representation of marriage draws from several passages in the Pauline canon besides Ephesians 5:22–33. These include Romans 1:18–32 (on sexual perversion and idolatry), 1 Corinthians 7 (on marriage, celibacy, and divorce), and, in *The Winter's Tale*, 1 Corinthians 8 and 10:14–22 (on the ethics of eating meat sacrificed to idols). These passages also include the famous statement of Pauline universalism in Galatians 3:28: "There is nether Jewe nor Grecian: there is nether bonde nor fre: there is nether male nor female: for ye are all one in Christ Jesus." The views expressed in Romans, Galatians, and 1 Corinthians are not necessarily those of the author of Ephesians. The institution that Paul of Tarsus reserves for the relief of lust, the author of Ephesians champions as the vehicle of Christian citizenship. This book allows these different biblical voices—Paul's and "Paul's"—to inform the analysis of marriage in Shakespeare's plays.[28] The theological contradictions and tensions inherent in this thing called "biblical marriage" are often visible in Shakespeare's work, and I suggest that Shakespeare scholars might accordingly look to the field of biblical studies in order to elucidate them. Given their canonizing treatment as secular scripture, Shakespeare's work might even offer an especially valuable source for elucidating these contradictions and tensions.[29]

IV

Further informing this book's response to the concept of biblical marriage is the recently successful movement within the United States to redefine state-sanctioned marriage by opening it to same-sex couples.[30] This redefinition has been quite rapid over the course of this book's composition. In 2012, when a version of chapter two first appeared in print, so-called gay marriage was legal only in a handful of states, most of them nestled in the blue Northeast. On July 26, 2015, the Supreme Court of the United States found, in *Obergefell v. Hodges*, that under the Fourteenth Amendment marriage was a right illegitimately denied to same-sex couples.[31] To many apologists for traditional marriage, this expansion of the right to marry constituted nothing less than an offense against God. To advocates of expanding marriage rights, however, these conservative arguments ignored both scripture and history. Historicizing marriage within biblical, church, and cultural tradition would not be possible were the institution not always in the process of redefinition. Moreover, the history of marriage is in large part one of contesting criteria for access.[32] Centuries after the Reformation, Catholics and Protestants continue to differ over the sacramental status of marriage and marriage's attendant impediments; and it is fully possible to argue from a Christian perspective that marriage should be available to gay couples.[33] Much like earlier controversies in the United States surrounding interracial marriage, controversies about gay marriage rights have revealed entrenched and persistent disagreements over marriage's purpose, whether for love, procreation, rights of citizenship, or a wide set of financial, cultural, and political benefits. With so many reasons to marry, many liberals argue, allowing gay couples to access the institution does not undermine marriage or set us on a slippery slope to legalized polygamy. Increasing access may help strengthen an institution whose membership has been steadily declining.[34]

Although their arguments have not gained nearly as much cultural and political traction as those of the Christian right and the "marriage equality" left, many feminist and queer scholars and activists have also criticized the movement to legalize gay marriage. These critics take aim at the conjunction of numerous social, legal, and economic benefits with long-term coupling. Michael Warner has argued that expanding marriage rights to same-sex couples does nothing to address the more fundamental injustice of stigmatizing people whose sexual preferences do not conform to marital norms.[35] Lisa Duggan has characterized the marriage-equality slogan as self-contradictory. In the name of fairness, "marriage equality" actually calls for "a contraction of options," betraying the LGBT movement's original goal of expanding forms of politically and socially recognized relationships.[36] Judith Butler has argued that the reduction of gay rights to marriage rights "would constitute a drastic curtailment of progressive sexual politics."[37] I sympathize with these critiques, but the thrust of this book is not *against* marriage, gay or otherwise. While I am under no delusions that it will be, my argument regarding Ephesians 5 and biblical marriage would better inform a defense of plural marriage launched from within a cross-denominational Christian understanding of the institution. As a means of attaining membership in the body of Christ, the fleshly union of man and woman invites a reading of the pair as married to all in Christendom—a union of the multitude that subsumes and exceeds that of mere same-sex coupling.[38]

To claim that the "perversion" of plural marriage adheres in the model of marriage bequeathed to Christian tradition by Ephesians is not to claim that most Christians have actually been advocates of plural marriage all along. There is no secret history to uncover here, no massive conspiracy to unearth. Undoubtedly, the majority of Christians, now as in the Renaissance, understand their sacred text to prescribe long-term sexual fidelity to one spouse. They likewise understand espousal itself as a union of only two. To make the claim that the construction of marriage in Ephesians 5 queerly translates the one flesh of wife and husband into the communal flesh of Christ is instead to understand perversion structurally, as Jonathan Dollimore has elucidated it: a mode of desire, understanding, and action that emerges from within a norm, not outside it.[39] To make this claim about plural marriage and the body of Christ is to begin with Christian arguments for and endorsements of monogamy and to work backwards to understand what, within the same faith tradition, these arguments and endorsements react against. It is to locate fissures within the Christian tradition caused by different readings of the same book, and to analyze these fissures as generative of distinctions between orthodoxies (norms) and heresies (perversions). In short, it is to analyze representations of marriage within Christian cultural texts according to this structural understanding of perversion, and to do so with the aim of developing both queer and feminist Christian theologies.

V

What follows are readings of four Shakespeare plays. Occasionally, these readings venture outside Shakespearean boundaries for the sake of comparison. Directly addressing the question of what makes marriage a sacrament if it is one, the Epilogue examines the relationship between marriage and Christian citizenship in three non-Shakespearean utopian texts.

Chapter 1, "Paul in Ephesus: Self and Sexual Difference in *The Comedy of Errors*," pivots off Richard Strier's defense of *The Comedy of Errors* as a play celebrating the Protestant bourgeoisie. Critiquing the temporal and ideological strictures of Strier's analysis, I read *The Comedy of Errors* as a materialist farce that reduces all persons, in the language of Ephesians 5, to bodies. In Shakespeare's Ephesus, the fiction of indistinguishable twins couples with the commodification of personhood to deprive the play's characters of interiority. The body of Christ, *The Comedy of Errors* summarily suggests, is nothing more than a body. It is flesh without inwardness, an outside without an inside.

This thesis prompts familiar questions about Pauline universalism. To what extent are bodies within the body of Christ interchangeable? To what degree does the body admit differences in sex and status among its members? Galatians 3:28 arguably suggests that all such differences disappear in a body whose members are completely interchangeable. But more important than Galatians 3:28 to the universalist ethic of *The Comedy of Errors* is Ephesians 5:28, where the author of the epistle—a pseudo-Paul I call Paul of Ephesus, as opposed to Paul of Tarsus—enjoins husbands "to love their wives, as their own bodies." The instruction echoes with a difference the commandment to love one's neighbor as oneself; and this difference is not without consequence for the play's reduction of persons to bodies. In both first-century and Renaissance contexts, the translation of *neighbor* to *body* aids in the one-sex disappearance of the female within a male body that is both the husband's and Christ's. Shakespeare's materialist farce nonetheless invites us to read for the return of the repressed neighbor as the undomesticated dimension of the marital self. The first of these returned neighbors is Antipholus of Ephesus, whose effort to break into his own house codes the uncivilized act of wife-beating as an obscene display of Christ's sovereign authority. The second of these returned neighbors is

Emilia, whose "resurrection" as wife and mother flags the Pauline excision of women from the body of Christ.

Chapter 2, "Portia's Pauline Perversion: *The Merchant of Venice* and Romans 1," brings Paul of Tarsus's etiology of sexual perversion into orbit around the male and many-membered body of Christ imagined in Ephesians 5. Associating same-sex sexual activity with idolatry, Paul of Tarsus condemns penetrated men as emasculated. Later in Romans, however, he defends the multiply penetrated, crucified Christ as a man who uniquely proved his manhood through the defeat of sin. This sexed exception of Christ from the prohibition against bodily penetration vexes Shakespeare's *Merchant of Venice*, a comedy about the power of marriage to simultaneously masculinize and Christianize. Dressed as a boy, Jessica elopes with Lorenzo, and later argues that she has thereby become a Christian. Also cross-dressed, Portia saves her husband's friend Antonio from Shylock's emasculating excision of flesh. Other critics have argued that Portia shores up a masculinist model of Christian embodiment through her courtroom defeat of Shylock and her subordination of the bonds of homoerotic friendship to those of heterosexual marriage. I juxtapose contemporary queer biblical and Renaissance Protestant readings of Romans 1 to argue that Portia instead perverts this masculine model through her presentation of Christ in the character of Balthasar, a eunuch. As Portia/Balthasar's ring trick opens the dyad of the married couple to the triad of married couple and friend, the "Pauline" distinction between monogamous, marital, Christian sexuality on the one hand, and sodomitical, Jewish sexuality on the other, begins to erode.

The first two chapters of this book focus on the sex of the savior. The second two examine the marital consequences of the Pauline regard for the flesh as inherently corrupt or mired in sin. The "workes of the flesh are manifest," Paul of Tarsus writes to the Galatians, starting a list that includes "adulterie, fornicacion, unclennes, [and] wantonnes" (5:19). (See also Romans 6–7.) In Chapter 3, "Chaste Impossibilities: Adultery and Individuation in *Othello*," I maintain that Desdemona is guilty of adultery insofar as she is a creature of the flesh. Chronicling the recent turn away from the "saint or strumpet" debate about Othello's wife that runs through the first few centuries of the play's criticism, I maintain that the current critical construction of Desdemona as a chaste but sexual subject often amounts to an essentialist guardianship of her Christian virtue. This construction protects Desdemona from the self-adulterating consequences of her marriage—her race-mixing union in the flesh with a black man and arguably a Muslim. Just as often, this construction takes Desdemona's chastity as an object of critical certainty, ironically reinforcing the claim of so many Renaissance marriage moralizers that chaste wives must be transparent subjects—their thoughts and actions completely legible to their husbands who head the marital body. Whereas the first two chapters of this book treat adultery as the inevitable result of the marital body's incorporation into the communal body of Christ, this chapter treats adultery as the inevitable effect of a wife being both too much one with and too separate from her husband. Desdemona is simultaneously one flesh with a black body figuring the racial limits of marital incorporation in the body of Christ *and* a subject independent from Othello in both thought and action.

The final chapter, "The Ecology of Adultery: Flesh, Blood, and Stone in *The Winter's Tale*," queries how the resurrection of Hermione from stone answers to Leontes's paranoia about his wife's infidelity. Sourcing the play's creaturely imaginary to Genesis 1 and 2, as well as to Paul of Tarsus's typological conjunction of Christ and Adam in 1 Corinthians, I argue that Leontes operates on the premise that the human flesh to which he has joined himself in marriage is constitutively adulterated, most immediately with the flesh of his friend Polixenes. The aptly named Paulina works to repair this conviction of constitutive adulation. Rewarding Leontes's reinvestment in the fantasy of human sexual purity, Paulina's presentation of Hermione as a statue gives artistic "life" to Othello's suggestion that the only chaste woman would be a work of "monumental alabaster" (5.2.5). Yet the resurrection of the body from the stone cannot repair the Pauline fractures in Paulina's theater of paradise regained. Prompted by the king's exclamation, "If this be magic, let it be an art/Lawful as eating" (5.3.110–11), I trace Leontes's anxieties about bodily purity to Paul of Tarsus's remarks in 1 Corinthians about believers who eat food sacrificed to idols. Paul's instructions on this matter are as contradictory as Leontes's remarks are enigmatic. Even the real apostle speaks with two different voices, one of which holds that knowledge (Leontes's "art") is no protection against demonic pollution of the body of Christ. Whereas numerous recent readings of *The Winter's Tale* concern themselves with the contours of the faith that Paulina makes a requirement of Hermione's resurrection, I contend that Shakespeare's romance is ambiguous about faith's connection to redemption. Instead of taking a Protestant, Catholic, or even secular approach to faith, Shakespeare's play stages a series of redemptive possibilities—among them the possibility that marriage alone, not faith at all, offers the unbeliever membership in the body of Christ.

PART I

Neither Male nor Female

CHAPTER 1

Paul in Ephesus: Self and Sexual Difference in *The Comedy of Errors*

In the final scene of *The Comedy of Errors*, Shakespeare resurrects Christ on stage as the abbess Emilia—wife of Egeon, the condemned man from neighboring Syracuse, and mother to the Antipholus twins, whom she pronounces "deliverèd" (5.1.404) after "Thirty-three years . . . in travail" (5.1.402). The Duke immediately begins the work of interpreting Emilia's self-revelation as the "same Emilia" (5.1.346) whom Egeon "once called Emilia" (5.1.343). And like one of Christ's apostles, the Duke does so in accordance with older testament: "Why, here begins his [Egeon's] morning story right:/These two Antipholus', these two so like,/And these two Dromios, one in semblance" (5.1.347–49). The Antipholus and Dromio twins are each identified as four separate men consequent to the self-identification of an abbess who herself figures Christ dead and resurrected at age thirty-three—as mother, minister, and spouse to multiple bodies delivered from error. In the parlance of modern evangelicalism, this family and its servants have been "born again" (John 3:3). In the parlance of the play's principle apostolic source, the epistle to the Ephesians, this family and its servants are no longer "strangers and foreners" to each other or in

Ephesus. They are now "citizens with the Saints, and of the housholde of God" (Ephesians 2:19).[1]

Promising to "make full satisfaction" (5.1.401) on all the day's mistakes of one body for another, Emilia issues an invitation inside the abbey that formerly separated the saintly and the seekers of sanctuary from the rest of the citizenry:

> The Duke, my husband, and my children both,
> And you the calendars of their nativity,
> Go to a gossips' feast, and joy with me.
> After so long grief, such festivity! (5.1.405–08)

Or really "such nativity"—which is the Folio's rendering of line 408, emended by the Oxford editors to "such festivity."[2] Although the emendation avoids the repetition of "nativity" in lines 406 and 408, I wager that the Folio's "error" is correct. In this comedy of confounded selves and signifiers, where words wander between misidentified and mystified bodies, the emendation to "festivity" mutes the ideological work of "nativity": a signifier that seals—*and awkwardly seals again*—this company's union in Christ.

If not purposeful, the repetition of "nativity" is at least symptomatic of the term's figural density. Doubled like a set of twins, "nativity" references four different events in the life of the incarnated Son of God. It references the first nativity, or Christ's birth in Bethlehem. It references the baptism, an event often followed in early modern England with a "gossip's feast."[3] It references the resurrection, or the rebirth of Christ's body after a three-day span that Shakespeare elides with the age of Christ at his death (thirty-three).[4] And it references the second coming, or the future return of Christ to deliver those still wandering in error.[5] Here at the play's end, this doubled "nativity" unites these four events with the simultaneous rebirth of the household and neighborhood as a single political and religious body. Glossing Ephesians 2:19's jointure of citizens and saints, Julia Lupton emphasizes that the Pauline "politico-religious body" contains "persons from diverse backgrounds, likely with continuing multiple memberships."[6] Among its members in *The Comedy of Errors* are men and women, masters and servants, wives and husbands, brothers and sisters, merchants, an abbess, a courtesan, an executioner, sundry officers, and a prince. They collectively hail from cities including Ephesus, Syracuse, Corinth, and Epidamnum. Furthermore, this body's members seem located at once in Plautine (third to second century BC) and Pauline (first century AD) antiquity, (post-)Reformation-era urban England,

and a Catholic Ephesus shaped by an English Protestant imagination. The clunky doubling of "nativity" indexes this dense coexistence of so many differences—the strained unity of person, place, and time—in Christ.

This chapter attempts to make further sense of this labored Christological nativity in terms of the play's frequently discussed Pauline politics of marriage. At stake in most of these discussions is the tension between the unmarried Luciana's Pauline posture of strict female subservience to men's headship and Adriana's "shrewish" frustration with her husband's truancy and seeming lunacy.[7] The strange redundancy of "nativity," its insistence on the Christian life cycle of birth, death, and resurrection, suggests that questions pertaining to Christian embodiment subsume, or provide a larger Pauline context for, this specific conflict over women's household roles. Put another way, this strange redundancy of "nativity" focuses the play's titular *comedy* about household roles and marital offices on the body of Christ and the fungibility of its members.

In what follows, I argue that *The Comedy of Errors* queries the extent to which membership in the body of Christ mitigates differences in status and sex. This argument engages recent conversations about Pauline universalism via a historicist reminder that the Pauline body is teleologically male and resolutely hierarchical. This argument further implicates the one-flesh model of the body in the eruption of domestic violence, and implicates adultery in the expansion of the Christian body politic through marriage. Because this chapter offers the most detailed exegesis of Ephesians 5, I position it first in this book. Honing in on the one-sex model of the body, this chapter also sets this book's pattern of reading Shakespeare's female Christ-figures as characters who engage, through their bodies, with Paul's texts. Through Emilia, *The Comedy of Errors* resists the disappearance of the female body within the Pauline body of Christ.

I

In the spirit of awkward resurrection, let me begin again, this time with Richard Strier's compelling effort in *The Unrepentant Renaissance* to make a singularly Renaissance and Protestant sense out of Emilia's nativity. The subject of two separate chapters in that book, *The Comedy of Errors* constitutes a key text in Strier's overall challenge to New Historicist narratives about the period's anxious subordination of the material to the spiritual. For Strier, *The Comedy of Errors* offers Shakespeare's "most wholehearted evocation and celebration of bourgeois life"—and *Protestant* bourgeois life especially.[8] Inviting the whole neighborhood inside for a gossips' feast, Strier contends, Emilia repurposes her abbey in a way that endorses the Protestant dispersal of holiness among all lawful earthly affairs, including business and marriage. The abbess becomes a wife again, the abbey opens to the reunited household, and the promise of "satisfaction" (5.1.401) through storytelling mutes any Catholic ring on the term as an element in the sacrament of penance. As opposed to the reading of Emilia's resurrection that I have just proffered—a reading wherein the apparent error of the second "nativity" sounds the strains of so much temporal, geographic, and personal union in Christ—Strier sets the textual crux beside the point that Shakespeare "seems to merge the 'rebirth' [of the twins] . . . with the birth that defined Christianity."[9] This merger holds regardless as to whether the second "nativity" should read "festivity." Nativity *is* festivity, and at error's end it matters not which word is correct. Or, as Strier puts this point using another pair of synonyms, the ending is "happy" and "holy" for Shakespeare's audience, very few of whom could even remember a time when abbeys functioned as politically separate, Catholic institutions.[10]

I find this argument doubtlessly right for some immeasurable portion of the play's late-sixteenth-century audience; on the level of its possible English Renaissance reception, Strier's reading of *The Comedy of Errors* as something like red meat for the Protestant bourgeoisie is completely plausible. At the same time, Strier's reading is so totalizing, so invested in contesting New Historicist representations of the *repentant* Renaissance, that it obscures the conflicting Christological figuration of Emilia available from the medieval, Catholic traditions of female monasticism the play cites by rendering her an abbess.[11] Strier acknowledges that Emilia would likely be required by canon law to remain a nun, and Egeon encouraged to join a religious order.[12] Yet Emilia says she will "gain a husband" (5.1.341), so Strier simply dismisses this legal likelihood in favor of reading the play's ending as a Protestant testimony to the holiness of the bourgeois family. This dismissal does more than elevate Protestant fantasy over any Catholic reality. It ignores Shakespeare's representation of Christ as a *woman*—as a mother and spouse.[13] At the end of *The Comedy of Errors*, Emilia is the Christ whose "deliverance" of her children generates the Eucharistic image of her as a nursing mother at a gossips' feast. She resembles the Christ who appears to Julian of Norwich as one who "may fedyn us with Himselfe, and doith full curtesly and full tenderly with the blissid sacrament that is pretious fode of very lif."[14] Strier's error is to overlook, in the name of theological coherence, *The Comedy of Errors*' summoning of this medieval, Catholic Christ onto the "Protestant" stage. In Shakespeare's theater, Emilia stands for the birth that defines Christianity. She simultaneously stands for the medieval past and the sexual business it left unfinished with the creative destruction of the English Reformation.

Shakespeare's theater of strained religious and temporal union also exaggerates the identicalness of identical twin brothers. Strier makes little room for this exaggeration other than to note the play's indebtedness to Plautus's *Menaechmi*. Shakespeare lifts the basic plot of his play from Plautus, doubling the divided twin pairs. Yet approaching *The Comedy of Errors* as a play about the hyperbolic sameness of twin brothers further encourages a reading attentive to theological conflicts within the play's own Christian environs. *The Comedy of Errors* asks its audience to believe the impossible: not merely that the Antipholus and Dromio brothers are two pairs of identical twins who can successfully pass for their siblings (for they apparently dress and style themselves exactly the same). It asks us to believe that not even their most intimate—their nearest, most proximate—companions can discern the difference between them. This shared identity is entirely superficial, a matter of looks and names rather than personality or disposition.[15] Adriana cannot tell the difference between the melancholic, wandering foreigner Antipholus of Syracuse and her successful merchant of a husband. Neither Antipholus can tell the difference between the witty Dromio of Syracuse and the frequently abused Dromio of Ephesus. The fact that these twin brothers *are* the same person in the eyes of others highlights the familiar thesis that any concept of selfhood in this play emerges only through a complicated relay of reflections.[16] But considering Strier's reading of the play as unapologetically Protestant, I would add that this relay of reflections does not readily lend itself to the recognition of any dimension of the self we would designate as "interior" or "inward," and associate with Pauline, Protestant subjectivity. Reformation climates of salvational scrutiny and denominational allegiance doubtlessly intensified a Pauline bifurcation of the self into inside and outside, visible and invisible. But little in *The Comedy of Errors* suggests that its characters are divided by anything other than a difference between who they believe themselves to be and who others see them to be. Against its own Pauline backdrop—the city of Ephesus—selfhood in *The Comedy of Errors* is absurdly one-dimensional.

The apparent exception to this claim about the play's hyperbolic rejection of interiority is Antipholus of Syracuse's brief self-reflection, offered in soliloquy at the outset of his urban adventures:

> I to the world am like a drop of water
> That in the ocean seeks another drop,
> Who, falling there to find his fellow forth,

Unseen, inquisitive, confounds himself.
So I, to find a mother and a brother,
In quest of them, unhappy, lose myself. (1.2.35–40)

Antipholus of Syracuse's comparison of himself to a drop of water seems deep enough (pun intended). Both substantively and grammatically, however, this comparison actually refuses the interiorization of the self, and with it any differentiation of the self predicated on a claim of inwardness. The ocean of Antipholus's description functions as what Steve Mentz calls a "massive containing wholeness"; it disperses and circulates selves at the moment of their conjunction.[17] The first sonic half of that "whole"—line 37's "Who"—refers most intelligibly back to the line 35's "I." But given its syntactical location, "Who" can also reference line 36's immediately antecedent "another drop." Antipholus's simile thus admits of two readings: The first drop falls into the ocean to find his fellow drop, and/or the first drop seeks another drop that itself drops into the water in search of "his fellow" who may or may not be the first drop. To whom or what, we might then ask, is the "I" of line 39 compared: the first drop, the second, both, or the whole body of water? The grammar of the self is confounding. What is clear is only that Antipholus of Syracuse fears his self-loss as a consequence of his lack of difference, not his irreducible difference, from other drops. All drops of water are basically the same. Furthermore, when Antipholus of Syracuse "finds" himself at play's end, he does so not by looking to anything like Hamlet's famous—and famously Protestant—"that within which passeth show" (1.2.85).[18] He finds himself through self-identification as his servant's superior: "*I am* your master, Dromio" (5.1.413, emphasis added).[19]

The Comedy of Errors further flattens surface/depth models of the self through its rendering of demonic possession as illusory. The Paul of Acts 19 spends much of his time in Ephesus exorcising demons—making the shared and split self one again by expelling the body of its unwelcome spiritual inhabitant. Antipholus of Syracuse gestures toward Ephesus's reputation for demonic possession when he worries about "Dark-working sorcerers that change the mind,/ [and] Soul-killing witches that deform the body" (1.2.99–100). By repeatedly predicating charges of demonic possession on misrecognition, however, *The Comedy of Errors* parodies the Pauline assumption of a self with an inside to be inhabited.

The play even parodies Acts 19's own exorcist comedy of errors. According to 19:13, "certeine of the vagabonde Jewes" in Ephesus adopt Paul's exorcist practice, driving out demons in the name of Jesus and the apostle alike. When one demon questions the identity of his interlocutor—"Jesus I acknowledge, and Paul I knowe: but who are ye?" (19:15)—the exorcists apparently have no good answer, for then "the man in whome the evil spirit was, ran on them, and overcame them, and prevailed against them, so that they fled out of that house, naked, and wounded" (19:17). Antipholus and Dromio of Ephesus's attack on Doctor Pinch sends up this demonic attack. Whereas the evil spirit of Acts 19:16 shames the exorcists by beating them and stripping them of their clothes, Antipholus and Dromio shame their exorcist with a perverse rendition of Pentecostal descent and baptism. They singe off Pinch's beard and douse him with "pails of puddled mire" (5.1.174). The comedy is simple inversion: Antipholus of Ephesus is not actually possessed, nor, as far as we see, is Shakespeare's Ephesus actually peopled with sorcerers and witches. As Strier maintains, the play endorses a Protestant vision of the world in which supernatural intervention has ceased.[20] It does so by making a fool out of figures like Pinch, who betrays his Catholic (rather than Jewish) identity when he orders Satan out "by all the saints in heaven" (4.4.52).[21] And it does so by having its characters, Protestant and Catholic alike, repeatedly and obviously (to the audience) mistake accidents for spiritual mysteries.[22]

Yet Shakespeare's coupling of this Protestant vision of the disenchanted world with a Plautine one of confounded selves makes *The Comedy of Errors* something other than the unequivocal celebration of Protestant mercantilism that Strier describes. This coupling makes the play a Plautine farce on the Pauline imagination of Christian universality—the union of all Christians in the body of Christ, ultimately figured on stage as Emilia, and, in Ephesians' own mixed metaphor (from 2:19), as her house, the abbey. This universalist imagination is polytemporal, extending back from the 1590s to medieval Christendom, to the first recipients of the gospel, and to before the birth of Christ. This imagination is heterotopian—oriented around the spatial conjunction of difference rather than the creation or celebration of the good.[23] Pace the play's ostensible celebration of the Protestant bourgeoisie, this imagination is finally economic. *The Comedy of Errors* is hyperbolically materialist; it trades in what Curtis Perry has described as a commodifying reduction of "people to near objects."[24] We may relate all these observations about the play's universalist imagination to still another episode from Paul's efforts in Ephesus: the riot of the craftsmen in Acts 19:23–41. Triggered by a silversmith upset over Paul's anti-idolatrous claim that "they be not gods which are made with hands" (19:26), this riot turns on the economic threat that conversion to Christianity poses to the local worship of Artemis. A city clerk dispels the rioters by encouraging them to take legal recourse against Paul. But the apostle soon thereafter departs, escaping the conflict between his missionary work and the health of the local, pagan craft economy. That this conflict would even need resolution would most likely come as a surprise to the author of Acts (traditionally Luke, although he does not identify himself). Like most early Christians, this author probably believed in the imminent return of Christ. A millennium and a half later, however, *The Comedy of Errors* would close the gap between economic and religious "good," or material and spiritual prosperity, by making materials of everyone. In Shakespeare's Ephesus, there are no Jews and Gentiles. There are Protestants and Catholics. But mostly there are just things.

Even the ocean conceit participates in this materialist construction of selfhood. It emphasizes the whirling circulation of selves elsewhere marked metonymically by their possession of goods like a gold chain, a ring, and a rope; and synecdochely by physical "marks" or bruises that pun on money as the means of exchange. "I have some marks of yours upon my pate," Dromio of Ephesus complains to Antipholus of Syracuse, "Some of my mistress' marks upon my shoulders, / But not a thousand marks between you both" (1.2.82–84). The market provides *The Comedy of Errors* with a discourse for structuring selves without interiority. At the same time, the physical liability of this lack—and the lack itself—becomes apparent in the misrecognitions that ensue. Through the beatings of the Dromios, Shakespeare's mercantilist comedy repeatedly marks the poverty of one-dimensional selfhood on the only level of the self it recognizes: the body.

Returning us to the letter of the text, Dromio of Ephesus's pun on *marks* indexes the materialist dimensions of *The Comedy of Errors*' Plautine play on Ephesians' guarantee that all Christians are one in Christ—"of his bodie, of his flesh, and of his bones" (5:30). Members of this body occupy different, marked positions as husbands, wives, children, servants, et cetera. To borrow a term from Elisabeth Schüssler Fiorenza, this body is *kyriarchically* structured (from *kyros*, meaning *lord* or *master*); it anatomizes social positions of domination and subordination.[25] *The Comedy of Errors* simply adds that members of the body of Christ must thereby be reduced to bodies—devoid of any interiorized, individualized essence that would resist kyriarchical incorporation.[26] In Shakespeare's farce, to be of Christ's body is to be only a body or, synecdochely, a body part. It is to subordinate, dominate, and depend on other parts. It is occasionally to share a part: "We came into the world like brother and brother," Dromio of Ephesus concludes the play, "And now let's go *hand in hand*, not one before the other" (5.1.426–27, emphasis added). But to be of the body is sometimes to compete for parts—especially the part of the head. "If you will jest with me," Antipholus of Syracuse warns the confused Dromio of Syracuse, "know my aspect, / And fashion your demeanour to my looks, / Or I will beat this method in your sconce" (2.2.32–34).[27] Such violence against the flesh enforces kyriarchical distinctions that otherwise seem vulnerable to dissolution.

In a similarly minded reading of *The Comedy of Errors*, Jane Hwang Degenhardt argues,

> if St. Paul explicitly defined Christian universalism against the bodily distinctions and social divisions privileged by ancient Jewish laws governing diet, exogamy, and circumcision, *The Comedy of Errors* considers and ultimately resists the evisceration of contemporary social customs that divide individuals on the basis of determinants such as gender and class.[28]

I will argue in the last section of this chapter that the play's resistance to the evisceration of gender (or sexual) difference depends entirely on how one makes sense of Emilia's Christology. I nonetheless agree with Degenhardt with respect to class (or status). Adriana's ability to order and abuse Dromio testifies to the kyriarchical organization of bodies "according to the flesh" (Ephesians 6:5), wherein a wife may be the head of a servant while at the same time subordinating herself to the headship of her husband. What unites bodies of different sexes and statuses as one in the household of God is nothing more or less than the fact that they are all bodies.

II

So far unrecognized in criticism on *The Comedy of Errors* is the fact that the play's plot-driving error of confounded selves is an error that modern biblical scholars have also identified in the categorization of Ephesians as an epistle by the apostle Paul. Most biblical scholars now agree that the letter is deutero-Pauline, authored by someone impersonating Paul, or borrowing Paul's hand—someone I will call, apropos *The Comedy of Errors*, Paul of Ephesus, as opposed to Paul of Tarsus.[29] The New Testament contains several deutero-Pauline epistles. Pseudo-Pauls probably authored Colossians, 2 Thessalonians, 1 Timothy, 2 Timothy, and Titus. Also dubious is the traditional attribution of Pauline authorship to the anonymous Hebrews. Shakespeare would almost certainly not have known about any question surrounding the authorship of Ephesians or any Pauline epistle. Erasmus briefly raises doubts about Ephesians' authorship in his annotations of 1519, remarking that the "style differs so much from the other Epistles of

Paul that it could seem to be the work of another person did not the heart and soul of the Pauline mind assert clearly his claim to the letter."[30] Otherwise, Ephesians' authorship remains uncontested until the late eighteenth century and the advent of higher criticism in biblical studies. Shakespeare would therefore have derived his sense of Pauline universalism in part from an epistle erroneously attributed to the real apostle.

Both Paul of Tarsus and Paul of Ephesus speak of the body of Christ. Paul of Tarsus cites this body when explaining to the Corinthians the distribution of different spiritual gifts: "For as the bodie is one, and hathe many membres, and all the membres of the bodie, which is one, thogh they be many, yet are but one bodie: even so is Christ" (1 Corinthians 12:12). He says much the same in his epistle to the Romans: "For as we have many members in one bodie, and all members have not one office, So we being many are one bodie in Christ, and everie one, one anothers members" (12:4–5). In both cases, Paul of Tarsus emphasizes the unity of the body in the multiplicity of its members. He does not align body parts with particular gifts or partition body parts according to any explicit hierarchy. That Paul nonetheless conceives of this body as male becomes evident elsewhere, most explicitly in 1 Corinthians 11:3: "Christ is the head of everie man: and the man is the womans head: and God is Christs head."[31]

As many recent scholars have argued, Paul also sexes the body of Christ as male in what has somewhat ironically become the rallying cry of Pauline universalism, Galatians 3:28: "There is nether Jewe nor Grecian: there is nether bonde nor fre: there is nether male nor female: for ye are all one in Christ Jesus."[32] Alain Badiou may account this verse a "genuinely stupefying statement" by the "rules of the ancient world" that insist on making and maintaining differences in status, ethnicity, and sex.[33] But it is simply not true that the verse was incomprehensible or even necessarily radical in its ancient context. Within Paul's one-sex model of the body, sexual difference disappears in the teleological realization of the body as male. The Geneva Bible most likely captures Paul's original meaning when it glosses "neither male nor female" as "all one man."[34]

In the previous section of this chapter, I argued that *The Comedy of Errors* farcically equates Pauline subjects with Plautine ones, reducing these subjects to bodies. I argue in this section that Paul of Ephesus shares his predecessor's one-sex model of the body, albeit with an eschatological difference that bears on Shakespeare's representation of the marital body in *The Comedy of Errors*.[35] Paul of Tarsus does not invoke the body of Christ to justify marriage. His overarching concerns are more immediately apocalyptic. He states in 1 Corinthians 7:8 that he would prefer the single and the widowed to remain unmarried. He imagines marriage only as a prophylactic against sin, conceding that "it is better to marie then to burne" (7:9). (About mutual society and reproduction, those hallmarks of companionate and biopolitical marriage, Paul of Tarsus has nothing to say.) This ambivalence about marriage is easy to understand in terms of the apostle's eschatology. The "time is short," he reminds the Corinthians, and soon "they which have wives, be as thogh they had none" (7:29). The married and the unmarried also have different priorities: "The unmarried careth for the things of the Lord, how he may please the Lord. But he that is married, careth for the things of the worlde, how he maie please his wife" (7:32–33).[36] By contrast, Paul of Ephesus seems less certain that the end of the world is so immanent, and more concerned with the earthly problem of managing the expanding Christian church.[37] Paul of Ephesus expresses no concerns about divided loyalties or the evanescence of temporal union. Nor does he begrudgingly justify marriage on the basis of avoiding sin. Instead, he enlists for church purposes the classical concept of the family as a building block of the polis. For Paul of Ephesus, *not* Paul of Tarsus, marriage constitutes a means of joining the church and becoming one with the body of Christ.

The correlation of the marital body with Christ's body is particular to Paul of Ephesus's theology. Paul of Tarsus may mark Christ and men as heads, but otherwise he draws no relationship between marriage and the church. In his instructions to wives and husbands, Paul of Tarsus grants each spouse power over the other's body: "The wife hathe not the power of her owne bodie, but the housband: and likewise also the housband hathe not the power of his owne bodie, but the wife" (1 Corinthians 7:4). This shared right of bodily access follows from Paul of Tarsus's statement that the only purpose of marriage is "to avoide fornication" (7:2). It makes no sense to withhold sex from one's spouse when one is espoused for the sole purpose of having sex. Paul of Ephesus, on the other hand, prioritizes the husband's body in describing marriage's conjunction of two bodies to the body of Christ. Paul of Ephesus instructs wives to submit to their husbands: "For the housband is the wives head, even as Christ is the head of the Church, and the same is the saviour of his bodie" (Ephesians 5:23). He then orders husbands not to mutually submit to their wives, but to love their wives as they love their own *bodies*. These verses from Ephesians 5 are worth quoting again:

> (25) Housbands, love your wives, even as Christ loved the Church, and gave him self for it, (26) That he might sanctifie it, and clense it by the washing of water through the worde, (27) That he might make it unto him

> self a glorious Church, not having spot or wrinkle, or anie suche thing: that it shulde be holie and without blame. (28) So oght men to love their wives, as their owne bodies: he that loveth his wife, loveth him self. (29) For no man ever yet hated his owne flesh, but nourisheth and cherisheth it, even as the Lord doeth the Church.

Although Paul of Ephesus states that husbands should sacrifice themselves for their wives like Christ sacrificed himself for the church, his concept of the marital flesh entails the primary expectation of female self-sacrifice. Frances E. Dolan describes this "Pauline" expectation as that of a wife's relinquishment of "her own will, her own ideas and interests" to her husband, lest the one self "devolve[] into two fractious persons."[38] Building on Dolan's work, I submit that the tension between these sacrificial expectations—female submission and male love—identifies Paul of Ephesus's "body" as a one-sex body. The marital body and the body of Christ are both male bodies that subsume the female in the process of growth and perfection.

Instrumental to the construction and maintenance of this one-sex economy of the body of Christ is the translation, in Ephesians 5:28 and 33, of the law of Leviticus 19:18: "love thy neighbour as thy selfe." The Synoptic Gospels agree that Jesus elevates this law to the status of the second greatest (Matthew 22:39, Mark 12:31, and Luke 10:27). Paul of Tarsus also elevates the law, arguably making it the only one: "For all the Law is fulfilled in one worde, which is this, Thou shalt love thy neighbour as thy self" (Galatians 5:14).[39] (See also Romans 13:8: "Owe nothing to any man, but to love one another: for he that loveth another, hathe fulfilled the Law.") In Paul of Ephesus's translation, however, the command is not to love a neighbor. The command in 5:28 is to love a body (*soma*), apparently equivalent to 5:33's "self" ("let everie one love his wife, even as him self"). Some modern commentators have argued that the embedded quotation of Genesis 2:24 in Ephesians 5:31 anticipates this translation, given the symmetry of body and flesh. Ernest Best additionally notes that the word *body*, in Greek, "does not necessarily carry a strong physical or anatomical connotation"; a less misleading translation for the modern reader might be *person*.[40] I nonetheless want to stake a claim for the significance of this translation of *neighbor* to *body* with respect to *The Comedy of Errors*. This translation at once helps explicate the play's reduction of persons to bodies, and evokes political-theological arguments regarding the relative egalitarianism of neighborly (as opposed to master/servant, sovereign/subject) relations. In Kenneth Reinhard's words, the "figure of the neighbor . . .

materializes that uncertain division between the friend/family/self and the enemy/stranger/other"; the neighbor "bears within it . . . the kernel of *jouissance* that is both foreign, strange, and unrecognizable in the other and intimate to me."[41] Guided by *The Comedy of Errors*, I read Paul of Ephesus's translation of *neighbor* to *body* as a gendered disavowal of this uncertain division, a repudiation of the neighbor whose presence connotes a horizontal (identical) rather than vertical (differential) axis of relation between self and other. For Paul of Ephesus, the wife-as-neighbor becomes the wife-as-body in order to be incorporated within a one-sex economy that posits the male as both all and half of the self.

Psychoanalysis provides the theoretical frame for most of these political-theological arguments. And within psychoanalysis, of course, the horizontal plane of neighbor-love has always had bumps—symptoms of the disavowal inherent in the original command to love one's neighbor as one's self. Freud famously found the command an offense to love, a perverse insistence that one ignore the differentiating criterion of merit: "My love is something valuable to me which I ought not to throw away without reflection. . . . If I love someone, he ought to deserve it in some way."[42] Lacan averred that Freud simply "stop[ped] short in horror at the consequences of the commandment," protecting himself from "that fundamental evil which dwells within this neighbor . . . this unfathomable aggressivity."[43] For Lacan, what makes the command to love one's neighbor as oneself so traumatic is its insistence that one love one's *worst* self—the self necessarily repressed in the civilizing process. Slavoj Žižek has more recently argued that the law chafes against the liberal humanist universalism it ostensibly promotes. The law demands the neighbor's "ethical domestication," the translation of the neighbor into a "Man" or a "human person" at the expense of "subjectivity."[44] For Žižek, this neighbor is no real neighbor at all. Like the cleansed bridal church of Ephesians 5:26–27, this neighbor has been domesticated. "One should hear in the term [*neighbor*]," Žižek continues, "all the connotations of horror fiction: the Neighbor is the (Evil) Thing which potentially lurks beneath every homely human face."[45]

Anyone seeking Shakespearean examples of this Neighbor (now capitalized to distinguish it from its more innocuous fellow) will easily find them in the tragedies. The Neighbor is Iago, lurking behind the face of honesty; Macbeth, lurking behind the face of a loyal subject; King Hamlet, lurking behind the face of Hyperion; and Edmund, lurking behind the face of a dutiful son. One will also find ready biblical figurations of the Neighbor as Satan. The Neighbor is the snake (traditionally identified as Satan) in the garden, luring Eve with the promise of knowledge; and the devil in the desert, tempting the Son of God to flex his divine muscle. Here, however, the psychoanalytic critique of the second-greatest commandment turns the conversation about the body of Christ in *The Comedy of Errors* to the scene of neighborhood disturbance at the beginning of Act 3. When Antipholus of Ephesus returns home to find the door locked against him, the play takes what Žižek would describe as a decidedly *obscene* step in rendering the Neighbor as both husband and Christ alike.

We should read this scene with all the Christological connotations it invites, beginning with the name of the house, the Phoenix, the first-century sign of Christ's death and resurrection. At the door of the Phoenix, Dromio inverts the gentle command of Jesus in Matthew 7:7—"knocke, and it shalbe opened unto you"—when he enjoins his master to "Knock the door hard" (3.1.58). This hard knocking gains Antipholus no admittance. The bridegroom has returned home to find himself unwelcome, and his reaction is violent. He orders Dromio to bring him a crowbar so he can break the gate open. That Antipholus has designs on beating Adriana might well be inferred from his later efforts to do so. Battery is presumably the reason he orders Dromio, in 4.1, to purchase a rope. In a fever pitch of rage in 4.4, Antipholus then charges his wife with being a "Dissembling harlot . . . false in all," and threatens to pluck out her eyes (4.4.96). The stage directions indicate that he "reaches for Adriana," who "shrieks," but Antipholus is bound before he can make good on his word. Back in 3.1, Balthasar, whose name helps draw the analogy between Antipholus and Christ insofar as Christian legend attributes to one of the magi who visits the Christ child, marvels at his neighbor's transformation from civilized businessman to potential domestic abuser: "Have patience, sir. O let it not be so! / Herein you war against your reputation" (3.1.86). Balthasar adds that this transformation threatens to draw Adriana's "honor" into "the compass of suspect" (3.1.88–89). (That is neighbors might wonder if Adriana has done something to provoke him.) To read 3.1. as a bit of sacramental theater, however, is to draw into the compass of suspect the self-sacrificial God of Ephesians 5:25–29. As husband and neighbor, Antipholus morphs into this God's self-same other. He becomes the Neighbor-God enraged by his household members' refusal to believe that he is who he says he is. Antipholus of Ephesus becomes in this comedy of doppelgängers the monstrous bridegroom incarnate—an *un*domestic abuser accordingly barred from the household of God.

Paul of Ephesus's translation of *neighbor* to *body* might be theologically insignificant in its first-century context, but *The Comedy of Errors* renders it a particularly significant accident nonetheless. Shakespeare's play suggests that by writing of selves as bodies, Paul of Ephesus tries to do away with that wild dimension of subjectivity upsetting to marital harmony—the dimension of both the wife (the female) and the wife-beater (the uncivilized male). *The Comedy of Errors* further suggests that the reduction of the self to a one-sex body in Ephesians 5 engenders the violent return of the Neighbor as the Christ-like husband who demands recognition of his headship. This latter suggestion is theologically obscene. A civilized (happily bourgeoisie) marriage necessarily excludes the brutal, authoritarian savior from the house set up in his name. I will argue in the final section of this chapter that the play's consequent representation of the neighborhood nun Emilia as Christ is no less obscene a response to the "Pauline" theology of the marital body. At present, however, I want to suggest that the need to excise the Neighbor from the marital body helps explain why almost no one in the Renaissance comments on Paul of Ephesus's translation.

As compared to modern commentaries on Ephesians, I have found few mentions of the second greatest commandment in the many glosses, homilies, sermons, and manuals on marriage that refer to Ephesians 5.[46] Silence on this translation cedes discursive authority to the otherwise commonplace distinction of marital love from neighbor love, examples of which abound in early modern drama. In the 1608 play *The Family of Love* (once attributed to Thomas Middleton, but now of uncertain authorship), a wife (Mistress Glister) asks her husband's apprentice (Club) about the play's titular, heretical sect:

> **MI[STRESS] GL[IS]T[ER]:** And I pre thee Club what kind of creatures are these Familists, thou art conversant with them.
>
> **CLUB:** What are they? With reverence be it spoken, they are the most accomplish Creatures under heaven, in them is all perfection.
>
> **MI GLT:** As how good Club?
>
> **CLUB:** Omitting their outward graces, Ille show you only one which includes all other: they love their neighbors better then themselves.
>
> **MI GLT:** Not then themselves, good Club.
>
> **CLUB:** Yes better then themselves, for they love them better then their husbands, and husband and wife are all one; therefore better then themselves.
>
> **MI GLT:** This is logick.[47]

Club's "logick" depends upon the routine figuration of the neighbor as a potential threat to the bond of marriage. The allegedly orgiastic members of Family of Love adhere so strictly to the second greatest commandment that they can justify adultery. Shakespeare's Rosalind cites this same figuration of the neighbor when she chides Orlando's "Wit, whither wilt?":

"Nay, you might keep that check for it till you met your wife's wit going to your neighbor's bed" (*As You Like It*, 4.1.143–45). *The Winter's Tale*'s Leontes marvels at any husband ignorant of the fact that "his pond [has been] fished by his next neighbor, by/Sir Smile, his neighbour" (1.2.196–97). In all these examples, the neighbor is a potential home-wrecker—not Christ, and not an unruly wife, but an extramarital lover.

Henry Smith's 1591 *Preparative to Marriage* offers a telling exception to this general Renaissance silence on Paul of Ephesus's translation of *neighbor* to *body*. Smith reasons that "if God commaunded men to love their neighbours, as themselves, much more are they bound to love their wives as them selves, which are their next neighbors."[48] This statement edges toward gender egalitarianism—an equality of male and female selves. But like most marriage reformers, Smith checks gender egalitarianism by qualifying it from two ends. First, he takes pains to angle the plane of spousal neighbor-love, prefacing this definition of the wife as an intensified form of the neighbor with a lengthy discussion of a husband's headship. Second, he enlists this construction of the wife as the "next neighbor" in his argument against domestic abuse—an argument for civility that nonetheless must tacitly admit the neighbor as a provoking subject whose bids for headship solicit repeated domestication.[49] Given these qualifications, it is not surprising that most English Renaissance discussions of Ephesians 5:22–33 simply do away with the figure of the neighbor altogether, focusing instead on what the translation of *neighbor* to *body* helps facilitate: the domesticating prescription of a wives' subordination to her husbands' Christ-like, sovereign authority. Indeed, the Homily on the State of Matrimony references Ephesians 5 only for verses 22–23, which it translates straightforwardly enough: "Here you understande, that GOD hath commanded, that ye [wives] should acknowledge the authoritie of the husbande, and referre to hym the honor of obedience."[50] In the Ephesians model of marriage, the peaceful Christological union of both bodies in one flesh depends upon the subjugation of the female to the male. Marriage has no room for neighbors.

The same prescription holds in many of today's "complementation" Christian marriage advice manuals, which navigate the treacherous waters of feminism and "the culture" by steering couples to the distinct roles that God has ordained for husbands and wives. According to the logic of kyriarchy, these roles mirror others one might simultaneously play. In *Night Light: A Devotional for Couples*, for example, Focus on the Family–founder Dr. James Dobson and his wife Shirley gloss Ephesians 5:22 by universalizing submission: "Each of us submits to a higher authority. Consider the boss at work or the IRS agent at tax time." The Dobsons allow that husbands and wives, like employees and bosses, are "equal people," but they insist that this equality does not compromise the chain of command.[51] Leader and subordinate are the complementary roles that, respectively, husbands and wives play in marriage. Spouses may therefore be "one flesh," but as Dolan demonstrates of both reformist and complementation models of marriage, this one flesh should have no more than one head. In *The Comedy of Errors*' farcical rendering of this doctrine, this Christological flesh should also be nothing more than flesh. It should harbor nothing or no one "inside" to upset the sacramental scene of a wife subordinated to her husband's authority. It should reflect only a husband's self-reflexive love of his own body that Paul of Ephesus, apparently unacquainted with the death drive, imagines "no man ever yet hated."

III

This biblical construction of husband and wife as one flesh that informs the comedy of domestic violence in *The Comedy of Errors* also informs the play's comedy of adultery. Much of this comedy turns on unanswered, even unanswerable questions about who has sex with whom—Antipholus of Syracuse with Adriana, and Antipholus of Ephesus with the Courtesan. In Plautus's *Amphitryo*, Shakespeare's source for the possible dinner affair of Antipholus of Syracuse and Adriana, the "husband" (Jupiter in disguise) and wife Alcmena both eat and sleep together. Alcmena is relatively unambiguous on this point: "You had dinner with me and went to bed with me."[52] Shakespeare's Adriana also hints at sex when she teases Antipholus with punishment and orders Dromio to give her and her husband privacy:

> Husband, I'll dine above with you today,
> And shrive you of a thousand idle pranks.—
> Sirrah, if any ask you for your master,
> Say he dines forth, and let no creature enter. (2.2.207–10)

How much to read into this shriving has nevertheless proven debatable. Strier argues against any conclusion that Adriana and Antipholus of Syracuse sleep together, citing as evidence what Antipholus of Syracuse later says to himself about Adriana: "She that doth call me husband, even my soul / Doth for a wife abhor" (3.2.156–57). Strier then comes to the rather startling conclusion that marriage in *The Comedy of Errors* is a "matter of finding a 'soul-mate.'"[53] I have argued that the play's politics of the flesh bend in precisely the opposite direction, toward the denial of the soul. Antipholus of Syracuse's libidinous soul-stirrings sound this play's spoof on the very idea of soul-mates.

In 3.2, Antipholus of Syracuse is also more enamored with Luciana than with her sister, and what he says about Adriana needs to be heard in this context. He neither affirms nor denies that he slept with Adriana, however much he may "abhor" her now. *The Comedy of Errors* likewise leaves open the question of whether Antipholus of Ephesus is having sex with the Courtesan—perhaps a prostitute, perhaps an innkeeper, or perhaps both.[54] To conclude that sex does or does not take place between Antipholus of Syracuse and Adriana or Antipholus of Ephesus and the Courtesan may therefore be to miss the point of these open questions. The point is not that adultery, understood as illicit sex, does or does not take place in violation of marital commitments. The point is that whether all these bodies are already adulterated to the extent that they are mixed (up) with others.

Adriana's Act 2 complaint against Antipholus of Syracuse, whom she mistakes for Antipholus of Ephesus, locates the crime of adultery in the body shared between spouses and their lovers:

> I am possessed with an adulterate blot;
> My blood is mingled with the crime of lust.
> For if we two be one, and thou play false,
> I do digest the poison of thy flesh,
> Being strumpeted by thy contagion. (2.2.140–44)

Adriana balks at Pauline restraints on women's liberty (2.1.1–26) and her sister Luciana's admonishments of patience (2.1.32–41). She nevertheless takes quite literally the doctrine of one-flesh marriage upon which Paul of Ephesus expounds in Ephesians 5. She also takes literally Paul of Tarsus's claim that "coupling" alone makes two bodies one: "Do ye not knowe," the real apostle asks, "that he which coupleth him self with an harlot, is one bodie? for two, saith he [Moses, presumably], shalbe one flesh" (1 Corinthians 6:16).[55] Adriana would seem to assume that sex makes husband and wife one flesh, and that sex outside of marriage can accordingly pollute the marital flesh with the flesh of a third person. Moving from body to body, what Adriana calls the "adulterate blot"—the mark of the marital self that contains more than one husband and one wife—provokes her initial charge that her husband is "estrangèd from [him]self" (2.2.120), or diluted. This charge seamlessly unfolds into one of marital estrangement, of one flesh formally "undividable, incorporate" (2.2.122), now "tear[ing]" (2.2.124) apart as the result of an unwelcome addition.

We miss the theological import of Adriana's complaint if we regard it simply as mistaken (because her husband is not actually sleeping with anyone else) or misdirected (because she is speaking to the wrong brother). To take literally, as Adriana does, the fleshly mixture of bodies united through marriage and sex is to expand the marital body to include more than two people, husband and wife. This body now includes not only those other people with whom one has sex (the Courtesan, etc.), but also all those people with whom one is *already* "one flesh" through other vectors of kinship. In the Plautine environs of *The Comedy of Errors*, the most immediate vector of fleshly oneness is of course identical twinship. Adriana's misdirected address, her "mistake" of one brother for another brother as her flesh, argues that she shares her flesh with her husband *and* his brother. So does her uncanny echo, in the same complaint, of her brother-in-law's comparison of the self to a drop of water:

For know, my love, as easy mayst thou fall
A drop of water in the breaking gulf,
And take unmingled thence that drop again
Without addition or diminishing,
As take from me thyself, and not me too. (2.2.125–29)

Figuring the marital body, like Antipholus of Syracuse does the familial body, as a mixture of drops from which extraction of the single individual is impossible, Adriana unwittingly admits that Antipholus of Ephesus need not sleep with the Courtesan or anyone else to introduce another person into the union of husband and wife. Antipholus simply needs a twin.

Or perhaps he simply needs a sibling. Adriana's mistake of Antipholus of Syracuse for Antipholus of Ephesus raises the question of how to distinguish as one individual someone who already shares his or her flesh with both an identical twin and a spouse. Antipholus of Syracuse's effort to seduce Luciana complicates this question by adding several measures of difference between one of the sibling pairs. Adriana and Luciana are not identical twins. They neither look the same nor have the same personality. Shakespeare nonetheless explores the extent of their identity with each other and with the Antipholus twins by giving the sisters polysyllabic rhyming names (Ad-ri-an-a and Lu-ci-an-a) and entertaining their substitution as the object of Antipholus of Syracuse's desire.

When Antipholus of Syracuse woos Luciana, the word *sister* variously differentiates and consolidates the identity of the siblings:

LUCIANA: Why call you me "love"? Call my sister so.
ANTIPHOLUS S.: Thy sister's sister.
LUCIANA: That's my sister.
ANTIPHOLUS S.: No;
  It is thyself, mine own self's better part,
  Mine eye's clear eye, my dear heart's dearer heart,
  My food, my fortune, and my sweet hope's aim,
  My sole earth's heaven, and my heaven's claim.
LUCIANA: All this my sister is, or else should be.
ANTIPHOLUS S.: Call thyself sister, sweet, for I am thee. (3.2.59–66)

In this quick calculus of selfhood, the object of Antipholus of Syracuse's "love" swerves from Luciana to Adriana ("my sister"), back to Luciana ("Thy sister's sister"), back to Adriana ("my sister"), to Luciana *and* Antipholus ("thyself, mine own self's better part"), back again to Adriana ("my sister"), and back yet again to Luciana and Antipholus ("Call thyself sister, sweet, for I am thee"). As Freud would remark of this exchange, love often discriminates, even among persons who are in many respects the same; it matters to both Antipholus of Syracuse and Luciana that she is *not* Adriana. (*The Comedy of Errors* previews this scene of inexplicable preference among the identical when Egeon notes that the storm-tossed Emilia was "more careful for the latter-born" of her twin sons [1.1.78].) At the same time, Antipholus of Syracuse's expletive construction of the one-flesh doctrine—"*It is* thyself, mine own self's better part"—grammatically overrides love's discrimination to yoke four different bodies in one gender-neutral pronoun: Luciana is Adriana is Antipholus of Syracuse is Antipholus of Ephesus. The comedy of this exchange turns on this play of conflation and differentiation, the alternating coincidence and opposition of identities.

This claim that marriage and siblinghood work in tandem, if not without friction, to assemble the many into the one raises a further set of questions about Christian sexual ethics. If spouses are one flesh, and siblings are too, why may a husband not sleep with his sister-in-law, a wife with her brother-in-law, a brother with his brother, a sister with her sister, or everyone with everyone? Why does mutual membership in the body of Christ not override restrictions on sexual relations? And how can an adulterate blot mark a moral failing when its possession is the inevitable result of a shared self? I am not the first to hear *The Comedy of Errors* ask these questions about sexual license. Thomas Luxon hears them as well, concluding that Antipholus of Syracuse's preference for Luciana rather than

Adriana "shift[s] threatening images of illicit desire (the brother's wife, thy brother's flesh) into something more licit: brothers marrying sisters, not their own of course, but each others."[56] This reading is incisive, and like Strier's, surely right for some measure of the play's audience. Yet I am not so convinced that "the play tucks safely away the very specters of incest (both hetero- and homoerotic) and narcissism it evokes."[57] For one reason, the specter of incest is an old haunt of Christianity; the charge trailed early Christians in part because they referred to one another as brother and sister.[58] The argument that the play can so easily lay to rest a charge it so hyperbolically activates assumes a universal audience of ready ghost-busters. For a second reason—and this one comes from the future—the specter of incest that *The Comedy of Errors* conjures will even more literally be fleshed out on the Jacobean stage. This stage includes the Shakespeare play Marc Shell places at the center of his own study of incest and universal siblinghood: *Measure for Measure*. It also includes John Ford's *'Tis Pity She's a Whore*, wherein Giovanni obscenely reasons that he and his twin sister Annabella are "one soul, one flesh, one love, one heart, one all"—a point he ultimately seeks to prove by cutting that heart from her chest.[59]

Upholding the Christian law of sexual propriety against this obscene logic of license is the task that befalls *Comedy*'s Luciana, who shares with *Measure*'s Isabella a libidinal attachment to the law. Luciana contrasts her "practise to obey" (2.1.29), which Adriana derides as "servitude" (2.1.26), to the "troubles of the marriage bed" (2.1.27), implying that obedience to the law is better than sex. Isabella eroticizes martyrdom as "Th'impression of keen whips" she would "wear as rubies" (2.4.101), in contrast to the "shame" of yielding herself to Angelo (2.4.104). Like Isabella, Luciana's attachment to the law is so strong that it would seem to lead her into moral contradiction. After holding forth on male mastery in conversation with her sister at the beginning of Act 2, Luciana admonishes (the wrong) Antipholus to at least be more circumspect with his infidelity: "Apparel vice like virtue's harbinger./Bear a fair presence, though your heart be tainted" (3.2.12–13). Enlisting what little distinction between the self's inside ("heart") and outside ("presence") the play recognizes, Luciana asks Antipholus to be, in effect, less *Neighborly*: "Comfort my sister, cheer her, call her wife:/'Tis holy sport to be a little vain/When the sweet breath of flattery conquers strife" (3.2.26–28). This advice may seem hypocritical for one so devout. But Luciana offers it to Antipholus for the same reason that she admonishes Adriana to have patience: because the moral law that she follows predicates marital peace on the Pauline orthodoxy of a wife's subordination to her husband and a husband's loving treatment of his wife.

Whatever perverse turns obedience to this law may take—namely, licensing secret infidelity—she will follow.

At the same time, Luciana is Isabella's sister in the Shakespearean "romance of orthodoxy" that forces both sisters to reckon with the Christian legality of incest.[60] "Is't not a kind of incest," Isabella asks Claudio, "to take life / From thine own sister's shame" (3.1.140–41)? As Shell has argued, the answer is yes: Claudius is effectively using his sister's body for sex, trading his life for her virginity. Moreover, the threat of incest does not vanish with the bedtrick, which only plays further on the motif of substitution that *Measure for Measure* shares with *The Comedy of Errors*. Through the bedtrick, Isabella dubiously scruples a way to save both her virginity and her brother, paradoxically avoiding incest through its apparent commission. In comparison, Luciana briefly glimpses the legality of incest along the vector of siblinghood. Her words of retreat from the man she supposes to be her brother-in-law are ambiguous: "O soft, sir; hold you still; / I'll fetch my sister to get her good will" (3.2.69–70). Luciana could simply mean that she is running to fetch her sister; the next time we see her, in 4.2, she informs Adriana of Antipholus's advances. Only her lines admit another interpretation. This orthodox sister at least wants her sister's permission before romancing her brother-in-law. She wants Adriana's "good will."

IV

If it has not been obvious up to now that I have been talking about gay marriage, let me go ahead and make this context explicit. To argue, as evangelicals do, that "Christian marriage" is heterosexual is to misunderstand profoundly Paul of Ephesus's own metaphor. Paul of Ephesus does not order wives to love their husbands as their own bodies. Rather, he understands membership in the body of Christ to fill the deficit of the female body by supplying that body with a head. Man and wife are one flesh, and that flesh is the husband's. In Ephesians 5:22–23, one finds both the theological basis for the legal doctrine of coverture and the obscene exposure of Christian marriage as a wholly masculine and masculinizing affair. The question remains whether Shakespeare so obscenely imagines marriage in *The Comedy of Errors*—whether Shakespeare, in figuring marriage's universal impulse in relation to the union of bodies in Christ, also figures the body of Christ as finally, teleologically, male.

The play hardly lacks for comedy that denigrates the female body. While the marks of the beaten Dromio of Ephesus most concisely encode the debts incurred by the reduction of selves to bodies, two of the play's female characters translate those debts into an excessively fleshy corporeality. Following Luciana's retreat from Antipholus of Syracuse in 3.2, the first of these women enters the play via Dromio of Syracuse's description. The name of this "kitchen wench . . . all grease" (3.2.94–95) is Nell (3.2.108), or perhaps Luce. The Folio identifies Luce as the Phoenix servant who, in 3.1, enters to see about the commotion outside. For continuity's sake, however, the Oxford editors, and the Norton editors following them, emend Luce to Nell, possibly making two servants into one. In 3.1, Nell/Luce does not seem the least illustrative of the grotesque figure that the name Nell suggests: "an ell and three-quarters," Dromio of Syracuse quips, "will not measure her from hip to hip." (3.2.109–10). The Nell/Luce of 3.1 is not the figure Patricia Parker reads as a literary fat lady whose "dilated body stands in some sense as a figure for the dilation (and errors) of *The Comedy of Errors*."[61] When understood as the same person, however, Nell/Luce's fatness figures her conjunction of bodies, even as her "hot" pursuit of her future brother-in-law Dromio of Syracuse raises the same heretical questions about sibling spouse-swapping and flesh-sharing as Antipholus of Syracuse's wooing of Luciana. In Dromio of Syracuse's description, Nell/Luce bodies forth the fleshy excess of the human. Like the Neighbor repressed in the formation of the marital body, Nell/Luce figures the inhuman inside the human. She is, by Dromio's own account, a "beastly creature" (3.2.88–89) whose inversion of the sexual order of things translates him into a "woman's man" (3.2.76).[62]

Strier might well read Nell as a carnivalesque component of *The Comedy of Errors*' Protestant praise of robust engagement with the uncloistered world. To be sure, Dromio describes Nell/Luce as "spherical, like a globe" (3.2.113), her body a map of the world that he and Antipholus chart by likening European countries to body parts. Dromio's fear of "a fat marriage" (3.2.93) further merges this carnival comedy with the Protestant celebration of marriage. But this merger does not work towards an unequivocal celebration of either God's creation of the world or the institution that God provides for humans to lawfully exercise their sexual desires. In Dromio's depiction, Nell is so fat that no marriage could quench her Pauline burning. Likening her body to a candle, Dromio quips that Nell's burning will last past the end of days: "If she live till doomsday, she'll burn a week longer than the whole world" (3.2.97–99). In this exchange between master and servant, Nell/Luce figures the expansion of the world through marriage as grotesquely female—the emasculating threat of which Dromio and Antipholus of Syracuse work to neutralize through a series of misogynistic fat jokes.

The second of these excessively embodied women is Emilia, who bears the burden of what a Protestant theology of Pauline universalism often remainders—the Catholic and the female. As wife, mother, and Christ, Emilia describes herself as extremely pregnant, finally delivering two children after thirty-three years, and their servants and father besides, through the resurrection of bodies presumed lost or dead. The eschatological revelation of her identity reunites the household according to a Rabelaisian-inflected Christology of the flesh. I argued above that Emilia's redundant use of the word "nativity" signals the play's crowded discomfort with the Pauline Christology she embodies—the sacramental conjunction of so much sexual, class/status, temporal, geographic, and religious difference in one body. I further argued that Antipholus of Ephesus's appearance as Christ is no less symptomatic an indication of the Pauline remaindering of the Neighbor in the translation of selves to bodies. Both arguments about the limits of Pauline universalism now help explain why Emilia *herself* effects the play's final Christological act of bodily salvation. As this neighborhood's cloistered medieval Christ-wife, Emilia figures the remainder of the universal within Pauline Protestantism. She is the one upon whose gendered disavowal Paul of Ephesus's own universal image of the body of Christ depends. Anticipating *The Winter's Tale*'s Paulina, whose ministrations transform stone to flesh, Emilia is also Paul of Tarsus—a "man" who tropes himself, quite unlike Paul of Ephesus, as the bearer of what Adriana calls a wife's "weight of pain" (2.1.36). "I travaile in birth againe," Paul of Tarsus writes to the Galatians, "until Christ be formed in you" (4:19).[63] Like Emilia and Paulina, Paul of Tarsus plays the role of an evangelical mother.

To discount the difference Emilia's sex makes to *The Comedy of Errors*' staging of salvation is to repeat the very gesture of disavowal that occasions her return in Shakespeare's sacramental theater. As I will explore more fully in the next chapter, on *The Merchant of Venice*, Shakespeare's transvestite theater makes such a disavowal particularly easy. One might well be tempted to claim that the body beneath Emilia's habit finally determines the truth of her sex. Like all the other women on stage, Emilia is played by a man, or a more accurately a boy, on his way toward becoming a man. Perhaps the play's conclusion offers nothing less than a Pauline wet dream in which women transition (back) into men or soon-to-be men. The last scene of *The Comedy of Errors* allows for another reading, however—one for which I would rather stake a claim of stasis against the move out of representation and into the actors' "real" bodies. There is no indication that Shakespeare means for us to follow these characters out of character—no Rosalind-like epilogue, for instance. The play provides no warrant, in its own world, for reading Emilia as anything other than how she presents herself—as a Rabelaisian Christ who confounds male and female, Protestant and Catholic, earthly and the spiritual, living and dead. By not gesturing outside the play, Shakespeare asks us to stop truth at this moment. He asks us to linger with both the female character and the male actor; with reformed and unreformed worldviews; and with the strains of a Christian universalism in its encounter with so much difference. As Emilia sounds and sounds again Christ's nativity, Shakespeare asks us to stop truth at this moment when Christ is both Neighbor and wife. And I submit we leave her there, the bride of Christ as Christ herself—the one who is more than one, who answers Paul of Ephesus with Paul of Tarsus's and Christ's own labor pains.

CHAPTER 2

Portia's Pauline Perversion: *The Merchant of Venice* and Romans 1

Several years after Emilia associates the rebirth of her household with the birth of Christianity, Shylock's daughter Jessica seizes on marriage as a vehicle of Christian citizenship. Looking forward to her evening flight from her father's house, Jessica soliloquizes:

> Alack, what heinous sin is it in me
> To be ashamed to be my father's child!
> But though I am daughter to his blood,
> I am not to his manners. O Lorenzo,
> If thou keep promise I shall end this strife,
> Become a Christian and thy loving wife. (2.3.15–20)

Nowhere in *The Merchant of Venice* does Jessica offer testimony of her new faith. Much less does she fall down on her knees and accept Jesus Christ as her personal Lord and Savior. Becoming a Christian and becoming Lorenzo's wife are, for Jessica, one in the same act—an act that she undertakes in disguise as a boy.[1] This cross-dressed elopement enacts the becoming-male of Christ's body discussed in the previous chapter. It enacts, too, the causal logic of Ephesians 5:30–31 discussed in the Introduction. When Lancelot later informs Jessica that she is damned for being Shylock's daughter, she cites this causal logic in defense of her conversion: "I shall be saved by my husband. He has made me a Christian" (3.5.15–16). Having left her Jewish father, she has become one with her husband and the body of Christ.

Then again, perhaps the verse Jessica has in mind when she makes this claim to Christian citizenship is not Ephesians 5:30–31, but rather 1 Corinthians 7:14: "For the unbeleving housband is sanctified by the wife, and the unbeleving wife is sanctified by the housband."[2] If so, as we will see in Chapter 4, Jessica confuses Paul of Tarsus's argument against divorce with an argument for marriage. She also mistakes Paul's distinction between sanctification and salvation. But is Jessica nonetheless right to claim that she has become a Christian through marriage? The play makes it difficult to determine. Lorenzo's response to Lancelot's charge that "there is no mercy for [Jessica] in heaven because [she is] a Jew's daughter" (3.5.27–28) is less than theologically confident: "I shall answer that better to the commonwealth than you can the getting up of the Negro's belly. The Moor is with child by you, Lancelot" (3.5.31–33). Instead of offering further scriptural support for his wife's conversion, Lorenzo quips that the union of Christians and Jews as one flesh constitutes a more socially acceptable form of miscegenation than the union of Christians and Moors. The problem for any reading of Jessica as a member of the body of Christ therefore remains that the blood she admits to sharing with her father ("I am daughter to his blood") may no more respond to Christian cleansing than the dark skin of the proverbial Ethiop.[3] "I say my daughter is my flesh and my blood," Shylock asserts (3.1.32), prompting a retort by Salerio fuelled more by anti-Semitic venom than genetic acumen: "There is more difference between thy flesh and hers than between jet and ivory; more between your bloods than there is between red wine and Rhenish" (3.1.33–35). Compounded by Shylock's forced conversion to Christianity at the end of Act 4, the play's internal argument about the mutability of Jewish flesh and blood, the restrictive and nonrestrictive characteristics of Jewish and Christian bodies, is never settled.

In this chapter, I build on this brief argument regarding Jessica's tenuous claim to membership in the body of Christ to suggest that Portia's transvestite intercession in the Venetian courtroom hauls theological questions about Christ's sex into the controversy over Jewish conversion to Christianity. Both the subplot and the main plot of *The Merchant of Venice* concern hazardous exchanges of the flesh that alternatively demarcate or erase distinctions between Jewish and Christian bodies. The subplot restricts this exchange to one between a husband and wife. The main plot employs a Jewish moneylender to exacerbate the Christian cultural conflict between monogamous marital union (Bassanio and Portia) and possibly sodomitical and effeminate same-sex friendship (Bassanio and Antonio, Portia and Nerissa). Within *The Merchant of Venice*, conversion to Christianity signifies as both religious and sexual. It marks a turn away from two signifiers often linked in the early modern mind: the Jewish and the female.[4] When Jewish conversion to Christianity is not regarded, pace Lancelot, as impossible, it may signify in the play as an act of supersession (once Jewish, now Christian; once female, now male) or accommodation (part Jewish and part Christian, part male and part female). The tensions among these models of conversion focus *The Merchant of Venice*'s much discussed biblical allegory on the extent to which, through marriage, the body of Christ admits women, Jews, and same-sex friends.[5]

Taking up this question about the limits on membership in Christ's body, this chapter thereby begins where the previous one concluded in its analysis of Emilia's excessively fleshy and female Christlikeness. With its unique interest in the bodily problem of Jewish conversion to Christianity, however, this chapter shifts attention away from Christ's nativity to "his" crucifixion, and to the (homo)erotics of the event that marks the transition from old (Jewish) to new (Christian) covenants in so much Christian theology. Before Christ was resurrected, victorious over a death Christian anti-Semitism lays at Jewish feet, he was crucified in the flesh—nailed to the cross in an act of voluntary suffering that Paul of Tarsus worries was also emasculating. Comically equating the Jewish demand for Christ's life with Shylock's demand for a pound of Antonio's flesh, *The Merchant of Venice* implicates the potentially sodomitical erotics of the crucifixion in its Pauline conjunction of two or more bodies as one flesh.

I

To perceive *The Merchant of Venice*'s engagement with the potentially sodomitical erotics of Christ's crucifixion, we must turn from Paul of Ephesus's household codes to Paul of Tarsus's letter on Jewish/"Christian" relations. In the first chapter of Romans, Paul of Tarsus draws a sharp contrast between his lack of shame in the gospel and the shameful lot of sexual perverts who knowingly reject God. Often cited in evangelical condemnations of homosexuality as unnatural and sinful, this contrast actually contains a strange and, to most modern ears, historically foreign etiology of sexual perversion. These verses are therefore worth quoting in full:

> (16) For I [Paul] am not ashamed of the Gospel of Christ: for it is the power of God unto salvation to everie one that beleveth, to the Jewe first, and also to the Grecian. (17) For by it the righteousnes of God is reveiled, from faith to faith: as it is written, The juste shal live by faith. (18) For the wrath of God is reveiled from heaven against all ungodlines, and unrighteousnes of men, which withholde the trueth in unrighteousnes, (19) For asmuche as that, which may be knowen of God, is manifest in them: for God hathe shewed it unto them. (20) For the invisible things of him, that is, his eternal power and Godhead, are sene by the creation of the wordle, being considered in his workes, to the intent that they shoulde be without excuse: (21) Because that when they knewe God, they glorified him not as God, nether were thankeful, but became vaine in their imaginations, and their foolish heart was ful of darkenes. (22) When they professed them selves to be wise, they became fooles. (23) For thei turned the glorie of the incorruptible God to the similitude of the image of a corruptible man, and of birdes, and foure foted beastes, and of creeping things. (24) Wherefore also God gave them up to their hearts lustes, unto uncleanes, to defile their owne bodies betwene them selves: (25) Which turned the trueth of God unto a lie, and worshipped and served the creature, forsaking the Creator, which is blessed for ever, Amen. (26) For this cause God gave them up unto vile affections: for even their women did change the natural use into that which is against nature. (27) And likewise also the men left the natural use of the woman, and burned in their luste one towarde another, and man with man wroght filthines, and received in them selves suche recompense of their errour, as was mete.

Unlike modern evangelicals, Paul does not attribute perverse sexual activity to personal choice, much less to a genetic defect. The sexual activity he denounces in verses 26 and 27 is also not a discrete practice by persons with a particular sexual orientation.[6] This activity is rather a divine response to the worship of idols. It results from God's resignation of men and women to their natural depravity or "hearts lustes" following their willful exchange of the Creator for the created.

In the Renaissance, these verses were routinely read as references to sodomy—that "utterly confused" discourse of criminal intimacies often, but not always, homoerotic, and often, but not always, extramarital.[7] Several examples will illustrate this common reading. In his commentary on Romans, Martin Luther likens the "vile affections" of Romans 1:26 to the "sin" of "Sodom," taking women's "natural" relations to mean "intercourse with men in matrimony." Luther notes that Paul avoids detailing "the character of these [unnatural] relations, whether it is mutual abuse or lying with animals and demons." Paul is also vague about what the men of Romans 1:27 are doing; Luther can deduce only that "they deal with each other in mutual disgrace."[8] In any case, the point is that these acts are sodomitical because they are not marital. They take place outside the boundaries of the institution God established for the legitimate exercise of sexual desire.

The popular *Annotations upon All the Books of the Old and New Testament*, first published in 1645, likewise directs the reader of Romans 1:27 back to Genesis 19:5, where the men of Sodom ask Lot to bring his two angelic visitors "out unto us that we maie knowe them," and Leviticus 18:22: "Thou shalt not lie with the male as one lieth with a woman: for it is abominacion."[9] This triangulation of Romans 1:27 with Genesis 19:5 and Leviticus 18:22 does not clarify what Paul means by "natural" and "unnatural." Genesis 19:5's "know" and Leviticus 18:22's "lie" both leave room for a considerable variety of bodily interactions. But the triangulation of verses leaves little doubt that, for the authors of the *Annotations*, the acts performed by the men Paul condemns are the same acts that result in the destruction of Sodom and the same acts that God prohibits among the Jews.

The English cleric Andrew Willet agrees, adding that the women of Romans 1:26 are also sodomites. Willet hears Paul referring to women who change "the organe and instrument of generation." Then, as if to clarify that he is talking about anal sex between men and women, he adds, "or [the women] companied with men, as Sodomites," meaning that "males abused . . . that part of the bodie in the female, which was not appointed for generation."[10] Willet additionally reads the men of Romans 1:27 as sinning "actively, in forcing upon others unnaturall acts of uncleanness; and passively, in suffering others to doe it."[11] With his concern for active and passive roles in sex, Willet's reading approaches what many biblical scholars agree is Paul of Tarsus's actual antipathy toward the exchange of gender positions. Bernadette J. Brooten argues, for instance, that in verse 26, Paul references sex between women that perverts their cultural designation as naturally passive and penetrable. Brooten's Paul likewise refers in verse 27 to males who play the passive part in sex (i.e., bottoms), as well as men who help them do so (i.e., tops).[12] Yet Willet's Paul forges a backwards link to the story of Sodom that Brooten's Paul does not: "This [exchange of natural for unnatural roles] was the sinne of Sodome, for the which they were destroyed," Willet writes.[13] Considering that no one in the Bible glosses the destruction of Sodom and Gomorrah as a consequence of their citizens' fondness for anal sex, Paul would probably have found this connection bizarre.[14]

Still another cleric, Thomas Wilson, departs from Willet's gloss of Romans 1:26 as a reference to women who let themselves be anally penetrated by men. He also seems to disregard Luther's suggestion that the deviant men of Romans 1:27 are coupling with animals or demons. Wilson nevertheless agrees with Willet, Luther, and the authors of the *Annotations* that the male and female subjects of Paul's condemnation are sodomites. A character in Wilson's 1614 dialogue on Romans explains that Paul denounces "the monstrous impurity of both sexes, both women and men in the act of generation, going against the naturall course ordained of God, for propagation and encrease of mankinde." "Sodomitry," this character continues, violates the "naturall course" through an "uncleanness betweene them of one sexe."[15] Once again, it is not clear of what this "uncleanness" consists. What is clear is that for Willet and Wilson, if not also for Luther and the authors of the *Annotations*, Paul is chiefly concerned in Romans 1 with nonreproductive sex, be it "heterosexual" or "homosexual" (or "interspecies"). This reading of Paul's verses is one to which most modern biblical scholars would object. As Dale Martin states, the apocalyptic Paul, certain of Christ's imminent return, "shows no concern for procreation whatsoever."[16] In contrast, the Renaissance discourse of sodomy makes procreation paramount. This discourse hitches a Pauline preoccupation with natural gender roles to a decidedly non-Pauline preoccupation with biological increase.

As is well known, the exchange economies of the Renaissance theater underwrote numerous antitheatrical complaints about its production of idolaters and sodomites. These complaints flowed from the pens of puritanical clergy incensed by the theater's transvestite productions and its attraction of prostitutes and gamblers. Abundant scholarship on antitheatricality has demonstrated that Shakespeare, like most early modern playwrights, was not deaf to such Pauline moralizing about sodomy or idolatry. Nor does Shakespeare's rejection of such moralizing go without saying. If, to take just one example, a comedy like *Twelfth Night* advances an antitheatrical argument from inside the theater by dramatizing "the containment of gender and class insurgency," as Jean E. Howard has argued, *The Merchant of Venice* may well have done the same by encouraging the displacement of antitheatrical censure onto a villainous Jew.[17] In what remains of this section, I want to map out the logic of this displacement, which doubles down on Paul's efforts in Romans 1 to distinguish the righteous from the unrighteous by troping the latter as religiously and sexually depraved. I emphasize that I develop this reading *strategically*, seeking as I do so to bolster as a critically pervasive account of *The Merchant of Venice* as an anti-Semitic drama of Christian sexual virtue. In the next section of this chapter, however, I argue that the play actually frustrates, in its last act, this same anti-Semitic displacement of the Pauline opposition to idolatry. Contrasting Paul's remarks in Romans 1 about perverse exchange with his anxiety about the erotics of the crucifixion, I argue that *The Merchant of Venice* blurs the boundaries between Christian marriage and friendship, on the one hand, and Jewish sodomy on the other.

Crucial to the audience's displacement of Paul's censure of perverse exchange onto Shylock is the commonplace association of Jews with usury and usury with sodomy. Medieval and Renaissance Christians typically regarded usury as a perversion in the reproductive order of things. Like the male sodomite exchanging the vagina for the anus or the mouth, the human for the nonhuman, or generally putting his seed to any purpose other than reproduction, the usurer confuses the animate and the inanimate by growing money rather than using it for trade.[18] Thomas Pie's 1604 tract *Usuries Spright Conjured* borrows the language of nature in Romans 1 to explain this connection:

> The usurer perverteth that end and use of money, which is . . . agreeable to nature: namely commutation, for commutation was the end wherefore money was ordained in humane societie; and the use of it, which naturalle use the Usuerer turneth into that which is against nature. . . . Therefore it is called a kinde of Sodomie.[19]

If money was "ordained" for the purpose of facilitating the exchange of goods and services, the usurer perverts this use by trading money for more money. On this analogy of sex and money, the charge of sodomy works in Renaissance culture to distinguish licit from illicit exchanges. Terming semen "love's *use*," for instance, the speaker of Shakespeare's Sonnet 20 deflects the charge of sodomy away from his relationship with the addressee ("Mine be thy love") and onto the addressee's relationship with women ("and thy love's use their treasure") (l.14). The speaker is not interested in the addressee's penis or semen—these things are "to [his] purpose nothing" (l.12). Thus his love, according to this strained logic, is not sodomitical.[20] *Merchant*'s Antonio likewise tries to deflect onto Shylock the charge of sodomy that critics frequently note he attracts as Bassanio's close friend: "If thou [Shylock] wilt lend this money," Antonio insists, "lend it not/As to thy friends; for when did friendship take/A breed for barren metal of his friend" (1.3.27–29)? Read alongside his pledge to Bassanio—"My purse, my person, my extremest means/Lie all unlocked to your occasions" (1.1.138–39)—Antonio's rhetorical question conflates the economic and the erotic so as to differentiate the "free gift" of Christian exchange between friends from the sodomitical breeding practices of avaricious Jews.[21]

In a fine essay arguing that Antonio wagers his flesh for Bassanio in competition with the official rites of marriage, Arthur L. Little Jr. notes that "Antonio conjures and rejects the ability of usury, of sodomy, to speak for queer friendship and desire."[22] I would add that a Jewish presence in the play encourages audience endorsement of this rejection. Bassanio and Antonio attract the charge of sodomy in what Little describes as *The Merchant of Venice*'s "encroaching heterofantasy world," which pits the viability of their friendship against the viability of male-female marriage.[23] Bassanio and Antonio also attract the charge through their treatment of marriage as a financial investment plan. Bassanio raises the eye of the Pauline moralizer when he accounts Portia not as the future mother of his children or as his helpmeet in a life of Christian virtue, but instead as the solution to his financial problems: "In Belmont is a lady *richly* left" (1.2.161, emphasis added). For Bassanio, already indebted to Antonio "in money and in love" (1.2.131), as if they were the same thing, the "worth" (1.1.167) Portia harbors is principally monetary, no less valuable or material, he adds, than the "golden fleece" for which Jason sailed (1.2.170). Bassanio's venture confounds the distinction between licit, mercantile hazarding and illicit throws of the dice. It amounts to a considerable gamble with Antonio's money and flesh. It also amounts to a considerable gamble with his own heterofantasy future. According to the rules of this game, if Bassanio chooses the wrong casket, he can never marry.

Portia invites the charge of sodomy, too, when she dons a male disguise and does not even have the decency to regret it. Whereas *Twelfth Night*'s Viola judges herself a "poor monster" (2.3.33) in her disguise as Cesario, Portia seems only to revel in the sexual deceit she undertakes with her suspiciously intimate waiting-woman. (Portia even tries to gamble on the success of her makeover: "I'll hold thee [Nerissa] any wager,/When we are both accoutered like young men/I'll prove the prettier fellow of the two" [3.5.62–65].) Her reasons for following Bassanio to Belmont are likewise as financially tainted as Bassanio's reasons for courting her. Plying Lorenzo with what he calls her "noble and true conceit/Of godlike amity"

(3.4.2–3), Portia prefaces her fiction of retreating to a monastery by explaining that Antonio and Bassanio are basically the same person:

> . . . for in companions
> That do converse and waste the time together,
> Whose souls do bear an equal yoke of love
> There must needs be a like proportion
> Of lineaments, of manners, and of spirit,
> Which makes me think that this Antonio,
> Being the bosom lover of my lord,
> Must needs be like my lord (2.3.11–17).

On the terms of such likeness in body and soul, Portia's intervention on Antonio's behalf constitutes an intervention on Bassanio's behalf as well; the difference between husband and friend is minimal. Yet the precision with which Portia negotiates the legal system makes it possible to read her motives as less related to this mystified discourse of egalitarian friendship than to monetary exigencies. Having just learned that her new husband is not the wealthy man he pretended to be, Portia may follow Bassanio to protect her financial investment.[24] One need not be a Puritan to recognize that the love between both friends and spouses in *The Merchant of Venice* is a thoroughly economic affair. Antonio's bond of his flesh only epitomizes the play's relentless commodification of persons, which rivals that of *The Comedy of Errors*. What nonetheless protects the Christians of the letter from the charge of sodomitically trafficking in "barren metal" is the presence of a Jew whose confusion of the animate and the inanimate is *so* pronounced, *so* gratuitous, that, in Solanio's hearsay report, he can barely distinguish between the fruit of his loins and lifeless coins—"My daughter! O, my ducats! My daughter" (2.7.15)!

Another Pauline term for this confusion of the animate with the inanimate is idolatry—and in several ways besides his usurious lending practices, Shylock fits the mold of the idolater as well as the sodomite. First among these ways is the plain fact that he is a Jew. In Romans 1:16, Paul identifies the Jews as the initial recipients of the gospel: "the Jew first, and also to the Grecian." Jews in Rome were the original audience of Paul's letter, and they most likely took the perverts of Paul's subsequent condemnation to be Gentiles. Dale Martin argues that Paul was "enticing" his Jewish audience "to nod in agreement with this traditional Jewish indictment of Gentile corruption" before turning, in subsequent chapters, on Jewish moralists.[25] From the perspective of most Renaissance Christians, however, the Jews rejected the gospel en masse. The subjects of Paul's subsequent condemnation were thus read as Gentiles and Jews alike.

We may look to the commentaries already cited for examples. Andrew Willet writes of Roman 1:23, "This grosse idolatrie of the heathen in worshipping the images of creeping things, and beasts with such like, did not containe it selfe among the heathen onely: But the Israelites also learned to follow the Gentiles."[26] Willet cites as evidence for this claim Ezekiel's discovery of the Elders' painted idols (Ezekiel 8:10–11), but one could easily point to the Israelites' worship of the golden calf (Exodus 32) and that sin's initiation of the Jewish routine of forgetting the One True God and falling in with the idol-worship of neighboring tribes. The authors of the *Annotations* also look to the chosen people of the Old Testament for evidence that God gives idolaters up "to their hearts lusts, unto uncleanes, to defile their owne bodies betwene them selves" (Romans 1:24) They cite the Israelites' worship of Baal and "whoredome with the daughters of Moáb" (Numbers 25:1), as well as King Asá's destruction of his father's idols and his driving "away the Sodomites" (1 Kings 15:12).[27] Each of these citations illustrates Jewish exchanges of the Creator for the created, with the *Annotations* making the additional Pauline connection to sexual perversion. For an audience steeped in such an anti-Semitic reading of scripture, Shylock is susceptible to the combined charge of idolatry and sodomy simply for belonging to such a wayward tribe.

Further coding Shylock as idolatrous is the fact that Jews were commonly represented in the Renaissance as worshippers of wealth, and the city that tolerated them, Venice, was itself represented as an idolatrous city—one too mercantile and worldly for Christian comfort. In Thomas Luxon's reading, *The Merchant of Venice* "suggests that blindly promoting merchant law . . . may make a city rich and beautiful, but it may also unintentionally give rein to the merciless and idolatrous lusts of unchristian beasts like Shylock."[28] To the play's original English audiences, Shylock likely represents this idolatrous city. He does so notwithstanding the fact that, as a Jew, he is technically "an alien," as Portia points out (4.1.344). For original English audiences, too, Shylock likely provides a distraction from the knowledge that the play's Christians are Catholics, themselves no strangers to charges of idolatry. *The Merchant of Venice*'s high-stakes theological game pits Christians against Jews, not Protestants against Catholics. Yet as James O'Rourke remarks, "the very frequency with which the Venetians are called 'Christians' indicates the stress borne by the word as it tries to persuade a Tudor audience to see Italian Catholics standing in for the same values as English Protestants."[29] As a part of this effort at persuasion, Shylock absorbs the charge of idolatry that would otherwise attach to Venetians who presumably do not, as Paul writes in that most important of Reformation verses, "live by faith" (Romans 1:17).

For any or all of these reasons, Shylock can be read as an idolater—a Jewish usurer driven by what Paul of Tarsus would call his "hearts lusts," or his lust for Antonio's heart, as a result of his rejection of the gospel. This reading takes seriously the possibility that *The Merchant of Venice* stoked the flames of English anti-Semitism by scapegoating Shylock. Cued to Romans 1, this reading also supplements the play's well-known allegory of Christian salvation in which Portia/Balthasar turns the courtroom into the site of transition between old and new covenants, Jewish law and Christian mercy. This reading adds that Portia brings the wrath of the Christian court down on the idolatrous sodomite in their midst. As Janet Adelman maintains, Portia's courtroom victory completes the emasculation of Shylock already implicit in Jessica's theft of his "stones" (2.8.20) and his earlier claim of "suff'rance" as "the badge of all our tribe" (1.3.106).[30] Whereas Antonio stood to lose his manhood under the Jewish knife, Portia turns the tables and subjects the previously "impenetrable cur" (3.3.18) to the exacting cut of the very law he so passionately "crave[s]" (4.1.201). The immediate death sentence of this idolatrous sex pervert willfully deaf to the rightness of Portia's gospel teachings might therefore seem meet. After all, the subjects of Paul's condemnation warrant execution (Romans 1:31). Any pardon they receive, the apostle later adds, comes only from the economy of free gifts they reject: "For the wages of sinne is death: but the gift of God is eternal life through Jesus Christ our Lord" (Romans 6:23). This gift is the one more or less forced upon Shylock at the end of Act 4.

If Portia's courtroom victory completes Shylock's emasculation, as Adelman so cogently argues, Portia "herself" figures Christ as so much of a man that his femininity vanishes from the theological scene. In other words, far from being the "active" woman whom Paul almost certainly condemns in Romans 1:26, Portia is the Christ whose femininity—*like his Judaism*—vanishes in his phallic fulfillment of the law. As Adelman further argues, Jessica's transvestism differs in significance from Portia's insofar as the latter actually achieves this female vanishing act. Jessica's transvestism "makes her a stand-in for the gelded and effeminized figure of her father," but Portia's transvestism "function[s] in exactly the opposite way." Portia's female body disappears between the male character of Balthasar and the body of the boy actor playing him; and through this disappearance, Portia's transvestism "repairs the suspicion that there is something too feminine in

Christianity."[31] As Christ, Portia saves Antonio from being unmanned by the idolatrous Jew with a lust for Christian flesh. As Christ, Portia makes a markedly manly business out of Christian salvation.

II

This Christian allegory of one-sex salvation falters, of course, on any insistence that the Pauline ironies surrounding Portia's courtroom performance do not disappear so easily. Under the rubrics of hypocrisy, bad faith, and injustice, many of these ironies have been well explored in the critical conversation surrounding the play's religious politics. As ubiquitous as observations about the sodomitical contours of Bassanio and Antonio's friendship are observations about Portia's "Jewish" legalism, her Jacob-like gamesmanship in outwitting Shylock through an even more rigorous reading of the law. One rarely explored point at which Portia's performance as Balthasar intersects with her performance as Christ, however, is her denial of Antonio's own attempt to play the role of sacrificial savior. Antonio figures himself as a castrated ram ready to die for his friend: "I am a tainted weather of the flock," he tells Bassanio, "Meetest for death" (4.1.113–14). When Shylock's courtroom victory seems likely, Antonio instructs Bassanio to interpret his sacrifice according to the doctrine of substitutionary atonement: "Repent but you that you shall lose your friend, / And he repents not that he pays your debt" (4.1.273–74). Eric Mallin appropriately calls Antonio a "conspicuously failed Christ figure" who "wishes to repeat Christ's strategy of incurring infinite debt by offering an unanswerable sacrifice."[32] Only Antonio does not get the chance. As the bearer of the good news that the Jew has misread the law, Portia saves Antonio's life, rescuing the body of the Christian who seeks to enact the most extreme of *imitationes Christi*.

Portia's cross-dressed prevention of Antonio's masochistic sacrifice cues us to Paul of Tarsus's labored efforts to gender masculine the multiply penetrated body of Christ. In reading these efforts, I follow biblical scholar Stephen Moore. Confronted with the potentially effeminizing sexual spectacle of the crucifixion—the sight of the naked and bloodied messiah who wills himself over to bodily violation—Moore's Paul takes recourse in another element of the Greco-Roman sex/gender system: the equation of masculinity with death-defying self-mastery. "Death hath no more dominion over him," the apostle declares, "For in that he dyed, he dyed once to sinne: but in that he liveth, he liveth to God" (Romans 6:10). Paul rescues the crucified Christ from decent into womanhood by configuring sin as deadly enslavement to the passions. In Moore's words, "Paul's Jesus, as the one who uniquely overcame sin, is implicitly held up as the supreme exemplar of masculinity for Jew and gentile alike—a hypostatized Masculinity, if you will, to which all human beings can now aspire, whether or not they have been blessed with male genitalia."[33] *The Merchant of Venice* cites Paul's salvation of Christ's masculinity through Portia/Balthasar's display of mastery over Shylock and his passionate enslavement to the law. This display contributes to scapegoating Shylock as effeminate and disappearing the female within the body of Christ. Yet the rub is that this Christ-like performance of mastery entails a concomitant denial of the Pauline proposition that masculinity is at all indexed to self-sacrifice as the act that overcomes sin. Antonio does not die for Bassanio at Shylock's hand, and Portia does not die saving Antonio. Instead, *The Merchant of Venice* splits Christ in two—into Portia and Antonio, the first a cross-dressed, boy-acted woman, and the second a melancholic, male masochist. The play then keeps both alive, as if pointing to the crucifixion as the crux in Paul's efforts to make a man out of the savior of "mankind."

If the courtroom scene of 4.1 distracts from this crux through its scapegoating of Shylock, the remainder of the play draws attention to this crux through the bawdy comedy of the ring trick. Portia establishes the marital significance of the ring when she first gives it to Bassanio: "This house, these servants, and this same myself/Are yours, my lord's. I give them with this ring" (3.2.170–71). The ring is readily legible as a wedding ring—a sign of spousal possession as well as the endless, circular commitment of husband and wife. As an object traded among Catholics, however, this ring also picks up on Puritan criticism of it as a relic of the sacramental construction of marriage and an idol of the spouse.[34] Like the slaves Shylock cites in protest of Christian hypocrisy (4.1.88–97), the ring testifies to the Venetian commodification of the self. Portia uses it to test Bassanio's willingness to trade her wealth and body (the same thing) to other men. When Bassanio summarily fails the test by giving the ring to Balthasar as payment for his courtroom services, Portia continues the conflation of the erotic and the financial by glossing the transgression as an act of sexual infidelity, threating to respond in kind: "I will become as liberal as you./I'll not deny him anything I have,/No, not my body, nor my husband's bed" (5.1.225–57). If Bassanio betrayed Portia by giving Balthasar the ring, Portia claims the right to betray Bassanio with Balthasar, too.

The ring trick belies my and Adelman's claim that Portia's femininity disappears, like Judaism from the Christian body politic, at the end of *The Merchant of Venice*. The revelation of the ring trick forces Bassanio to realize what we the audience have already known, and could well have kept in mind during the courtroom scene—that Balthasar was Portia, a woman and Bassanio's wife, all along; that the harbinger of the gospel was not a man but a woman dressed as a man. Lest we forget, Bassanio and Graziano's gratuitous remarks about their willingness to sacrifice their wives to save their friend remind us of the gendered stakes in Portia's intervention (4.1.276–82, 285–87).

At the same time, I would complicate even this claim by pointing out that the ring trick also confounds rather than clarifies the difference between the bodies of Portia, Balthasar, and the boy actor playing them. For both the characters in the play and the play's original Renaissance audiences, distinguishing these bodies by sex becomes difficult if not impossible. Portia's threat to "have that doctor for my bedfellow" (5.1.232) first collapses male and female bodies into a single self-copulating body. Portia then announces that she has already made good on this threat—"For by this ring, the doctor lay with me" (5.1.258). Nerissa seconds this admission: "For that same scrubbèd boy, the doctor's clerk, / In lieu of this last night did lie with me" (5.1.260–61). These images of adulterous self-copulation evoke Andrew Willet's description of sodomy's offense to the institution of marriage:

> By Gods ordinance, in lawfull copulation by marriage, two became one flesh, both sexes were joined together in one: by this Sodomiticall uncleannes, the same flesh is divided into two, the men with men working uncleannes with women, and so serve in stead of two sexes.[35]

Whereas marital sex joins a male and a female body into one flesh, sodomy both splits one body into two and multiplies bodies. One becomes three, two male bodies and a female. How this math works I am not entirely sure. Willet may be explicating the process of adulterous contamination I discussed in the previous chapter. The husband mixes his flesh with another male and passes the "adulterate blot" along to his wife.[36] Shakespeare's play nevertheless offers an alternative interpretation. Gesturing toward their Venetian selves and the bodies beneath their clothes, Portia's and Nerissa's dirty jokes split their own bodies into a similar triad of bodies, two men and one woman: Portia and Nerissa (two women), the doctor and the doctor's clerk (two men), and the actors beneath (two more men, if not more ambiguously gendered *boys*).

The subsequent resolution of this crisis of monogamy crisscrosses the line between marital and sodomitical eroticism no less than the ring's materialization of the self and these jokes about adultery. After Antonio guarantees that Bassanio "Will never more break faith advisedly" (5.1.252), Portia gives Antonio the ring to give to Bassanio: "Give him this, / And bid him keep it better than the other" (5.1.253–54). Antonio does so, ordering Bassanio to "swear to keep this ring" (5.1.255), which Bassanio immediately recognizes as "the same [he] gave the doctor" (5.1.256). This circuit of exchange is odd. If rings signify the espousal of those who trade them, who is (re)marrying whom? And to whom is Bassanio supposed to swear? Are Portia and Bassanio effectively renewing their vows? Or are they renewing their vows while also expanding their union to include Antonio? Echoing a common conclusion about Portia's success in sidelining Antonio, Arthur L. Little Jr. argues that the friend loses his fleshy competition with the rites of marriage to the "patriarchally and homophobically empowered" wife.[37] Portia divides her husband from his friend to claim the former as her flesh rather than Antonio's. Yet I suggest that Bassanio's ambiguous vow to keep the ring and the strange path of the ring through three hands signal not any obvious victory for heterosexual marriage over queer friendship. They signal a conjunction of marriage and friendship that belies either union's restriction to a dyad. If I hesitate to call Portia a homophobe or a guardian of patriarchal marriage, and if I hesitate to echo the critical commonplace about Antonio's status as the odd-man-out of the play's marital pairings, I do so because the vow Portia orders and the exchange she initiates suggest still another threesome—one in which husband and wife, husband and friend, and friend and wife, are all one flesh.

Further contributing to the sodomitical erosion of sexual distinctions in this plural marriage is the anal, not merely vaginal, significance of the ring (from the Latin pun on *anus*). As Laurie Shannon notes, the "suggestion of anality in Bassanio and Gratiano 'giving the rings away to men' leaves the ultimate sex(es) of this ring's bodily reference, so to speak, an open question."[38] Indeed, the anal erotic joke with which Graziano closes the play further ensures that the question remains open. After asking Nerissa whether she would like to consummate their marriage now or the next evening, Graziano concludes:

> But were the day come, I should wish it dark
> Till I were couching with the doctor's clerk.
> Well, while I live I'll fear no other thing
> So sore as keeping safe Nerissa's ring. (5.1.303–06)

In Graziano's fantasy, Nerissa's ring is her vagina, the clerk's anus, and her anus. The pun bypasses the suggestion of gynosodomy—or the "heterosexual" anal sex of Willet's disapprobation—to collapse the vagina and the anus into a single, indistinct orifice.[39] Like Portia's gift of the ring to Antonio rather than Bassanio, this joke forecloses any final distinction between sodomitical and marital erotics. Graziano can sleep with Nerissa and the doctor's clerk, for they are one and the same person; and he can have sex with Nerissa as he would with the doctor's clerk, regardless as to whether that sex is vaginal or anal. The same may be said of sex between the mirroring couple Bassanio and Portia. Following Portia's revelation that she was Balthasar, Bassanio signals that he gets her jokes about an adulterous three-way when he addresses her as the "doctor" and tells him/her, "you shall be my bedfellow. / When I am absent, then lie with my wife" (2.1.283–84). I have argued elsewhere that this collapse of the anus and the vagina is routine in early modern anal erotic discourse, and that the ends of this collapse are often misogynistic.[40] I would nonetheless like to suggest here that Graziano is not simply speaking the language of the grotesque feminine, or coding the vagina as an anus to make heterosex more palatable for this typically misogynistic Renaissance man.[41] In the queerest possible spirit of Galatians 3:28, Graziano is looking forward to a kind of sex outside a heterofantasy world—a sex in which penetrated orifices do not index sexual difference.[42]

The ring trick and Graziano's joke confound both the modern logic of sexual difference and the pre- and early modern logic of the one-sex body. At the play's end, male and female bodies are not clearly distinct, and nothing suggests that the male body has ontological priority as the more perfect version of the female body. Whereas Portia's Pauline effort to save Antonio from the Jewish knife and displace her own and Antonio's femininity onto Shylock requires her male disguise, the ring trick and the jokes that gloss it code her own body, both female and male, as equally penetrable. The ring trick and the jokes sever the historically pervasive association of penetrability with femininity, confounding the Pauline narrative of masculine salvation from bodily violation that climaxes in the courtroom scene. Considering the deep entanglement of misogynistic, sodomitical, and anti-Semitic discourses in *The Merchant of Venice*, the ring trick and Graziano's joke further suggest that, while Shylock has been left behind in Venice, the body part indexed by Shylock's name (a shy lock) might still be read as the Jewish part.[43] This part becomes the locus of Judaism on the Christian body insofar as it—not the foreskin or even the heart—becomes the focal point for anxieties about penetration. This focalization draws upon cultural associations of Jews with women and anality, but it also works toward collapsing the "us versus them" binaries of male/female, vagina/anus, and Jew/Christian that otherwise structure the play's representation of conversion. At this end of *The Merchant of Venice*, the displacement of the feminine, Jewish *something* in the Christian body politic falters on the teasing evocation of penetrated, sexually indistinct bodies—"nether Jewe nor Grecian—. . . nether male nor female."

III

In tracing the difficulty of Jewish conversion to Christianity to the fact that all people have anuses, I have made an implicit distinction between the religious conservatism of Act 4 and the queer radicalism of Act 5. I have done so because most readings of the play's Christian allegory, including Janet Adelman's, function as if that allegory concludes with Portia's courtroom victory. But this distinction now needs undoing, for ridding the Christian body politic of its wandering Jewish part is itself an endeavor that the two incidents of transvestism in the play sufficiently frustrate. Jessica's transvestism facilitates her marital conversion into the otherwise masculine community of Venetian Christians, and equates religious and sexual difference with sumptuary difference. As Adelman remarks, however, Jessica and Lorenzo's reception in Belmont makes "clear that Jessica's status as a no-Jew is as evanescent as her disguise as a gilded boy."[44] I concur, albeit with the caveat that Portia's disguise as Balthasar only further frustrates Christian efforts at Jewish purgation.

The name *Balthasar* is multivalent. As we saw in the previous chapter, Christian legend attributes it to one of the magi who visited the Christ child. More relevant here, however, is the fact that Balthasar is also the Babylonian name for the Old Testament prophet Daniel, whom many Renaissance Protestants read typologically as a figure for Christ. As Thomas Luxon points out, Daniel represents the "new" sacrifice in the "old" context. He is Jesus before his time, a figure Portia embodies when lecturing the recalcitrant Jew about the relationship between justice and mercy.[45] My additional claim is that as Daniel and Christ, Balthasar evokes the "unmanning" of the Christian body—or, in classical terms, the perverse translation of men into creatures less than men. Jonathan Walters describes these unmen as "men in sex, but not in gender," neither male nor female, but not outside the Greco-Roman sex/gender system either.[46] Unmen include eunuchs and slaves, children and foreigners, barbarians and bottoms. Somewhere between male and female, these unmen are akin to the Renaissance figure of the boy: a creature neither female nor (yet) male, one of whom is playing Portia.[47]

In a Jewish hermeneutic tradition that Jerome translates into Christianity, Daniel was one such unman. As a servant to the "chief of the Eunuches" (Daniel 1:7), Daniel was a eunuch. Yet Renaissance Christians (in contrast to early ones) tended to argue away or ignore the testicular implications of this designation.[48] Attuned to what Kathryn Ringrose describes as the reinvention of the eunuch as "a perfect servant," the authors of the *Annotations*, for example, gloss away any genital meaning to Daniel 1:7. In their first edition, they account a "eunuch" as "one whom the king nourished, and brought up to be ruler over other countrys afterward."[49] By the printing of the second edition in 1651, their denial is more explicit. They assert that Daniel was not a eunuch "in the strictest sense; as the mind of some is."[50] This aversion to the strict sense also shows itself in the Geneva translation of Matthew 19:12, where Jesus responds to the disciples' question about the good of marriage by replying that some people have made themselves eunuchs (*eunoucoi*) for God.[51] The Vulgate preserves the vexatious word: "Sunt eunuchi qui se ipsos castraverunt propter regnum caelorum." The King James does, too: "There be eunuchs, which have made themselves eunuchs for the kingdom of heaven's sake." The Geneva Bible avoids the castrating implication of such asceticism, however: "There be some chaste, which have made them selves chaste for the kingdome of heaven." This translation of eunuchry to chastity in the Geneva's Matthew, and a eunuch into a not-eunuch in the *Annotations*' Daniel, has much to do with the emasculating implications of castration for the body of Christ. When Portia disguises herself as Balthasar, she embodies these implications. If her phallic supplement risks coding her as one of the women Paul condemns in Romans 1:26, her phallic lack also makes her, even more perversely, most typologically fit to play the role of savior.

At stake in Portia's courtroom disguise and the ring trick is nothing less than the sex of the savior. Stephen Moore argues that Paul of Tarsus saves Christ from feminine degradation by making him a model of male self-mastery. I have suggested *The Merchant of Venice* resists this salvation through its representation of the savior's body as sexually undifferentiated and penetrable. Part of the biblical allegory one witnesses in *The Merchant of Venice* is the allegory of Christ's sexual contortions on the cross. He is both top and bottom, master of sin and multiply penetrated. Citing Richard Rambuss's work on the homoerotics of Renaissance devotional poetry, Moore notes that not every penetrated male body is perforce feminized: "Are male bodies without their own orifices?"[52] Moore's Paul answers this question with a "defensive clenching" while celebrating his submission to

Jesus as Jesus submits God: "Jesus submits himself obediently to God's excruciating demands. Paul submits himself to Jesus in turn, opens himself utterly to Jesus, is entered and possessed by Jesus. And throughout this steamy scene, there is not a single female face in sight, not to mention a female orifice."[53] The ring trick and Graziano's joke reopen Moore's question, however, carrying the body of Christ beyond sexual difference altogether, and inviting us to behold the "unnatural" act at the core of the Christian salvation narrative: the abomination of men turning into women, and women turning into men, with no end to the turning.

PART II

The Works of the Flesh

CHAPTER 3

Chaste Impossibilities: Adultery and Individuation in *Othello*

> OTHELLO: Are you not a strumpet?
> DESDEMONA: No, as I am a Christian.
> If to preserve this vessel for my lord
> From any other foul unlawful touch
> Be not to be a strumpet, I am none.
> OTHELLO: What, not a whore?
> DESDEMONA: No, as I shall be saved. (4.2.84–89)

In *The Merchant of Venice*, Jessica stakes her claim to membership in the body of Christ on her marriage to the Christian Lorenzo. In *Othello*, Desdemona stakes her claim to membership in the body of Christ on her chastity—the preservation of her body "from any other unlawful touch." Drawing on the deep historical construction of marriage as a vehicle for God's extension of grace, Shakespeare's tragedy places Othello and Desdemona's union at the crossroads of salvation and damnation. At this crossroads, Desdemona's fidelity to her husband ostensibly testifies to her Christian citizenship, if not also to her status as a Christ figure, the "pearl" to Othello's "base Judean" (that "Judean" being either Herod or Judas, 3.2.356).[1]

Meanwhile, Othello's *lack* of faith in his wife's chastity testifies to his status as both a religious and racial outsider. Robert N. Watson has argued that Othello's tragedy is a particularly Protestant one; the sacramental draw of Othello and Desdemona's marriage notwithstanding, *Othello* allegorically propagandizes for the doctrine of salvation by faith alone.[2] Huston Diehl has analogized Othello to Doubting Thomas, the apostle who sought "ocular proof" (3.3.365) of the resurrected Christ, only to receive it with rebuff: "Blessed are they who have not seene, and have beleved" (John 20:29).[3] Jane Hwang Degenhardt has most recently argued that Othello's anxieties about his wife's infidelity answer to early modern Christian anxieties over Muslim conversion to the true faith.[4] Whether indexed to the Catholic rejection of solafidianism, the severance of faith from ocular proof, or the difficulty of converting black bodies, Othello's exclusion from the body of Christ accords in these readings with his failure to believe that his wife is no foul strumpet.

Circling around Shakespeare's interracial couple are questions about unions of the flesh—black and white, Muslim and Christian—that potentially signify as adulterous (from *adulteration*, or illicit mixing).[5] These questions are complex political and theological ones about the geographic and biological reach of Christendom, the common heritage of Christianity and Islam, and the limits of Pauline universalism in stubborn differences of the flesh.[6] Within the considerable body of scholarship on Othello's lack of faith, it has nonetheless become routine to address these questions by placing Desdemona's chastity beyond doubt. Indeed, for most critics of the play, there is simply no good reason to credence the allegation of infidelity that, after all, we watch Iago and Othello manufacture. Undoubtedly chaste and Christian (for they are the same thing) despite Othello's "blackening" accusation of infidelity, Desdemona becomes, in Shakespeare's tragedy, the victim of dually racist and misogynistic anxieties about the "infidel." I aim in this chapter to contest this reading, but not to purge Desdemona or Othello from the body of Christ. I claim that critical certainty about Desdemona's chastity often pits an essentialist definition of the virtue against the racist association of miscegenation with adultery. In so doing, these claims of certainty perform an ahistorical rescue of Desdemona's reputation. They also diminish Desdemona's independent existence as a desiring subject—her equally adulterous withholding from the marital body her husband supposedly heads.

In the previous two chapters, I argued that any ostensible idealization of marital monogamy in *The Comedy of Errors* and *The Merchant of Venice* gives way under the dynamics of group embodiment. In this chapter, I shift my analysis away from group embodiment and toward the problem of individuation, or the persistence of difference between two or more people joined as one flesh. With this shift comes a new inflection on the Pauline flesh, which "works," in the words of Galatians 5:19, to divide bodies as well as join them. This flesh—the flesh of Paul of Tarsus rather than Paul of Ephesus—adulterates and fornicates. It is unclean and wanton. Its possession, I argue, is incommensurate with chastity, which explains why Othello equates chastity with disembodiment. "Yet I'll not shed her blood," he says on entering her chamber, "Nor scar that whiter skin of hers than snow, / As smooth as monumental alabaster" (5.1.3–5). For Othello, the only "white," which is to say chaste, woman is a dead woman, her skin not skin (flesh) but stone.

Offering a reading of *Othello* by way of a reading of its criticism, this chapter begins by demonstrating that Desdemona's chastity has only recently become a critical given. The cessation of critical condemnation of Desdemona largely accompanies a late-twentieth-century critical turn toward Othello's psychology—a move away from her obvious wantonness and toward her husband's vulnerability to deceit. For feminist and critical race scholarship on the play, this shift has been especially salutary, affording rich explorations of the misogynistic, racist, and sex-negative ideologies propelling *Othello* to its tragic end. At the same time, this shift has been guided by a recalibrated understanding of chastity as a virtue of abstinence from particular illicit sex acts—namely, extramarital genital intercourse—rather than, as Iago and Othello conceive of it, a racialized virtue of abstinence from illicit acts *and thoughts*. Because chastity is a highly mobile fantasy, I argue that one is not necessarily wrong to consider it primarily a matter of cognitive or racial integrity. Nor is one necessarily wrong to use this same standard to deem Desdemona unchaste. One is wrong, however, to assume that chastity according to this standard is even possible. Predicated on the one-sex model of the marital body, this standard demands a wife's complete relinquishment of mind and body to her husband and thus her complete transparency to the same.[7] It insists on a form of self-abdication that Desdemona inevitably fails to effect, as Othello recognizes when he decries the "curse of marriage, / That we can call these delicate creatures ours, / And not their appetites" (3.3.272–74).

I

Common in recent criticism on *Othello* is the assertion that Desdemona never commits adultery. For the first several centuries of criticism on the play, however, the case of Desdemona's chastity was hardly so clear. Othello's wife has been tried and found wanting for sins including elopement, elopement with a Moor, joking about sex with Iago, advocating on Cassio's behalf, advocating *adamantly* on Cassio's behalf, lying to Othello about the handkerchief, remarking on Lodovico's handsomeness, talking about adultery with Emilia, and, in one wildly speculative case, sleeping with Cassio before the action of the play.[8] These trials begin, at least in the critical archive, with *Othello*'s first critic, the Iago-ish Thomas Rymer. In his 1693 *Short View of Tragedy*, Rymer includes among his many objections to *Othello* that Shakespeare takes "a Venetian Lady to be the Fool." Although he professes equal bafflement by Shakespeare's choice of a Moor for the play's protagonist, Rymer justifies Othello's suspicion of his wife, declaiming Desdemona's audacity in running off with the Moor, "Bed[ding]" him on their wedding night, and then, the very next day, "importuning and teizing him for a young smock-fac'd Lieutenant."[9] Roughly a century later, US president and sometimes Shakespearean John Quincy Adams echoes Rymer when he proclaims Desdemona "little less than a wanton."[10] W. H. Auden only slightly more graciously suspects, still another century later, that had Desdemona lived, and spent more time with the likes of Emilia, she might soon "have taken a lover."[11] As late as 1974, Jan Kott hedges that "Desdemona is faithful, but must have something of a slut in her. Not *in actu*, but *in potentia*."[12]

To be sure, Desdemona has had what we might well call her defenders of the faith. A number of twentieth-century scholars, especially, reacted against her critical defamation not merely by affirming her virtue, but by elevating her to the status of a saint—the "divine Desdemona" of, ironically enough, Cassio's description (2.1.74). Robert B. Heilman argues in 1956 that Shakespeare "gives us devil and saint" (Othello and Desdemona, respectively) to dramatize "the extremes of hate and love."[13] Robert G. Hunter maintains in 1976 that Desdemona "is not only capable of goodness," but "*incapable of anything else*"—she is "a natural embodiment of grace apparently untainted by original sin."[14] Both Heilman and Hunter place Desdemona's goodness beyond all question; for both hagiographers, there is simply no argument to be made about the degree of Desdemona's virtue. But neither Hunter nor Heilman soars to such rhetorical heights in defense of Desdemona as A. C. Bradley. In 1905, Bradley fawns over

Othello's wife as "the 'eternal womanly' in its most lovely and adorable form"—

> simple and innocent as a child, ardent with the courage and idealism of a saint, radiant with that heavenly purity of heart which men worship because nature so rarely permits it to themselves. . . . [She] had no theories about universal brotherhood, and no phrases about "one blood in all the nations of the earth" or "barbarian, Scythian, bond and free".[15]

So saintly is Bradley's Desdemona that the complexities of Pauline universalism never occur to her. Untainted by racism or xenophobia, Desdemona is a creature sans flesh. She knows only a love so natural and strong—so *pure*—that it needs no foundation in "theory" and no prop in truisms about shared blood.

Early feminist Shakespeareans worked to find a way between these two critical extremes. Shirley Nelson Garner contends in 1976, for example, that "Desdemona is neither goddess nor slut."[16] Between these poles lies the figure of the "human"—a woman who, while not guilty of adultery, is still "capable of treachery." Garner's Desdemona has not cheated on her husband. But as we see when Desdemona discusses adultery with Emilia in 4.3, Desdemona does inhabit her body, with all the temptations and liabilities to which the body is heir.[17] Ann Jennalie Cook proposes in 1980 that Shakespeare structures his play in a way that makes us unsure of Desdemona's honesty "until it is too late."[18] Cook's universal audience suffers the constant elevation of suspicions, only to realize their error when Desdemona acquits herself with her famous last words, "A guiltless death I die" (5.2.132).

The year 1980 turned out to be something of a watershed for *Othello* criticism, with Cook's essay authorizing a doubt about Desdemona's honesty that would soon thereafter reflect poorly on the critic. Following quickly on the heels of Stanley Cavell's 1979 essay "Epistemology and Tragedy: A Reading of *Othello*," Stephen Greenblatt and Edward Snow published pieces whose influence partly consisted in turning the critical current away from the "saint or strumpet" debate altogether. With varying degrees of intention, each critic distances himself from condemnation or sanctification, resituating the binary as the product of the same erotic revulsion that drives Othello to kill. Snow is the most explicit in this endeavor, reading the "cause" (5.2.1) for which Othello murders Desdemona as the general's own "pathological male animus toward sexuality."[19] Greenblatt's Othello suffers an Augustinian fear of all sexual pleasure that leads him to construe even marital sex as a violation of the seventh commandment.[20]

Characterizing the accusation against Desdemona as "insanely false," Cavell finds Othello writhing in skeptical torment about his wife's independence as a desiring subject; Cavell's Othello *creates* the fantasy of Desdemona's infidelity as a response to the terrible fact of her individuation.[21] In each analysis, the division of Desdemona into saint or strumpet bespeaks a fatal problem of judgment—a problem the critic should recognize and resist repeating regardless as to his or her immediate alliance with any feminist cause.[22]

Published alongside Cook's essay in the 1980 issue of *Shakespeare Studies*, W. D. Adamson's "Unpinned or Undone?: Desdemona and the Problem of Sexual Innocence" most succinctly articulates the position on Desdemona's chastity that has become critically commonplace over the past thirty-five-odd years. Arguing that the standard binary amounts to a false choice, Adamson maintains that Desdemona's innocence coexists with a rich sexuality. The "conspicuous expression of her innocence," he writes, "is her vital exuberance, including the hot, moist hand of sexual vitality. She herself is a natural alternative to 'saint or strumpet,' which is all along a tragically false dilemma exploited by Iago."[23] For Adamson, Desdemona's fusion of innocence with vital exuberance—materialized in the hand Othello feels as "Hot, hot and moist" (3.4.37)—purifies the meaning of her most seemingly incriminating statements, including the long-damning "Lodovico is a proper man" (4.3.34). Regarding the doubts about Desdemona's honesty that bedevil even feminist critics like Garner, Adamson stakes out an admittedly "absolutist" position:

> She *must* be read as having been unwaveringly faithful to the Moor—though we may not be absolutely assured of this until just before her murder—or Iago begins to seem correct in principle when he makes obscene slanders against her, Othello begins to appear justified in murdering her as an unfaithful wife, and the play's entire structure of meaning collapses like a house built of sand.[24]

I bracket Adamson's assumption that an unfaithful wife might well deserve murdering to emphasize his imperative replacement of doubt with faith. We may not know that Desdemona has been faithful until she acquits herself in the final scene, but we have to read her as such anyway.[25] Otherwise there is no tragedy. In the decades since, the corollary idea that Desdemona is both a sexual agent and innocent of infidelity has helped most critics produce a wife who clearly never cheats on her husband. The hermeneutic mandate is no longer necessary.

Here are several statements of the obvious from some of the most significant modern critics of *Othello*. In 1985's *Broken Nuptials in Shakespeare's Plays*, Carol Thomas Neely argues that Othello needs some "realistic grounding in the facts of sex."[26] Whereas Desdemona "consecrates herself to [her husband] physically and spiritually," never breaking faith with him, Othello suffers "contempt for women, disgust at sexuality, terror of cuckoldry, [and] the preference for literal death over metaphorical 'death.'"[27] In 1992's *Suffocating Mothers*, Janet Adelman diagnoses Othello with a "diseased imagination" of women as inherently promiscuous, yet she distinguishes *Othello* from the earlier *Troilus and Cressida* by arguing that Desdemona, unlike Cressida, is "innocent not only of the crime Othello imagines, but also of the fantasies that infect him."[28] In 2002's *Shakespeare, Race, and Colonialism*, Ania Loomba remarks that the audience knows Desdemona's "honesty" as a matter "of course," and maintains that this knowledge helps tie the play's Gordian knot of racial and sexual politics: "Any sympathy for Othello reinforces the misogynistic sentiments mouthed by some characters, and any sympathy for Desdemona endorses the view that Othello is a 'gull, a dolt, a devil.'"[29] Introducing his 2006 Oxford edition of the play, Michael Neill inserts a parenthetical reminder of Desdemona's honesty as he puzzles over the play's discourse of occluded monstrosity: *Othello*, he writes, "taunts its audience with the possibility that (despite Desdemona's fidelity) Iago only discovers what was always there beneath the Moor's civil manners, advertised by the blackness of his skin—the barbarous and 'malignant' alien."[30] I take Neill's seemingly nonrestrictive assertion of chastity's certainty to illustrate what has come to function as a structuring paradox in these recent decades of *Othello* criticism. The play casts all truths about gender, race, and religion in doubt, except the truth of Desdemona's gendered and racialized Christian chastity.

Such certainty about Desdemona's chastity—synonymously termed her fidelity, honesty, constancy, and innocence—indeed proves curious for a number of reasons frequently explored in contemporary *Othello* criticism. First, from its opening line, "Tush, never tell me!" (1.1.1), *Othello* sets in motion dizzying dynamics of revelation and occlusion in which Desdemona's honesty, like Iago's, is inextricably bound. Following Brabanzio's warning to his new son-in-law, "She has deceived her father, and may thee" (1.3.292), Othello sets his "life upon her [Desdemona's] faith" immediately before turning to address "Honest Iago" (1.3.293). If my reader will pardon me still more literature review, it is worth demonstrating that these dynamics of revelation and occlusion have themselves become critical commonplaces since their "discovery" in the late 1980s and early '90s. In an essay that first joined feminist and critical race scholarship on the play, Karen Newman argues that these dynamics form a "scopic economy that privileges sight"; they structure the "spectacular opposition of black and white" and motivate "Othello's demand for ocular proof of Desdemona's infidelity."[31] Patricia Parker reframes this scopic economy as one of dilation—of opening, especially, the "secret female place to show."[32] Michael Neill reads the bed on stage in Act 5 as the "grimly material form" of this deep structural "tension between secrecy and disclosure"—the "hideous" revelation, finally, of the marital consummation scene the play has teased but not shown.[33] ("This object poisons sight," Lodovico says of the bodies on the bed. "Let it be hid" [5.2.374–75].) To conclude amidst all this grim teasing and upset sight that Desdemona has certainly not had sex with Cassio or with anyone other than her husband—or even with her husband, as Neill points out—is to reach a conclusion despite the play's Iago-like insistence that it will never tell.

This conclusion is likewise curious because fugitive chastity cuts a readily familiar figure across the stage of early modernity. As Laura Gowing writes, "Bodies rarely furnished reliable testimony of chastity or unchastity. Even pregnancy and childbirth were often impossible to prove."[34] While irreducible to the dubious standard of an "intact" hymen, virginity was supposed to evince itself visually, at the moment of its loss, as blood on the wedding sheets. This blood may or may not spot the sheets Desdemona orders Emilia to put on her bed. This blood may or may not be figured, too, by the strawberries on the play's most notorious symbol of loss, the handkerchief. (According to Othello, the strawberries were dyed in the fluid of mummified "maidens' hearts" [3.4.73]—the hearts of women who, in a possible anticipation of Desdemona's fate, died, pun intended, with their hymens intact.) Outside the bedroom, virginity was supposed to show itself in modest deportment and rare, quiet speech. These qualities were often regarded as signs of sexual integrity, as "outward, visual manifestations," in Theodora Jankowski's words, of inner virtue.[35] Maidenhood was sometimes still further called upon to prove itself through urological and astrological analyses, as well as incredible exams like the one Thomas Middleton and William Rowley imagine in *The Changeling*—the consumption of a potion that makes the maiden coordinately gape, sneeze, and laugh.[36] (These tests were hardly foolproof, as *The Changeling* demonstrates when Beatrice-Joanna fakes the symptoms and pays Diaphanta to substitute for her in bed.) Of course, marital fidelity only proved more elusive than virginity. As the guarantor of children's legitimacy and, reflexively, a husband's proper performance of his watchful office, wifely chastity was a usual subject—especially in the theater—of suspicion and doubt.[37]

To be fair, not every single modern critic has placed Desdemona's chastity beyond doubt. Reading *Othello* against early modern legal standards of evidence, Katharine Eisaman Maus, for instance, remarks that Othello would do better to "accept a degree of uncertainty in his relation to Desdemona."[38] Similar advice is implicit in Newman and Parker. Critics have also not ignored how the charge of infidelity follows from the interracial quality of Desdemona and Othello's marriage. Michael Neill excavates this racist logic whereby miscegenation signifies as adultery and adultery as miscegenation; and Lara Bovilsky enlists this same logic in her argument about Desdemona's legibility as a black woman.[39] Rarely considered, however, is the possibility that the charge of adultery is something more than the product of a dually misogynistic and racist imagination. Neill explicitly forecloses this possibility again when he substitutes a racist logic for a homophobic one, describing Iago's "seduction" of Othello as "the one *real* adultery of the play."[40]

In what follows, I argue that Desdemona has committed adultery—not simply through becoming one flesh with a black man, but also through her continued existence apart from him as a separate human being with her own thoughts and actions, her own flesh. I make this argument in three stages. First, I draw on an especially strict construction of chastity as unimpeachable self-display of marital oneness to quite easily prove Desdemona unchaste. I therein aim to demonstrate that modern apologies for Desdemona often separate appearance from reality, or in the play's vocabulary "seeming" from "being," in order to rescue her from the accusation of infidelity. In the second section, I pivot off Neely's claim that Othello needs education in "the facts of sex" to argue that many of Desdemona's defenders implicitly reduce sex to genital intercourse—and this despite the play's more skeptical inquiry into the acts that occasion chastity's loss. In the third section, I maintain that the assumption of Desdemona's constancy has choreographed our acrobatic efforts to parse her final words. These efforts illustrate the persistence of a Bradley-like tendency toward dehumanizing Desdemona by denying her even the capacity for deceit.

II

The construction of marital chastity on which I want to draw to prove Desdemona unchaste encompasses both sexual action and sexual thought, and it coalesces around female self-display.[41] This construction sometimes appears in the form of praise. Edmund Spenser, for example, celebrates the chastity of his bride Elizabeth Boyle by noting that she keeps her gaze "still fastened on the ground," conscious that any "glaunce awry/ . . . may let in a little thought unsownd" (*Epithalamion*, 234, 236–37).[42] More ominously, this construction of chastity also circulates throughout Renaissance marriage manuals and sermons that instruct wives, like maidens, in the ways of Christian conduct.[43]

Juan Luis Vives is doubtless this construction's most influential early modern advocate. In his 1524 *Education of a Christian Woman*, the Valencian humanist admonishes wives to police their habitus, even more carefully than maidens do, for any sign of dishonesty, including inappropriate dress, speech, and facial expressions. To possess virginity, he writes, is to possess "integrity of the mind, which extends also to the body, an integrity free of all corruption and contamination."[44] The mind, he reiterates, is the first line of the body's defense: "The mind must be particularly fortified, lest it be defiled in a virgin body, so that all the treasures and beauty of integrity will endure there, firm and unassailable."[45] Marriage does not relax a woman's need for mental guardianship, moreover. In a chapter misleadingly entitled "What *Thoughts* Should Occupy the Mind of a Woman When She Marries," Vives maintains that a wife must think *only* on Genesis 2:24's "They shall be two in one flesh":

> To fulfill this law and express it manifest in her deeds will be her one thought night and day, conscious that no virtue will be lacking in the one who considers herself to be one with her husband. May she so live that she both plainly *appear to be and truly be one with him*. On the contrary, she who does not do this will be entirely without virtue.[46]

Throughout *Education*, Vives stresses the absolute connection between seeming and being, and the consequent loss of all virtue with any slip in thought and action.[47] What Iago deems "an essence that's not seen" (4.1.17) *must* be seen, according to Vives, in how a wife lives within the marital body her husband heads. She must live as one flesh with him—her thoughts one with her spouse, her actions an extension and complement to his.

This predication of chastity on the identity of a wife with her husband is one the Chorus cites in the third act of Elizabeth Carey's *Tragedy of Mariam*—a closet drama about adultery, jealousy, and race sometimes compared to *Othello*.[48] "'Tis not enough," the Chorus preaches, "for one that is a wife/To keep her spotless from an act of ill" (3.3.96–97).[49] The chaste wife must also "bare herself" of "will" to her husband (3.3.99), relinquishing all that will entails—her thoughts and desires, as well as any property—to her husband when she joins with him as one flesh. The questions the Chorus then asks about Mariam's willingness to speak her mind rather than her husband Herod's are rhetorical, posed as if their answers were common sense:

> When to their husbands they [wives] themselves do bind,
> Do they not wholly give themselves away?
> Or give they but their body, and not their mind,
> Reserving that, though best, for others' prey? (3.3.114–17)

Carey does not necessarily intend the Chorus to speak with final authority about Mariam's chastity. Sohemus has just addressed Mariam as "chaste queen" (3.3.87), and Mariam has just twice declared her own "innocence" (3.353, 362). Herod's former wife Doris deems Mariam an adulteress for the altogether different reason that Mariam replaced her: "You in adult'ry lived nine year together,/And heaven will never let adult'ry in" (4.8.53–54). As a statement of communal sentiment echoing Vives and numerous other marriage moralizers, however, the Chorus's judgment of Mariam is damning.

Also frequent in Renaissance discourses of chastity are claims that the loss of chastity tracks back to an adulteration of thought. As Alexander Niccholes writes in his 1615 *Discourse of Marriage and Wiving*, "True chastity doth not onely consist in keeping the body from uncleanesse, but in with-holding the minde from lust."[50] Similarly, Daniel Rogers, in his 1642 *Matrimoniall Honour*, distinguishes four interrelated types of chastity (spirit, prevention, bed, and body), but makes "the center of Chastity . . . the mind." Statements about the separation of mind and body are likely familiar to early modern scholars as wedges driven into accusations regarding the loss of chastity through rape. If chastity is a virtue of the mind, it may well survive the body's adulteration. At the same time, statements like Rogers's also admit a porous boundary between mind and body through which the adulterate blot may pass. Shakespeare's Lucrece asks about the mind/body connection after Tarquin rapes her: "May my pure mind with the foul act dispense,/My low-declinèd honour to advance?" (1704–05). Yet when her audience of lords declares that her "body's stain her mind untainted clears" (1710), Lucrece refuses the partition: "'No, no,' quoth she, 'no dame hereafter living/By my excuse shall claim excuse's giving'" (1714–15). By stabbing herself, Lucrece not only releases her "soul . . .

from the deep unrest/Of that polluted prison [the body] where it breathed" (1724–26). She attempts to foreclose any absolute separation of mind and body to which more dishonest women than her could appeal.

Daniel Rogers also refuses any absolute separation of mind and body: "If the thoughts bee impure," he explains, "they will betray the body to the eyes, eares, and companie of the uncleane, and Satan will play the Proctor, soone bringing one uncleane person to another."[51] This warning about Satan's quick acceptance of the invitation by impure thoughts could easily serve to gloss Iago and Desdemona's exchange about white, black, and witty women in 2.1. By engaging with Iago's bawdy, Desdemona betrays her own body, handing him a piece of her heart and mind. Yet comparing several actual glosses on this exchange illustrates how we as critics have come to hold Desdemona to a much less stringent standard of chastity that dismisses slippery-slope thinking as fallacious and excuses her otherwise unseemly show.

M. R. Ridley, editor of the 1958 Arden edition of *Othello*, speaks for many critics before him when he refers to Desdemona and Iago's exchange as "one of the most unsatisfactory passages in all of Shakespeare" and "a long piece of cheap backchat."[52] For Ridley, joking about whores is almost as disgraceful as being one. In his 1997 Arden edition, E. A. J. Honigmann queries whether such sour opinions "tell us more about the critics or about Desdemona."[53] Like the Chorus's questions about Mariam, Honigmann's question is rhetorical; the answer is supposedly obvious. But it is telling that to rescue Desdemona from such old-fashioned judgment, Honigmann also lifts her from history: "The purpose of 2.1.100ff, *we would say today*, is to portray Desdemona as aware of the way of the world."[54] If Honigmann's Desdemona suffers any fault, it is one of mere "overconfidence . . . that reflects an essential innocence."[55] Edward Pechter more forthrightly comes to Desdemona's defense in his 1999 survey of *Othello*'s critical history. Allowing that the scene seems written to instill doubt about Desdemona's chastity, Pechter points out that the scene also "goes out of its way to reassure us" through Desdemona's remark that she needs distraction from her concerns about her husband's ship: "I am not merry, but I do beguile/The thing I am by seeming otherwise" (2.1.125–26).[56] Muffling the uncanny echo of Iago's "I am not what I am" (1.1.65), Pechter concludes that all this worry over Desdemona's virtue amounts to much ado about nothing: "Surely it is not 'dirty' to understand sexual banter. A sexual nature doesn't make you a whore."[57] Yet the problem remains that having a "sexual nature" alone very well may. When held to one fairly pervasive standard of chastity presumably shared by more than a few in the play's early-seventeenth-century audience, and certainly more than a few throughout the play's history, Desdemona can be regarded as a whore simply for understanding Iago's jokes, to say nothing of urging them on.

Like Rogers's Satan, Iago turns this exacting standard of chastity to his own advantage in his ensuing exchange with Roderigo, whom he instructs in the art of reading Desdemona's "paddl[ing] with the palm of [Cassio's] hand" (2.1.245–46). Roderigo decriminalizes the gesture as "courtesy" (2.1.247). But Iago reenlists it as evidence of both past and future sin:

> Lechery, by this hand; an index and obscure prologue to the history of lust and foul thoughts. . . . When these mutualities so marshal the way, hard at hand comes the master and main exercise, th'incorporate conclusion (2.1.248–53).

In Iago's narrative, holding hands provides the front matter for a story ("history") of illicit thought and action—the "marshal" for the "main exercise," in the second metaphor. Simultaneously, holding hands provides evidence of what has *already* happened—the other meaning of "history," the "conclusion." Here we find a ready instance of the play's deployment of the trope of the *preposterous*, the collapse of *in actu* and *in potentia* underwriting Thomas Rymer's famous claim that *Othello* is a play "fraught . . . with improbabilities."[58] Yet what makes this particular deployment of the trope properly *Satanic*, apropos of Rogers's warning, is its correspondence with, or doubling of, Christ's own preposterous construction of adultery. When Desdemona betrays her impurity, through jesting, to the company of the unclean, Iago responds by playing Jesus.[59]

In the Gospel of Matthew, Jesus declares that "whosoever loketh on a woman to lust after her, hathe committed adulterie with her already in his heart" (5:28). Jesus's "already" equates "the main exercise" with the thought of the exercise, bracketing the question of whether one intends to act on one's thoughts. Jesus's "already" even more preposterously renders the act of adultery a *precedent* for thought. The paradigmatic man, in this standard so much more often deployed against women, has committed adultery before he looks. Both state and ecclesiastical courts throughout the Middle Ages and the Renaissance were obliged to distinguish intent, act, and desire, but the jurisprudential logic of Matthew's Jesus and Shakespeare's Iago (and both Roderigo and Othello under Iago's tutelage) insists on their consonance.[60] Every evidence of illicit thought is itself evidence of both simultaneous and previous action. There is no foul thought, no slight relaxation of the sensory guard, which is not already an act of adultery. Not long before he works himself into a vengeful fury, Othello implies this foregone conclusion about Desdemona's infidelity when he describes her "devour[ing]" his stories "with a greedy ear" (1.3.149, 148)—letting down her sensory defenses and opening her "appetite" to this man she has yet to marry.

For us as modern critics and audience members, this preposterous standard of chastity begs for the substitution of a more lenient one. Implying that Jesus, Vives, and Iago are simply wrong, we detach action from thought and potential, and find for chastity's presence or absence on grounds ostensibly more solid. In doing so, however, we often tacitly posit what chastity *really* is, arresting a fugitive construction. Furthermore, we do so even though *Othello* invites a critique of all such constructions through its focus on the problem of marital individuation—the persistent existence of difference between two joined as one flesh. Here we need to recall Stanley Cavell's reading. For Cavell, the truth Othello finds so intolerable is not that the other (Desdemona) does not exist, but that she does: "Nothing could be more certain to Othello than that Desdemona . . . is flesh and blood; is separate from him; other."[61] Cavell's Othello knows Desdemona to be innocent. Her fidelity, Cavell argues, is simply a more awful truth—the accusation of infidelity the general's response to the fact that Desdemona is "separate from him, outside, beyond command, commanding, her captain's captain."[62] To claim, as Cavell does, that Desdemona never commits adultery posits a standard of chastity that decouples thought from action and effectively shortens the extent of Desdemona's separation from the "knowing" audience. The claim implies that, despite all her time off stage—not to mention the fact that she is not even a real person—we know her every move, an impossibility that Brabanzio's ignorance of her elopement underscores. It also implies that unlike every other character in the play, and despite what she says about herself ("I do beguile"), Desdemona is simply incapable of dissembling. (In this respect she is also, paradoxically, nothing but a primitive stage character, too one-dimensional to deceive.) To do justice to Desdemona's individuality, I maintain, means recognizing it in action and thought. It means recognizing her as a creature of the flesh whose flesh is not merely adulterated through becoming one with the flesh of her black husband, but also through its resistance to the same.

III

W. D. Adamson's coupling of sexuality and innocence affords Desdemona the ability to think about sex, and even joke about it, without being unchaste. This uncoupling of thought from action, I have argued, underwrites assertions of Desdemona's honesty as a matter of course. It also underwrites the dominant view of *Othello* as a play about misogynistic misreading. Here, for instance, is Lena Cowen Orlin on the "simple and unarguable . . . fact . . . of Desdemona's innocence": "In Desdemona we find all the warning signs of unchastity that would have been recognized by Henry Smith, John Dod, Robert Cleaver, and a score of their fellow authors. *But here all those signs are wrong.*"[63] In this section, I would like to suggest that Othello and Iago's interrogation of what Carol Thomas Neely calls "the facts of sex" makes it all the more difficult to claim that all those signs are wrong. At stake in this interrogation is the availability of sex to knowledge: that is, both the definition of sex—namely, adultery—and the ability of sight and speech to offer proof of sex.[64] Iago succeeds in "deceiving" Othello in part because Iago so relentlessly questions the facts, plunging Othello into an epistemological crisis whose symptoms include a seizure and homicidal rage.

I focus on the first scene of Act 4. Repeating the play's initial drop of its audience into the discursive dynamics of secrecy and disclosure, this scene opens on Othello and Iago in the middle of a conversation:

> IAGO: Will you think so?
> OTHELLO: Think so, Iago?
> IAGO: What, to kiss in private?
> OTHELLO: An unauthorized kiss.
> IAGO: Or to be naked with her friend in bed
> An hour or more, not meaning any harm?
> OTHELLO: Naked in bed, Iago, and not mean any harm?
> It is hypocrisy against the devil.
> They that mean virtuously and yet do so,
> The devil their virtue tempts, and they tempt heaven.
> IAGO: If they do nothing, 'tis a venial slip. (4.1.1–9)

Stephen Greenblatt identifies this exchange as "a brutally comic parody of the late medieval confessional manuals with their casuistical attempts to define the precise moment at which temptation passes over into mortal sin." Iago assumes the "laxist position," goading Othello into becoming the more rigorous casuist who eventually executes the equally rigorous punishment of adultery with death.[65] I would add that this casuistry also affords a grim demonstration of the difficulty of determining the facts of sex. At issue is not simply whether Desdemona and Cassio have had genital intercourse—the act most critics equate with adultery when they excuse all of Desdemona's otherwise evident slips (joking with Iago, paddling Cassio's palm, remarking on Lodovico's handsomeness, etc.). At issue is whether a kiss is adulterous. What about a private kiss? An unauthorized kiss? Lying naked with one's "friend" in bed? Lying naked for an hour or more? The same act with criminal intent? What if the friends do not mean any harm? Are they lying to themselves while lying together? Does lying naked in bed count as "do[ing] nothing," and if so, why is this nothing still a venial sin?

The facts of sex become only more elusive as the exchange continues. The handkerchief briefly reenters this factual nebula as the "ocular proof" (3.3.365) of infidelity that Othello seeks and these questions about action unsettle: "He [Cassio] had my handkerchief" (4.1.22). But then the adulterous act the handkerchief is supposed to prove takes off again, as Othello demands that Iago's hearsay report of Cassio's supposed confession bolster the case against his wife:

> **OTHELLO:** What hath he said?
> **IAGO:** Faith, that he did—I know not what he did.
> **OTHELLO:** What, what?
> **IAGO:** Lie—
> **OTHELLO:** With her?
> **IAGO:** With her, on her, what you will.
> **OTHELLO:** Lie with her? Lie on her? We say 'lie on her' when they belie her? Lie with her? 'Swounds, that's fulsome! Handkerchief—confessions—handkerchief. (4.1.32–36)

What torments Othello is the fact that "with" and "on" may index the same illicit sex act while also being differently indexed to truth and falsehood. The identity of the two prepositions "with" and "on" is riven by the punning difference of the verb "to lie," meaning both "to sleep with" and "to speak falsely."[66] Iago's seemingly dismissive "what you will" thus clarifies a fact that he has been exploiting all along. There is no single way of determining what constitutes sex, and no way for Othello, much less an audience member or a reader, to know beyond a shadow of a doubt if Desdemona has committed any illicit acts or thought any illicit thoughts. Of course, Othello does not take the epistemological point. Infuriated by these "lies," he stammers, "Handkerchief—confessions—handkerchief," as question and answer to the facts of sex. He then "falls down into a trance" (4.1.41.1)—his body's response to the cognitive overload supplied by the insufficiency of the evidence to answer his demand for proof.

What makes Iago's "what you will" even more menacing as a statement of sex's flight from the facts is that he has already cued Othello to the insufficiency of even the most pornographic evidence: "Would you, the supervisor, grossly gape on, / Behold her topped" (3.3.400–401)? Iago postures as if such a sight would confirm Desdemona's infidelity, but he is quick to point out that "it is impossible [Othello] should see this" (3.3.407). Desdemona and Cassio are simply too careful: "Damn them then, / If ever mortal eyes do see them bolster / More than their own" (3.3.403–05). In Katharine Eisaman Maus's reading, Iago "pretends that the merely practical difficulty of surprising an illicit couple in bed represents a real epistemological limitation."[67] Iago's use of the word "topped," which recalls his earlier taunt of "an old black ram / . . . tupping [Brabanzio's] white ewe," nevertheless reminds us that the primal scene of sex is already wrapped in metaphor.[68] What precisely would Othello behold? "Topped" may reference penile-vaginal intercourse, and thereby prove Desdemona's infidelity through the spectacle of vaginal penetration. But even this proof arguably presumes the transparency of Desdemona's mental will. What if she is being raped? To what extent is Cassio coercing her? And how would one know given the visual scene alone? "Topped" may also reference a nonpenetrative configuration of bodies—Cassio lying *on* Desdemona, or *with* her, but not necessarily *in* her. Finally, how close would Othello have to be to Desdemona and Cassio to bear sufficient witness to this topping? He would have to be closer than he is to Iago and Roderigo later in the same scene, when he misconstrues their conversation about Bianca as one about Desdemona. He would also have to be closer than *Much Ado*'s Claudio and Don Pedro are to Hero's bedchamber. We miss the point of Iago's mobile army of sex metaphors if we account them as techniques for manufacturing pornographic evidence of a crime never committed.[69] Their pornographic *imprecision* points rather to the gap between the spoken, the seen, and the thing-in-itself—the caesura that menaces any effort to excuse Desdemona from the works of the flesh.

IV

The liabilities supposedly inherent in doubting Desdemona lead many critics to take her at her word, elevating her above suspicion by casting that suspicion as the product of Iago and Othello's misogynistic and racist conjuring. What therefore becomes unthinkable, the constant in our constructions of this tragedy as one of false accusation, is the possibility that Desdemona is simply lying when she answers the charge of "strumpet" and "whore" with an emphatic "No" and "No" (4.3.85, 89). Critics suspicious of Desdemona's virtue have heard her denials as the insufficient self-defense of a strumpet *in potentia* if not *in actu*. Defenders of her virtue, whether that virtue attains sainthood or remains that of a sexual but innocent mortal, take her denials at face value.

While refusing to hear Desdemona's testimony risks Othello's own misogynistic and murderous deafness, my brief closing argument is that Desdemona actually suggests her guilt through her own final words:

> EMILIA: Sweet Desdemona, O sweet mistress, speak!
> DESDEMONA: A guiltless death I die.
> EMILIA: O, who hath done this deed?
> DESDEMONA: Nobody, I myself. Farewell.
> Commend me to my kind lord. O, farewell. (5.2.132–34)

In her study of elegy, Diane Fuss uses these lines to pattern what she calls the "Desdemona complex" of "women who prove their love and fidelity by using their dying words not merely to forgive their abusive or jealous lovers, but, more often than not, to exculpate them."[70] Indeed, the assumption that these words *prove* fidelity is pervasive. Carol Thomas Neely claims that "Desdemona's refusal to blame and hurt Othello is at the heart of her loving virtue."[71] Joyce Green MacDonald likewise holds that Desdemona "ends by confirming her fidelity and bounty."[72] However understandable as feminist defenses of Desdemona against centuries of misogynistic condemnation, these claims assent to the equation of female virtue with chastity, and thereby risk reinforcing the moral foundation on which the accusation of chastity's loss builds its pile of bodies. They also resist hearing equivocation in these final words—any contradiction to Desdemona's claim that she dies a "guiltless death."

Without going so far as to accuse Desdemona of lying, another group of critics allows that Desdemona's paradoxical "Nobody, I myself" at least hints at a certain measure of complicity in her own demise. While describing Desdemona as an unqualified "truth-teller," Eamon Grennan wonders whether "I myself" means "my husband," with the reciprocal pronoun indicating "the absolute commitment she feels to the sacramental union of marriage."[73] Harry Berger Jr. hears Desdemona speaking in the discourse of injured merit and unjust desserts. The self-negating fragment, in his words, "edges toward self-accusation," an acceptance of "responsibility, but not culpability."[74] Equally "edgy" is Joel Altman's reading of "myself" as akin to Hamlet's "that within which passeth show" (*Hamlet*, 1.2.85)—"something immaterial, interior, unseen," as opposed to the material "body" or "person." Altman's Desdemona acknowledges "her own disruptive potentiality," the portion of herself "beyond her grasp that has been appropriated, actualized, and given a 'character' by her 'kind Lord.'"[75] Especially instructive vis-à-vis feminism's supposed inability to broker any ambiguous reading of these final words is Kaara Peterson's opposition of "feminist impulses" to the line's suggestion that Desdemona is "wrongly accused of sexual betrayal but on some level . . . still guilty of having an errant female pathology" (258).[76] All three readings are nuanced and compelling, but especially striking about each is that they mute an implication easily heard when we suspend our governing assumption that, notwithstanding whatever else she is saying, Desdemona is telling the truth.

In the play of doppelgängers, Desdemona's "Nobody, I myself" echoes nothing so much as the self-negating statement of her partner in the discourse of injured merit: Iago's "I am not what I am." To allow Iago's self-negation but deny Desdemona's only denies her the same capability of duplicity, the same ability to equivocate, that a critic like Garner might note is simply human. An alternative reading affords her the ability to be guilty and to know her guilt. This alternative reading affords her the rather basic ability to contradict herself—to refuse ("Nobody") and accept ("I myself") responsibility for the deed in her dying moment—without specifying what exactly she did and did not do. This alternative reading need not turn Desdemona into the "sweet body" Othello imagines "tasted" by the "general camp, / Pioneers and all" (3.3.350–52). This reading also does not imply that Desdemona is justly murdered. Quite the contrary, the standard of sexual and rhetorical purity to which most critics hold Desdemona does little justice to the play's pervasive deconstruction of that mutable ideal. If we grant the human ability of self-contradiction to Desdemona, her "I myself" simply chafes against her claim that she dies a "guiltless death," and edges toward an acceptance of culpability—a confession regarding some dishonesty behind the doing of the "deed."

Desdemona is not the only character in the play who offers impeachable testimony of her own chastity. Bianca does as well, albeit from the position of a woman widely regarded as unchaste.[77] Most editions of the play account Bianca a "courtesan." As with the eponymous character in *The Comedy of Errors*, "courtesan" commonly described a prostitute, but could also describe an innkeeper or a barmaid like the Henriad's Mistress Quickly. Iago's initial description of Bianca as a "hussy that by selling her desires / Buys herself bread and clothes." (4.1.92–93) conditions this editorial attribution. Cassio further casts Bianca as a prostitute when Iago asks him if he intends to marry her: "I marry!" Cassio explains, "What, a customer?" (4.1.117). (He also calls her a "bauble" [4.1.13] and a "fitchew"

[4.1.141], both slang for prostitute.) Cassio, Iago, and scores of editors may nonetheless account Bianca what she is not. When Bianca hears the charge from Emilia's mouth—"O, fie upon thee, strumpet!" (5.1.123)—she explicitly rejects it with her final words in the play: "I am no strumpet, but of life as honest/As you that thus abuse me" (5.1.124–25). Bianca might, of course, be lying, and not be honest at all. Alternatively, Bianca might be telling a truth that, like the moral content of her racialized name, is harder to imagine. As Marianne Novy notes, Bianca occupies "an unusual position as an unmarried woman who can entertain Cassio."[78] Reading this unusual position as one of a prostitute substitutes the familiar for the unfamiliar, the highly legible for the more inscrutable. To resist this substitutive reading, we need to entertain possibilities nearly lost in this play's discursive universe: that Bianca "entertain[s]" Cassio (whatever that might mean) without financial transaction; that she sleeps with him (whatever that might mean) without sleeping with the whole camp; and that she is, according to her own definition, honest without being a Venetian *cortigana honesta*.

Locating Bianca in the play's intertwined discourses of honesty and the flesh challenges our willingness and ability to imagine unmarried sex and female desire outside the enmeshed tropes of racism and misogyny. That we must risk such imagining seems imperative, however, if we are to think as capaciously about the ethics of sex and marriage as we do about the troubles of conversion. The tragic charge is no more to rescue Bianca from false accusation, to defend her word as the final, *honest* word, than it is to prove Desdemona's constancy. There is no way of knowing whether Bianca is telling the truth about herself, or what she would account as the truth. The tragic charge is to recalibrate our imagination of erotic life, especially women's erotic lives, in ways justly responsive both to the impossibility of closing the gap between self and other, and to the play of the signifier that guarantees honesty's fugitive status. "I hope my noble lord esteems me honest," Desdemona pleads with Othello in the lines that follow those I used as an epigraph for this chapter. Othello's reply turns on the plea's double syntax: "O, ay—as summer flies are in the shambles/That quicken with every blowing" (4.2.67–69). For Desdemona, there is no way to stop *honesty* from evoking the grotesque fleshiness of promiscuity. For us as critics, there is likewise no way—except through denying her the human capacity for dishonesty and double-speak—to claim she really is chaste. There is only the obligation to imagine an erotic life that rejects such honesty as the measure of its merit.

CHAPTER 4

The Ecology of Adultery: Flesh, Blood, and Stone in *The Winter's Tale*

In a recent essay on *Othello* and *The Winter's Tale*, Jennifer Waldron contends that the standard distinction between "perceiving a stone statue" and "perceiving a human subject" is "foreign to Shakespearean phenomenology."[1] Pivoting off Othello's exclamation that Desdemona "dost stone [his] heart" (5.2.68), Waldron maintains that the "mixing of nature and dramatic artifice" in the scene of Hermione's resurrection "tends to undo the very opposition between human and stone that was so central to Protestant thinking" about the sin of idolatry.[2] Tiffany Jo Werth similarly argues that this final scene of *The Winter's Tale* draws on the Genesis image of God breathing life into stone to stage the "fluidity between forms of matter."[3] Whereas God creates Adam from the "dust of the grounde" (Genesis 2:7), Paulina resurrects Hermione with the incantation, "Be stone no more" (5.3.99). Like much ecocritical scholarship, Waldron's and Werth's fine essays work to undo distinctions between different forms of creaturely life, as well as distinctions between the living and the dead, the animate and the inanimate. Their focus on the continuity of stone and flesh also supplements the larger ecocritical conversation about the relationship of humans to plants and animals in Shakespeare's romance. In this final chapter,

I enter this ecocritical conversation to ask how the sexual liabilities of inhabiting human flesh in *The Winter's Tale* underwrite Hermione's Christlike resurrection, an event marked in all four canonical gospels by the removal of stone (Matthew 28:2, Mark 16:4, Luke 24.2, John 20:1).

On the subject of sexual liability, *The Winter's Tale* has a somewhat stronger deconstructive tradition than *Othello*—a tradition owing mostly to Howard Felperin's 1985 essay "'Tongue-tied our queen?': The Deconstruction of Presence in *The Winter's Tale*." According to Felperin, there is no way to be sure that Hermione has been faithful to Leontes: "We are from the outset in a world of interpretation—the producer's and our own—where nothing can be either wholly dismissed or wholly believed, and nothing can be known for certain."[4] The fact that the play is riddled with notoriously cryptic statements, particularly on the part of the mad king, only immerses us more deeply in this world of interpretation. Although plenty of criticism on *The Winter's Tale* still proceeds as if Hermione is unquestionably innocent, I take for granted that Hermione's chastity is an open question. My concern in this chapter is therefore not, as it was with respect to Desdemona in the previous chapter, with impeaching Hermione's purity. My concern is rather with Paulina's effort to stage Hermione's exemption from the adulterated condition of the human flesh by first rendering her as stone and then resurrecting her from the same. Hovering over Paulina's effort is Antigonus's predication of every woman's chastity on Hermione's: "For every inch of woman in the word, / Ay, every dram of woman's flesh is false / If she be" (2.1.139–41). On the one hand, Antigonus's hyperbole testifies to his certainty that Hermione has been faithful to Leontes (a certainty he later reconsiders when interpreting his dream about Hermione as evidence that Apollo wants the newborn Perdita "laid / . . . upon the earth / Of its right father [Polixenes]" [3.3.43–45]). On the other hand, Antigonus's conjunction of one woman with all women as creatures of the flesh helps gloss what I will argue is Paulina's suggestion—originally Polixenes's suggestion—that the unadulterated human would not be human at all.

In the first part of this chapter, I tease out this suggestion by focusing on three figurations of the human as animal. These three animals—lambs, cattle, and fish—are by no means the only ones in *The Winter's Tale*'s bestiary. (Antigonus falls victim to one exceptionally famous bear.[5]) I focus particularly on these three animals because of their role in Polixenes's nostalgic fantasy of prelapsarian disembodiment—a life both outside, and anterior to, life in the fallen human flesh. Prompted by Hannibal Hamlin's observation that "*The Winter's Tale* is preoccupied with the Genesis story perhaps more than any of Shakespeare's plays," I spend some time with the creaturely stakes of that story, or rather *stories.*[6] Genesis 1 and 2 tell different tales of the first "man," and map out different ontological relationships between created kinds: stone, dirt, plants, humans, animals, males, and females. These differences variously inform early modern efforts to imagine prelapsarian life, such as Andrew Marvell's "The Garden" and John Milton's *Paradise Lost.* These differences also variously inform early modern imaginations of marriage as an institution that recalls the prelapsarian order of things. By connecting Polixenes's handling of the Genesis stories to Paulina's resurrection of Hermione from stone, however, I argue that the biblical center of gravity in *The Winter's Tale* is less Genesis than 1 Corinthians, one of two epistles wherein Paul of Tarsus typologically joins Adam to Christ.[7] *The Winter's Tale* stages the Pauline redemption of Adam through Christ, albeit with a gendered difference that exposes Paul's neglect of Eve in his one-sex model of Christ's body.

In the second half of this chapter, I move from the play's second scene to its final one, and from Paul's typological conjunction of Christ and Adam to his instructions in 1 Corinthians against eating the meat of animals sacrificed to idols. At issue in these instructions is the demonic animation of stone and flesh, and the consequent pollution of the body of Christ through the consumption of that flesh. When Leontes exclaims, "If this be magic, let it be an art/Lawful as eating" (5.3.110–11), he invokes this Corinthian controversy about the consumption of idol meat. Conjuring Paul's instructions against "communion" with body-adulterating devils, Leontes makes it difficult to distinguish between pure and adulterated bodies. Paulina tries to force the distinction by requiring her audience's "faith" (5.3.95). Most critics have therefore concluded that only through faith is Leontes redeemed from his sin of infidelity, or rewarded for reinvesting in the fantasy of Hermione's chastity. Following the scene's engagement with 1 Corinthians, however, I argue that his faith in her resurrection may be irrelevant. Leontes may be redeemed for the sole reason that he is Hermione's husband.

I

How many humans lived in Eden? And what sex were they? Depending on which version of the Genesis story one follows, the answer to the first question is one, two, or many; and the answer to the second is male or male and female. Let us take the second story first.

In Genesis 2, written c. 950 BCE by an author or set of authors biblical scholars term the Yahwist, God (*Yhwh*) forms man—*adam*, the masculine form of *adama*, meaning fertile soil—from the "dust of the grounde" and places him in the garden to "dresse it and kepe it" (2:15). This lithic creature is alone, a condition God concludes "is not good" (2:18). As a first attempt to remedy this man's isolation, God creates from "the earth everie beast of the field, and everie foule of the heaven" (2:19), bringing them to the *adam* for names and, it seems, potential companionship. Only when the *adam* finds "no helpe meete for him[self]" (2:20) among the beasts and fowls does God form a second lithic creature, woman (*ishah*), from the *adam*'s rib (2:21–22). The creation of woman from the bone of man (*ish*) doubles via the *adam*'s self-division the number of humans in the garden and differentiates their sex. As the *adam* concludes, "This now is bone of my bones, and flesh of my flesh. She shalbe called woman, because she was taken out of man" (2:23). The male *adam* and the new female are, at the same time, both one creature and two.

The story of "man's" creation found in Genesis 2 departs considerably from the version found in Genesis 1, composed some 400 years *after* the Yahwist's account by an author or a set of authors biblical scholars term the Priestly Writer. In this story of the seven days of creation, the origin of animals precedes that of humans. Creatures of the sea and the air appear on day five, "the beast of the earth . . . the cattel . . . and everie creping thing" (1:25) on day six. Man also appears on day six, although in this instance *adam* suggests plurality ("mankind") rather than singularity: "God (*Elohim*) created man in his image: in the image of God created he him: he created them male [*ish*] and female [*ishah*]" (1:27). In Genesis 1, there is no tale of the *adam*'s initial isolation in the garden. There is no garden. There is likewise no tale of God's effort to provide the first man with beastly company before creating woman. Instead, this first man seems to be androgyne, or rather a group of androgynes—undivided beings both male and female, as yet undifferentiated in the flesh.[8]

These two stories of "Adam" and the woman who will come to be known as Eve (Genesis 3:20) are stories about sexual difference and marriage, the (re)union of man and wife as one flesh. They are stories about the uniqueness of the *adam*, and the *ish* and the *ishah*, within the order of creation. They are also stories about agriculture, or the connection of humans to the land that feeds them. Renaissance rehearsals of "the" Genesis account were hardly ignorant of these intertwined concerns, however unaware their authors remained of the book's textual history. These concerns reappear in numerous Renaissance efforts to imagine "good" creaturely relations. For instance, resisting God's conclusion that the *adam* of Genesis 2 needs a human female companion, the speaker of Andrew Marvell's "The Garden" predicates true paradise on male isolation: "Such was that happy Garden-state, / While Man there walk'd without a Mate" (57–58).[9] This little bit of misogyny is well known, but the speaker's image of paradise depends just as much, if not more, on the near absence of animals. There are only two animals in Marvell's poem, and one of them is figurative: the bird to which the speaker compares his soul (52–53), and the bee, at the poem's end, that "Computes its time" (70). Reworking what Laurie Shannon calls "the zootopian constitution" of Genesis in which God first entitles mankind and all the animals to "everie grene herbe" (Genesis 1:30), Marvell's "The Garden" imagines the distinction of the human through the disappearance of women, animals, and their respective claims on the land.[10] "Man" emerges here as a single creature, who enjoys a unique erotic and alimentary relationship to the garden's abundant plant life: "No white nor red was ever seen / So am'rous as this lovely green" (17–18).[11] Line 70's pun on "time" as "thyme" suggests that the only animal in the garden is there by virtue of its horticultural necessity. This lone bee facilitates ("computes") the production of a green herb.

Granting Adam's need for companionship rather than idealizing his isolation, John Milton's *Paradise Lost* offers the period's most extensive literary handling of the Genesis creation accounts. Critics including Diane McColley and Ken Hiltner have discussed at length Adam and Eve's differing relationship to the garden.[12] Less has been written about Adam and Eve's differing relationship to animals, the serpent obviously excluded. For the purpose of setting the Shakespearean scene, I want to look briefly at *Paradise Lost*'s suggestion that the difference between humans and animals also bears on the construction of human sexual difference. While narrating both Genesis stories of creation, *Paradise Lost* struggles to account for what is uniquely human prior to the fall. *The Winter's Tale* does as well, but to be clear, my claim is not that Milton's epic responds in any direct way to Shakespeare's play. My claim is that the expansive treatment of the Genesis creation stories in *Paradise Lost* helps render legible the nexus of interrelated concerns about sex and species also present in *The Winter's Tale's* relatively truncated treatment.

In Book 7, Raphael tells Adam the tale of Genesis 1, culminating on the sixth day with the creation of "Man" (7.519). This man is not an androgyne: "Male he created thee [Adam], but thy consort / Female for Race" (529–30).[13] Following a common medieval and early modern exegetical practice, Raphael's clarification frames the Genesis 1 account of man's creation as an abbreviated version of the account in Genesis 2.[14] Narrating the unabridged version belongs to Adam in Book 8. Begging his divine guest to say and hear "My Storie" (8.205) following Eve's departure from the conversation, Adam tells a symptomatic tale of coming-to-consciousness and discovering his loneliness. The animals provide no sufficient company, for they are his "inferiour" (8.382). What Adam wants, he recalls telling God, is one of the same:

> Among unequals what societie
> Can sort, what harmonie or true delight?
> . . . .
> Of fellowship I speak
> Such as I seek, fit to participate
> All rational delight, wherein the brute
> Cannot be human consort[.] (8.383–84, 389–92)

In the creatures that surround him, Adam has discovered both what he is not (a "brute") and what he desires: an equal companion, another human.

Confirming Adam's intuition that one human is at least one too few, God says—or Adam says God said—that he (God) always knew as much. Whereas the God of Genesis 2 appears to be operating by trial and error, bringing the animals to Adam to see if one or more of them will alleviate this problem of being alone, Adam's God claims that the animal parade was but a test of Adam's self-knowledge. Adam's report of God's words warrants quoting in full:

> Thus farr to try thee, *Adam*, I was pleas'd,
> And finde thee knowing not of Beasts alone,
> Which thou has rightly nam'd, but of thy self,
> Expressing well the spirit within thee free,
> My Image, not imparted to the Brute,
> Whose fellowship therefore unmeet for thee
> Good reason was thou freely shouldst dislike,
> And be so minded still; I, ere thou spak'st,
> Knew it not good for Man to be alone,
> And no such companie as then thou saw'st
> Intended thee, for trial onely brought,
> To see how thou could'st judge of fit and meet:
> What next I bring shall please thee, be assur'd,
> Thy likeness, thy fit help, thy other self,
> Thy wish exactly to thy hearts desire. (8.437–51)

While it is not good for man to be alone, it is also not good for man to confuse himself with animals. Before "fellowship" with an "other self" comes knowledge of species difference—a difference all the more absolute because animals were not created, like man, in the image of God (a notion that belongs to Genesis 1:26, and not to Genesis 2). I call Adam's story, including his hearsay report of God's words, *symptomatic* because, as we learn at the end of Book 8, this first man is now confused about his relationship to Eve—the creature he claims in the language of Genesis 2:23 is "Bone of my Bone, Flesh of my Flesh, my Self/Before me" (8.495–96). (The enjambment is telling: Eve is both his "Self" and spatially separate, apart from him.) As I have argued elsewhere, Adam's request for fellowship, (re) made in the egalitarian classical language of friendship, is not necessarily a request for the "Creature . . . /Manlike, but different Sex" (8.470–71) whom God, the Son, Raphael, and Michael all insist is actually his inferior.[15] This request, which Adam (re)relates to an angel who has assumed male form, speaks to Adam's desire for what he wants and has been told he did not get: "Thy likeness, thy fit help, thy other self/Thy wish exactly to thy hearts desire" (8.450–51).

Adam's story of Eve's creation suggests that on some level he believes he is still the only human in the garden. Eve is to him a strange creature. He professes to "understand" that she is his "inferiour, in the mind/And inward Faculties" (8.540–42), and less expressive than him of "that Dominion giv'n/O're other Creatures" (8.545–46) because she is closer to them in the hierarchical order of creation than he is. At the same time, he confesses to Raphael, Eve appears "so absolute . . . /And in her self compleat" (8.547–48)—like God, whom Adam attributes with being "through all numbers absolute, though One" (8.421). The angel finds this numerical ambivalence about Eve disturbing, interpreting it as nothing less than a threat to the first man's humanity. If one unto herself, how can she also be his other half? Raphael accuses Adam of desiring Eve for "the sense of touch whereby mankind/Is propagated" (8.579–80), the same sense of lust "vouchsaf't/To Cattel and each Beast" (8.581–82). According to Raphael, Adam's capacity for "true Love" (8.589), as distinct from "carnal pleasure" (8.593), explains why "Among the Beasts no Mate for Thee was found" (8.594). Of course, Raphael may well be wrong about who Adam and Eve are; the angel is as partial and unreliable a narrator in Milton's poem as Adam. But right or wrong, Raphael's claim that Adam verges on becoming beastly through the improper management of his desire indicates how tenuous and interrelated distinctions between the sexes and the species are in Milton's Eden.

If it is difficult to determine how many humans there are in *Paradise Lost*, let alone how many men, it is no less difficult in *The Winter's Tale*.

The play references Eden several times as it moves through court gardens and the Bohemian countryside. These references begin with Polixenes's famous reminiscence of his childhood with Leontes:

> We were as twinned lambs that did frisk i'th' sun,
> And bleat the one at th'other. What we changed
> Was innocence for innocence. We knew not
> The doctrine of ill-doing, nor dreamed
> That any did. Had we pursued that life,
> And our weak spirits ne'er been higher reared
> With stronger blood, we should have answered heaven
> Boldly 'Not guilty,' the imposition cleared
> Hereditary ours. (1.2.69–77)

The male counterpart to Helena's lament over her and Hermia's past "childhood innocence" (3.2.203) in *A Midsummer Night's Dream*, Polixenes's nostalgic fantasy of "boy[hood] eternal" (1.2.66) has elicited considerable critical commentary. Janet Adelman hears Polixenes voicing male anxieties about the female body. In this story of paradise lost, "the sexualized female body is a sign of male separation and loss."[16] Stephen Orgel similarly hears a fantasy of presexual childhood—a fantasy in which Leontes himself seeks refuge when, shortly thereafter, he casts his son Mamillius as his boyhood self, "unbreeched" (1.2.157) and "dagger-muzzled" (1.2.158).[17] Walter Lim hears Polixenes boldly questioning the doctrine of original sin, the inherent corruption of the flesh through a first transgression understood since Augustine to be not just alimentary but sexual.[18]

Building on each of these observations, I want to stake a claim for the Christological importance of the twinned lambs in Polixenes's imagination of prelapsarian identity with his boyhood friend. Like *Merchant*'s Antonio wagering his body for his friend Bassanio, this image of twinship rivals the conjunction of husband and wife as one flesh. Like Antonio describing himself as "a tainted weather of the flock," ready to die for his friend, this image of Polixenes and Leontes as innocent lambs also recalls the figuration of Christ as the untainted "lamb of God" (John 1:29, 1 Peter 1:8–19). The prelapsarian setting of this innocence, however, further draws these lambs to Paul of Tarsus's image of Christ as the "last Adam": "As it is also written, The first man Adam was made a living soule: and the last Adam was made a quickening [i.e., life-giving] Spirit" (1 Corinthians 15:45). Figuring himself and Leontes as Edenic lambs of God, Polixenes imagines a state of human creation that *precedes* human enfleshment and heterosexual marriage. Polixenes and Leontes share this anterior state with a savior whose qualifications include his exemption from the sins of the flesh even in his incarnation—his lifelong righteousness (2 Corinthians 5:21, 1 Peter 2:22, Hebrews 4:15, 1 John 3:5) and, tautologically, his celibacy.[19]

In this prelapsarian state of ovine, Christ-like boyhood, there is no substantive difference between the two friends. There is no loneliness, no isolation in need of remedy. Polixenes and Leontes are through all numbers absolute, though One. What brings their perfect singularity to an end is only the pull of "stronger blood" on their "weak spirits." We may, of course, interpret this blood politically, as a synonym for royal responsibility. We may also interpret this blood biologically, as the maturation out of ungendered or third-gendered boyhood into male adulthood.[20] Yet the opposition of blood to spirit invites us to hear a Pauline exegesis of the two Genesis creation accounts. When Paul of Tarsus writes that "the first man Adam was made a living soule," he not only conflates what many of his fellow first-century Jews understood to be two distinct creatures: one a creature of spirit (Genesis 1), and the second a creature of the flesh (Genesis 2).[21] Paul also vanishes Eve from the prelapsarian scene, implying that Christ redeems Adam through his (Christ's) perfect maleness—his instantiation of ideal masculinity, unmarried and, with respect to women, chaste. Polixenes's account of paradise shares Paul's misogyny. There is no Eve here. But Polixenes's account deviates from Paul insofar as it relocates "the fall" to the moment *between* the creation of these two *adams*. For Polixenes, the fall of "man" becomes a fall *into* a sexually differentiated body whose material substance Paul condemns to the earth: "This say I, brethren, *the flesh and blood* can not inherit the kingdome of God" (1 Corinthians 15:50, emphasis added). To be fallen, according to Polixenes, is to be male and female, sexed creatures of the flesh.

Hermione is hardly deaf to Polixenes's gloss. She "gathers[s]" that the kings have "tripped since" (1.2.78–79), a supposition Polixenes confirms by equating his and Leontes's loss of innocence with meeting their respective queens:

> Temptations have since then been born to's:
> In those unfledged days my wife was a girl.
> Your previous self had not then crossed the eyes
> Of my young playfellow. (1.2.79–82)

With one word, "unfledged," Polixenes and Leontes are no longer lambs. They are small birds, trapped in the nest and unable to fly, and therefore all the more vulnerable to the serpents whose role in the story, Hermione deduces, she and Polixenes's wife have played:

> Of this make no conclusion, lest you say
> Your queen and I are devils. Yet go on.
> Th'offenses we have made you do we'll answer,
> If you first sinned with us, and that with us
> You did continue fault, and that you slipped not
> With any but us. (1.2.83–88)

Hermione assents to Polixenes's coding of the kings' fall as their slippage from the presexual state of ovine innocence into male bodies sexually drawn to female ones. (At the same time, Hermione's slippery syntax allows that each king may have also "slipped" with the other's spouse ["us"]. Leontes will soon thereafter ask, "Ha'not you seen, Camillo . . . or heard . . . or thought . . . My wife is *slippery*" [1.2.269, 271, 273, 275]?[22]) In the atonement theology of the Gospel of John, the lamb of God "taketh away the sinne of the worlde" (1:29) through his sacrifice of blood on the cross. The author of 1 Peter agrees: "Ye were not redemed with corruptible things . . . But with the precious blood of Christ, as of a Lambe undefiled, and without spot" (1:18–19). For Polixenes, in turn, this bloody exchange of ovine innocence for the sins of "man" provides the template through which he thinks his and his friend's own loss of Edenic identity: the exchange of a presexual, prehuman, preflesh *we* for a marital *us* that now includes two women and two men.

The fall is consistent for Polixenes with becoming human and becoming male, and not only for him, but for his former twin lamb as well. When Leontes turns to his son—"Mamillius, / Art thou my boy?" (1.2.121–22)—he tries to recuperate Polixenes's fantasy of Edenic twinship by exempting himself and his son from the human's flesh and blood:

> Hast smutched thy nose?
> They say it is a copy out of mine. Come, captain,
> We must be neat—not neat, but cleanly, captain.
> And yet the steer, the heifer, and the calf
> Are all called neat. . . .
> . . . How now, you wanton calf—
> Art thou my calf? (1.2.123–29)

Wiping dirt from Mamillius's nose, as he presumably does here, Leontes tries to purify the body that he and his son share. He tries to make that shared body like the lamb of 1 Peter, undefiled and without spot. But the effort at purification fails with the pun on *neat*. The pun collapses the body of the human with that of horned cattle (ready figures for cuckoldry), and realizes the suggestion of Milton's Raphael: that sin, and specifically sexual sin, turns the human into a beast, and specifically into cattle. The fact that humans use cattle for the production of milk—a maternal blood product in humoral physiology—additionally helps activate the etymology of Mamillius's name (from *mamilla*, or nipple). When Leontes later snatches Mamillius away from Hermione, his vicious reasoning echoes this bovine figuration of the human: "I am glad you did not nurse him./Though he does bear some sign of me, yet you/Have *too much blood* in him" (2.1.58–60, emphasis added). Like Hamlet blaming Gertrude for his inheritance of original sin ("frailty, thy name is woman!" [1.2.146]), Leontes imagines the adulterate blot passing to Mamillius through Hermione's body. Her blood contains the contaminant that pollutes her son's "neatness."[23]

As Stephen Orgel observes, Leontes's sudden paranoid turn on his friend and wife is explicable in terms of the Renaissance cultural rivalry between same-sex friendship and marriage.[24] It is also explicable insofar as Leontes assents to Polixenes's equation of prelapsarian existence with the perfect identity of boyhood friends and fallen self-division and adulteration with heterosexual marriage. Whereas Orgel holds that no "particular word or gesture is required to trigger Leontes's paranoid jealousy," I would note that Leontes's first words of jealousy contain the word *blood*: "Too hot, too hot/To mingle friendship farre is mingling bloods" (1.2.111). Within the fallen world's overlapping relational spheres of friendship and marriage, Hermione participates in Leontes and Polixenes's friendship not only through hospitable conversation, advancing her husband's friendly cause by entreating Polixenes to delay his departure. She more materially participates in Leontes and Polixenes's friendship because man and wife are one flesh, which is to say one blood. In Polixenes's retelling of Genesis 1 and 2, moreover, blood is the substance that he and Leontes likewise share. Returning briefly to that retelling, I read, as I suspect Leontes does, the possessive "our" before "weaker spirits" (1.2.74) as also governing "stronger blood" (1.2.75). The pronoun codes the blood as the substance of interconnected human beings, even as its associations with the fall simultaneously code it as the theological substance of self-polluting sin.[25] For Leontes, Hermione is an adulteress because she mingled blood with him—and his body, already far in friendship with Polixenes, was still one blood with his friend.[26]

Leontes's claim that spouses and their friends share blood further illuminates his soliloquy remarks on the "many a man" who

holds his wife by th' arm
That little thinks she has been sluiced in's absence
And his pond fished by his next neighbor, by
Sir Smile, his neighbor. (1.2.193–96)

This somewhat mixed metaphor renders the marital body as a body of water drained, or "sluiced," of water and/or fish. We have seen such aquatic metaphors of the marital body before, in chapter one, where I cited these lines to illustrate the commonplace Renaissance construction of the neighbor as a threat to the bonds of marriage.[27] Striking about these lines now is the way "sluicing" suggests bloodletting. (This interpretation has Shakespearean precedent. In *Richard II*, Bolingbroke accuses Mowbray of having "Sluiced out [Gloucester's] innocent soul through streams of blood" [1.1.98].) When Milton's Adam describes Eve's creation, he, too, speaks of blood and water, of "Life-blood streaming fresh" from his side (8.465). For Milton's Adam, bloodletting attends the creation of sexual difference through self-differentiation; bloodletting *engenders* marriage as the institution that reunites man and woman as one flesh. For Leontes, by contrast, bloodletting drains the marital body of its integrity. It diminishes that body through the adulterating (and obviously phallic) insertion of a drain or fishing line. By fishing in his neighbor's pond, the friendly Sir Smile—Leontes's "next," or most intimate neighbor, to recall Henry Smith's phrasing—has separated flesh from flesh, or siphoned blood from blood, in an obscene replay of God's original division of the *adam* into *ish* and *ishah*.

When Hermione and Polixenes take their leave of Leontes, it is therefore no accident of place that they go to walk "i'th garden" (1.2.179). A heterotopia crafted by the twinned instruments of art and nature, this garden, like many early modern gardens, evokes the first garden from which Adam and Eve were expelled.[28] Amy Tigner reads Leontes's royal garden as a medieval *hortus conclusus*—a fallen garden often associated with adulterous trysts.[29] Tigner further contrasts this royal garden with Perdita's, arguing that *The Winter's Tale* effects "the recuperation of paradise" through the juxtaposition of these gardens and their respective biblical, female archetypes: the fallen Eve and the virginal Mary.[30] For my purpose here, it seems equally significant to this fallen garden's biblical origins that Leontes floods it, rhetorically transforming it into a pond:

To your own bents dispose you. You'll be found,
Be you beneath the sky. [*Aside*] I am angling now,

> Though you perceive me not how I give line.
> Go to! Go to!
> How she holds up the neb, the bill to him,
> And arms her with the boldness of a wife
> To her allowing husband. (1.2.181–86)

Following the ecological trajectory of the first chapters of Genesis, Leontes's depiction of himself as a fisherman and his wife as a fish (her mouth a "neb" and "bill") carries the play from the garden to the deluge, from paradise lost to God's effort to punish the sins of the flesh by covering the earth in water.[31] Leontes functions in this allegory as the divine judge overseeing all creatures "beneath the sky." Again exempting himself from the flesh, he claims the right to punish fallen creatures. The irony of this allegory is that Hermione can survive the flood. Fish are largely immune to swelling waters.[32] But she will not survive it as a human. In *The Winter's Tale*, there are no "pure" humans, be they chaste or unique. There is, rather, a landscape of beasts, plants, and, finally, stone from which the play draws its many images of "man."

II

Polixenes's burst of Edenic nostalgia sets the terms by which Hermione must vanish into stone to rise again as Leontes's chaste wife. So far, I hope to have demonstrated why this inhuman figure cannot be an animal, so close in kind to humans that the Yahwist's God of Genesis 2 thinks one or another of them might be a suitable companion for Adam, and so close in kind to fallen humans that they, too, suffer the near extinction of the flesh wrought by the flood. This inhuman figure also cannot simply be a tree or plant. Although the play simultaneously develops fantasies of floral redemption, no more so than through Perdita (whom Gabriel Egan has keenly described as a seed cast on the shores of Bohemia), flora form part of the earth that God condemns in Genesis 3.17 ("cursed is the earth for thy [Adam's] sake") and drowns in Genesis 7.[33] To enact the redemption of her flesh, Hermione must first return to the bone from which she came. She must be drained of blood. She must become stone.[34]

No less than Polixenes's fantasy of eternal boyhood, Hermione's presentation as a statue orients numerous analyses of *The Winter's Tale*. More than one critic has argued that the statue answers to Leontes's anxieties about female infidelity and adulterous mixtures of the marital flesh. Gail Kern Paster, for instance, finds Hermione's sealed and stony body representative of an "evidently successfully, self-imposed discipline of shame."[35] No longer legible as the incontinent vessel Leontes condemned, Hermione has been sealed up and sealed off from the world. Reading Paulina's gallery as another of the play's gardens, and Hermione as a garden automaton, Amy Tigner maintains that the statue scene balances "the unbridled passions and controlled artful restoration of faithful matrimony"—bringing Hermione back to life as both a desiring subject and a chaste wife.[36] Other readings focus on the sectarian dimensions of Shakespeare's neo-miracle play. Julia Lupton has influentially contended that Hermione's reanimation "smashes the Catholic idols in order to extract their fascinating power" for a "secular theater."[37] Michael O'Connell contends that, in the final scene, Shakespeare endorses the radical Protestant association of "theatricality with idolatry" and thereby stages a "displaced [Catholic] religious ritual."[38] Jennifer Waldron argues that the scene draws on the Protestant location of the human body at the sacramental interstices of the spiritual and the material.[39] Sidestepping for the moment these questions of sectarianism and secularism, I would suggest that Leontes's strange expression of wonder upon seeing the statue animated—"If this be magic, let it be an art/Lawful as eating" (5.3.110–11)—gestures toward the controversy Paul addresses in 1 Corinthians 8 and 10. At issue in both chapters of the epistle is the permissibility of eating food sacrificed to idols. At issue in Leontes's allusion to this controversy at this moment of resurrection is the success of Paulina's efforts in staging the purification of Hermione's flesh.

I begin by excerpting a set of passages from Paul's discussion of sacrificial meat in 1 Corinthians 8:

> (1) And as touching things sacrificed unto idoles, we knowe that we all have knowledge: knowledge puffeth up, but love edifieth. . . . (4) [W]e knowe that an idol is nothing in the worlde, and that there is none other God but one. . . . (7) But everie man hathe not knowledge: for some having conscience of the idole, until this houre, eat as a thing sacrificed unto the idole, and so their conscience being weak, is defiled. (8) But meat maketh not us acceptable to God: for nether if we eat, have we the more: nether if we eat not, have we the lesse. (9) But take hede lest by any meanes this power of yours be an occasion of falling to them that are weake. . . . (10) For if any man se thee which hast knowledge, sit at table in the idoles temple, shal not the conscience of him which is weake, be boldened to eat those things which are sacrificed to idoles? (11) And through thy knowledge shal the weake brother perish, for whome Christ

> dyed. . . . (13) Wherefore if meat offend my brother, I wil eat no flesh while the worlde standeth, that I may not offend my brother.

As Dale Martin explains, the danger confronting the Corinthian church is the pollution of the body of Christ through one of its members' communion with an impure agent.[40] Like a cancer, this impurity metastasizes, spreading throughout the body of believers. This fear of pollution informs Paul's injunction against another form of communion—fornication—in the preceding chapter: "Knowe ye not that your bodies are members of Christ? Shal I then take the members of Christ, and make them the members of a harlot? God forbid" (1 Corinthians 7:15). This fear of pollution also informs Paul's insistence that women cover their heads "because of the Angels" (1 Corinthians 11:10)—spiritual beings, like the "Watchers" of Genesis 6, who might be tempted to have sex with human women.[41] Here in 1 Corinthians 8, this fear of pollution informs Paul's instructions to avoid eating meat sacrificed to idols. The church members whom the apostle casts as "strong" seem to contend that their knowledge of the one true God frees them from the popular superstition that ingesting meat sacrificed to an idol means ingesting something of that idol's divinity. The strong also seem to know that one's eating practices no longer have any bearing on their righteousness before God. The problem, Paul points out, is that different members of the church possess this knowledge in different degrees. The weaker among them risk being misled by the stronger into defiling their conscience, and thus the body of Christ, through what they understand to be a church-sanctioned exchange of the Creator for the created. To save their brothers in Christ, Paul admonishes, the strong Corinthians must refrain from an act of consumption that would otherwise be a matter of indifference before God.

Taken in isolation, this argument for acting out of brotherly love rather than knowledge is intelligible enough. The salvation of one's brother matters more than the origins of one's meat. What makes this argument complicated is Paul's return to the controversy two chapters later, where he compares eating the meat sacrificed to idols with the Eucharistic communion of believers in the body of Christ:

> (14) Wherefore my beloved, flee from idolatrie. (15) I speake as unto them which have understanding: judge ye what I say. (16) The cuppe of blessing which we blesse, is it not the communion of the blood of Christ? The bread which we breake, is it not the communion of the bodie of Christ? (17) For we that are many, are one bread and one bodie, because we are all partakers of one bread. (18) Behold Israel,

> which is after the flesh: are not they which eat of the sacrifices partakers of the altar? (19) What say I then? that the idole is any thing? or that that which is sacrificed to idoles, is any thing? (20) Nay, but that these things which the Gentiles sacrifice, they sacrifice to devils, and not unto God: and I wolde not that ye shulde have felowshippe with the devils. (21) Ye can not drinke the cup of the Lord, and the cup of the devils. Ye can not be partakers of the Lords table and of the table of the devil.

Speaking again to the strong ("them which have understanding"), Paul now appears to identify himself as one of the weak, contending that knowledge is no protection against demonic pollution. In verses 19 and 20, the apostle returns to his earlier claim that idols are "nothing." He adds that meat, too, is nothing. But devils, he insists, are something. They are as real as the one true God is real. And to eat the meat—the polluted flesh—sacrificed to idols is to commune with devils in the same way that to eat the bread and drink the wine is to commune with Christ.

Should one, therefore, not eat meat sacrificed to idols because one should act to protect the salvation of the weaker believer, or because eating this meat means communing with devils? Paul is not clear. Nor does Paul clear up what he means by "nothing." Are idols and their meat nothing in relation to the law?[42] Or are idols and meat nothing because they are inanimate objects—just so much stone and dead flesh—*which have nevertheless been demonically animated*? Either way, Leontes's anxious recognition of Hermione's animation as "magic" aligns him with the weak Corinthians who believe in the demonic animation of idols and their food.[43] This alignment is ironic considering that Leontes's "knowledge" puffs him up into a tyrant during the play's first three acts. There, Leontes's confidence in Hermione's infidelity serves as an entirely ineffective prophylactic against his simultaneous knowledge that his human body is a thing impure.[44] Now, after marveling at a stone statue so realistic that it seems its "veins did verily bear blood" (5.2.64–6), Leontes leverages the possible animation of both Christ's dead body and idol meat, human and animal flesh, in an attempt to distinguish licit from illicit fellowship: "If this be magic, let it be art / Lawful as eating."

The ambiguous results of Leonte's attempt reflect Paul of Tarsus's own. On the one hand, Leontes could mean that this resurrection *should* be an art as lawful as Christian communion; after all, those with understanding know that to eat the bread and drink the wine is to partake of the body of Christ. (*Art* in this context means an act undertaken with specialized knowledge.[45])

On the other hand, Leontes could mean that this resurrection should be an art as lawful as eating *anything*, for knowledge dictates that the divine is no longer concerned with the origins of one's food.[46] Either way, Leontes is expressing a wish, not stating a fact. And this wish for legality mires Paulina's "magic" in the demonic practice of idolatry, sullying the spectacle of Hermione's fleshly purification through its Corinthian suggestion that Leontes's "communion" with her body could again pollute his.

Leontes's ambiguous reaction to Hermione's resurrection suggests that his anxieties about the body-adulterating effects of marriage have not vanished, however much Paulina has done to convince him of his wife's "unparalleled" perfection (5.1.16). Indeed, Hermione's touted perfection might only heighten his anxieties, for now it is he who stands to pollute her by partaking of her body. Cleomenes avers that Leontes has committed "No fault . . . / Which [the king has] not redeemed, indeed, paid down / More penitence than done trespass" (5.1.2–4). Driven by Paulina's condemnation, however, Leontes continues to repent his adulterate blots, his "blemishes" (5.1.8). The redemption that does come with Hermione's resurrection is partial—incomplete and fragile. Mamillius remains dead. Sixteen years have passed. And although she embraces Leontes upon her resurrection, Hermione directs her only speech to Perdita—an act that arguably implies something less than immediate marital reconciliation. For most critics, this final scene of *The Winter's Tale* nevertheless reads as one in which the former unbeliever is rewarded for his faith with the restoration of his wife and daughter, as well as the marriage of his daughter to his friend's son.[47] Extending the connection between marriage and redemption, Leontes rewards the widowed apostle with a new husband of her own.[48] Like the final scene of *The Comedy of Errors*, however, the final scene of *The Winter's Tale* is densely overlaid with Protestant, Catholic, secular, classical, and comic scripts. My objective in what remains of this chapter is not to sort these scripts out or privilege one over the other. Instead, turning to the role that faith plays in this final scene, I want to further insist on the relevance of the scene's Corinthian script to its staging of marital redemption. What might we learn about *The Winter's Tale* by focusing this scene through Paul's specific writings to the Corinthians about marriage?

To answer this question, we need to return to a verse discussed briefly in Chapter 2: "For the unbeleving housband is sanctified by the wife, and the unbeleving wife is sanctified by the housband, els were your children uncleane: but now are they holie" (1 Corinthians 7:14). Much depends on the meaning of "sanctified," often rendered as "made holy." For modern biblical scholars, Paul's meaning is not hard to deduce. Paul refers to the covenant encompassing all Jews.[49] This covenant extends through the flesh from the Jewish believer in Christ to the Gentile believer in Christ, and through them to their children, who would otherwise be unclean, which is to say outside the covenant. A couple of verses later, Paul explicitly distinguishes sanctification from salvation, or membership in the Jewish covenant from the more exclusive membership in the body of Christ. He opposes divorce from nonbelievers with parallel rhetorical questions: "For what knowest thou, oh wife, whither thou shalt save thine housband? Or what knowest thou, oh man, whither thou shalt save thy wife?" (7:16). This distinction between Jewish covenantal sanctification and eternal salvation through Christ makes sense if Paul is understood as a messianic Jew, with a novel but still fundamentally Jewish message of deliverance from sin. Yet this distinction makes far less sense for later medieval and Renaissance Christians who regard Paul as one of them.

Augustine, for example, holds that what Paul means by sanctification is not clear. Paul could be referring to some "particular sanctification" regarding purity laws or some more general "sprinkling of holiness arising out of the close ties of married life and children."[50] Or 7:14 and 7:16 could be redundant, both ways of saying that "sometimes wives gain[] husbands to Christ, and sometimes husbands convert[] wives, while the Christian will of even one of the parents prevail[s] towards making their children Christian."[51] In any case, Augustine's Christianization of Paul puts him at pains to distinguish sanctification from membership in the body of Christ: "Whatever be the sanctification meant, this must be steadily held: that there is no other valid means of making Christians and remitting sins, except by men becoming believers through the sacrament according to the institution of Christ and the Church."[52] Still later readings take comparative pains with the grammar of 7:14. Without specifying exactly what sanctification is, the Geneva gloss makes marriage, not the unbelieving partner, the sanctified object: "The faith of the belever hathe more power to sanctifie marriage then the wickednes of the other to pollute it." Calvin similarly deduces that the marriage of the believer and the nonbeliever is "sacred and pure," but "this sanctification is of no benefit to the unbelieving party."[53] This hermeneutic shift to reading marriage rather than the nonbelieving spouse as the object of sanctification in 1 Corinthians 7:14 provides a way of accommodating the distinction between sanctification and salvation within a Christian theology disinclined toward recognizing Paul's Judaism. Meanwhile, the apparent paraphrase of the verse by Jessica in *The Merchant of Venice*—"I shall be saved by my husband. He hath made me a Christian" (3.5.15–16)—reminds us that this distinction between sanctification and salvation does not necessarily have popular hold. For Jessica, who might also base her claim to salvation on Ephesians 5:30–32, marriage to a Christian makes her a Christian. Marriage, not baptism or the Eucharist, is the sacrament that grants her membership in the body of Christ. And she is not necessarily wrong.

To witness the final scene of *The Winter's Tale* through Jessica's eyes is to witness Leontes redeemed through the Christ-like resurrection of his wife's body. It is to witness the union (even if only a hug) of the human body (Leontes) with the body of Christ (Hermione). It is not necessarily to witness any reward for Leontes's faith. Among contemporary critics, the faith upon which Paulina insists—"It is required / You do awake your faith" (5.3.94–95)—is often richly contoured, both denominationally and existentially. It is also not necessarily first-century or Reformation-era Pauline faith. James Kuzner hears Paulina speaking in the language of Alain Badiou's Paul; the faith she requires is not a "belief system" that comes with a set of factual propositions about the resurrection, but instead "the experience of being carried away."[54] Sarah Beckwith similarly hears Paulina proffering the Johannine thesis that "the credibility of the resurrection is bound to the credence of believers."[55] Richard McCoy accounts this faith a Romantic suspension of disbelief through which Leontes regains his faith in Hermione.[56] But so much critical emphasis on faith obscures a reading that a Christian like Jessica might well offer: Hermione "returns" to life (if indeed she does) without any regard to whether we, including Leontes, actually awaken our faith or not.[57] Paulina's resurrection show goes on despite what anyone believes or does not believe, and with no regard for how or whether any particular person distinguishes demonic from divine power, the live from the dead, the stone from the flesh. To be more precise, the show goes on once everyone has been *ordered* to be faithful. Anyone without awakened faith (whatever that might mean), or who does not want to bear witness, is expressly forbidden from leaving: "No foot shall stir" is Leontes's command (5.3.98). What Beckwith calls Shakespeare's "theater of faith" is not voluntary.[58] It is compulsory—and this compulsion helps mitigate the scene's more "heretical" suggestion that Leontes receives what redemption he does because he is Hermione's husband. He is one flesh with her, and by her own admission she has come back to life *not* for his sake but her own and her daughter's: "For thou [Perdita] shalt hear that I, / Knowing by Paulina that the oracle / Gave hope thou wast in being, have preserved / Myself to see the issue" (5.3.130). Leontes's redemption may be but a Pauline side-effect of this mother/daughter reunion.

We need not cynically reduce Paulina to a stage-managing manipulator of Leontes's credulity in order to be a bit less romantic about the faith she requires. Paul may have been a charlatan, and Paulina may be, too. But just as Shakespeare's scene of paradise partially regained holds open rather than resolves questions about flesh's relationship to stone, it also holds open rather than resolves the question of whether redemption comes through faith alone, through participation in one or more sacraments (the Eucharist or marriage), or through some combination of the above. Shakespeare's decision to gender both the apostle and the risen Christ as female offers another index of redemptive possibilities. Terming the mixed-genre romance a "mongrel drama" that "boldly—promiscuously—mingles the myths, beliefs, and historical details of various epochs and cultures," Huston Diehl reads the sex of the servant apostle and the resurrected savior as Shakespeare's response to antitheatrical misogyny.[59] Basing his own reading on Paul's deployment of *parrhèsia* (fearless speech) in 1 Corinthians, Randall Martin accounts "Hermione's and Paulina's performances as a Pauline challenge to Paul's own anti-female discourse."[60] I suggested earlier that Shakespeare's sexing of the apostle and Christ as female responds to Paul's excision of the female from the plot of man's redemption. If I now avoid enlisting this response to queer or feminist purpose, as I did in previous chapters, it is only to emphasize that the scene, like so many in Shakespeare, offers adulterated representations of Pauline Christianity, of Paul "himself," that the critical reduction of Leontes's redemption to a matter of faith risks consolidating for a particularly orthodox Christian disjunction of marital sanctification from personal salvation. My claim is that this scene is not singularly Protestant, Catholic, or secular. Much less is it blandly ecumenical. This scene stages competing, mixed models of redemption that track back to the multiplicity of Pauls in and after the first century.

Epilogue: Why (Again) Are the Utopians Monogamous?

For the most part, the texts that this book has considered belong to William Shakespeare. His interest in marriage and the body of Christ is obviously not unique among his contemporaries, however. I therefore want to close this book with a brief look at three non-Shakespearean texts: Thomas More's *Utopia* (1516), Francis Bacon's *The New Atlantis* (1627), and Henry Neville's *The Isle of Pines* (1668). Via their explicit interest in state planning and population management, these utopian texts lay bare the pre- and post-Reformation dependence of Christian citizenship on the institution of marriage.

As is well known, More's Utopians eschew private property. Unlike their neighboring states, as well as sixteenth-century Europeans ones, Utopia is communist. In one way, however, the Utopians distinguish themselves from their neighbors but accord with the Europeans. As Raphael Hythloday reports, "they only of the nations in that part of the world be content every man with one wife apiece" (91).[1] The Utopians reject plural marriage. They also believe that marriage should be permanent, "never broken but by death, except adultery break the bond, or else the intolerable wayward manners of either party" (91). Responding to More's (the author's) concerns about the political and social dangers that follow from the European commitment to private holdings of wealth, Hythloday's Utopian mirror reflects an opposing model of economic organization in which communal prosperity follows from the public holding of resources. Yet regarding marriage, Hythloday's Utopian mirror reflects identity with European practice—and it does so in some tension with both the ostensible foreignness of the Utopians and their requisite commitment to communism. If private property is anathema in Utopia, why do the Utopians practice what might well be called the private ownership of spouses? Why, on this point in particular, are the Utopians possessive individualists?[2]

I am not the first to ask this question. Janel Mueller asks it in a 1994 essay on Utopian women and the family, taking her cue from the fact that Utopians punish fornicators by forbidding them to marry. According to Hythloday,

> The offense is so sharply punished because they [the Utopians] perceive that unless they be kept from the liberty of this vice, few will join together in the love of marriage, wherein all the life must be led with one, and also all the griefs and displeasures coming therewith patiently taken and borne. (90)

Mueller finds Hythloday's explanation "in keeping with the pessimistic bent of commentary on generic human nature in the work": More's fallen humans need discipline.[3] At the same time, this explanation is altogether inadequate from an anthropological perspective, which implicitly would suggest that monogamous marriage goes hand-in-hand with private property as a means of guaranteeing the orderly production of legitimate heirs to inherit said property. But inheritance is not a Utopian concern. I would add to Mueller's objection that Hythloday justifies the punishment of fornicators by fallaciously begging the marital question. His explanation amounts to saying that the Utopians must commit to monogamy because otherwise they would not. Why life "*must* be led with one" remains unanswered.

For Mueller, only the preservation of the patriarchal family unit squares this circle of Utopian monogamy. The Utopians need monogamy to identify heads of household and maintain gender-hierarchal lines of instruction and discipline. In Mueller's words, "monogamy certifies that a given male is the father of a given woman's children, investing him with authority over them (and her)."[4] I agree that monogamy serves Utopia's interest in gendered structures of discipline, which ultimately overrides its interest in common holdings. Nevertheless, I want to press this question about Utopian monogamy further in light of the two later utopian texts by Bacon and Neville that make monogamous marriage a mark of Christian citizenship.

In Bacon's *New Atlantis*, a shipwreck brings a European crew into contact with the Bensalemites, a mostly Christian people whose moral rigor has been sustained in part by their lack of European contact. The Bensalemites incentivize population growth, celebrating in the publically funded Feast of the Family any patriarch who "shall live to see thirty persons descended of his body alive together, and all above three years old" (169). After hearing of this Feast, the European narrator of *New Atlantis* postures as Mueller's imagined anthropologist when he asks a Bensalemite Jew named Joabin whether the Bensalemites practice polygyny:

> And because propagation of families proceedeth from the nuptial copulation, I desired to know of him what laws and customs they had concerning marriage; and whether they kept marriage well; and whether they were tied to one wife? For that where the population is so much affected, and such as with them it seemed to be, there is commonly permission of plurality of wives. (173)

The narrator's knowledge of differing customs suggests that in pursuit of population growth, the Bensalemites would likely refrain from restricting the number of wives any one man may possess. Polygyny is only logical. Counteracting this logic, however, is the Bensalemite commitment to what can be called Judeo-Christian family values. Joabin explains that "there is not under the heavens so chaste a nation as this of Bensalem; nor so free from all pollution or foulness" (173). The Bensalemites believe that God instituted "the faithful union of man and wife" in Eden, and did so as "a remedy for unlawful concupiscence" (173). Their consequent commitment to chastity is so strong that "there are no stews, no dissolute houses, no courtesans, nor any thing of that kind" (173). Much less are there plural marriages of the type practiced by Joabin's own forefathers. This explanation of the Bensalemite commitment to sexual purity by a "good Jew" (174) amounts to a fantastical enfolding of Jewish and Christian marriage doctrines into one coherent religious tradition.[5] In Bacon's utopian fiction, the rejection of plural marriage marks Bensalem as a Judeo-Christian nation—one that pursues its goal of citizen production and patriarchal family preservation within the ostensible strictures of scripture.

Compared to Bacon's *New Atlantis*, Henry Neville's *The Isle of Pines* spins a more dystopian shipwreck tale in which rampant sexual depravity overcomes Christian restraints on reproduction and sexual partnership. The patriarch of the titular island, George Pine, fathers children with each of his four fellow female shipwreck survivors, whom he calls his wives. (There is no ceremony, only a sudden appellation.) His fecundity follows not from any felt need to establish a state or follow God's command to increase and multiply (Genesis 1:28, 9:91). The island's Edenic abundance of easy food simply makes him horny: "Idleness and a fullness of everything begot in me a desire for enjoying the women" (197). Pine's indulgence in turn begets both an enormous population and moral disorder. By the time Pine reaches the age of eighty, he and his children have peopled the island with almost two thousand inhabitants. So morally fragile is this polity that, following his death, it quickly descends into a Hobbesian state of nature:

> But as it is impossible, but that in multitudes disorders will grow, the stronger seeking to oppress the weaker, no tie of religion being strong enough to chain up the depraved nature of mankind, even so amongst them mischief began to rise. . . . Nay, not confining themselves within the bounds of any modesty, but brother and sister lay openly together; those who would not yield to their lewd embraces, were by force ravished, yea, many time endangered of their lives. (201)[6]

As a consequence of this rapacity, Neville's islanders break out in a civil war that concludes with the establishment of a new set of commandments—a series of laws answering to the want of "Christian instruction" (201). Locating the practices of endogamous and plural marriages in the island's implicitly Jewish past, this new Christian covenant outlaws rape and adultery alongside blasphemy and absence from monthly Bible readings. In *The Isle of Pines*, as in *New Atlantis*, the enforcement of monogamy answers to the state promotion of Christianity. Yet More's Utopian state has no such apparent interest, and it tolerates a comparative freedom of religion. Utopians shun only those who do not believe in the eternal life of the soul and the supreme government of providence. If the prohibition against plural marriage somehow indexes Utopian state Christianity, it therefore must do so *from the future*, from what that state has yet to become.[7]

Here we need to resituate Mueller's question about Utopian monogamy within Stephen Greenblatt's argument about the temporal situation of the Utopians. In *Renaissance Self-Fashioning*, Greenblatt treats the Utopian family as an institution disarticulated from any private concern with lineage, sexual fulfillment, or companionship, and made to serve the collective interest in the production of citizens. In short, "family strategies are entirely subsumed under state strategies."[8] Later in the same chapter, however, Greenblatt deduces that the Utopians are a people "who will in time join the fellowship of the Catholic faithful."[9] Whether by divine guidance or because it agrees with the majority belief in a supreme being called Mithras, the Europeans' word "of Christ, of his doctrine, laws, miracles, and of the no less wonderful constancy of so many martyrs" finds easy audience among these monogamous communists (107). For Greenblatt, the Utopians thereby become legible as More's "fantasy of a people for whom conversion would be no true trauma."[10] (Bacon offers another version of the same fantasy. His tricky association of religion with illusion notwithstanding, *New Atlantis* recounts the European discovery of a people who have already been converted, and whose commitment to Christian morality now exceeds that of the Europeans.) I suggest that the Utopian commitment to monogamy reads as another sign of the state's preparedness to enter Christendom. Expected of all Utopians except one sect of the Buthrescas, monogamous marriage sustains the existence of the state through the production of equally monogamous citizens. For the Utopians, monogamous marriage constitutes an issue, an obligation, of state citizenship, and of church membership, too, albeit avant la lettre.[11]

Fast-forward several decades from the publication of *Utopia* to the Council of Trent (1545–63) and one finds marriage explicitly framed as an issue of church membership. The Council's 1563 *Tametsi* responds unequivocally to Protestant efforts to change church membership requirements by removing marriage from the list of sacraments:

> Since matrimony in the evangelical law surpasses in grace through Christ the ancient marriages, our holy Fathers, the councils, and the tradition of the universal Church, have with good reason always taught that it is to be numbered among the sacraments of the new Law.[12]

The preceding several centuries of church history certainly support this statement, but the Council's "always" is still a bit misleading. Prior to the twelfth century, the church lacked a systematic theology of sacramental marriage; and only in the thirteenth century did the church begin to mandate acceptance of the doctrine among its members.[13] Entirely elided by the Council is early Christian antipathy toward marriage, the attitude Paul of Tarsus expresses in 1 Corinthians.[14] In the fifth century, Augustine influentially accounts marriage a sacrament on the basis of its indissolubility: "The essence of the sacrament (*res sacramenti*)," he writes, "is undoubtedly that the man and woman who are joined together in marriage should remain inseparable as long as they live."[15] During the doctrinal contests of the twelfth century, however, Gratian attributes marriage's sacramental status to consummation, while Duns Scotus argues that marriage is a sacrament because it is performed by a priest who blesses the couple.[16]

The orthodox position eventually became that the exchange of vows alone makes marriage a sacrament. In *Summa contra Gentiles* (1260–64), Aquinas returns to the Augustinian theme of indissolubility to emphasize that the permanence of marriage reflects the permanence of membership in the body of Christ. He also pivotally adds that, as a sacrament, marriage constitutes a vehicle for the extension of God's grace: "Since the sacraments are what they figure, it is to be believed that grace is conferred through this sacrament on the spouses, whereby they might belong to Christ and the church."[17] Focused on shoring up the rules of membership, the Council's assertion that marriage has "always . . . numbered among the sacraments" glosses over this complicated history of contestation about what makes marriage a sacrament, if it is one, and what significance the status of sacrament conveys.

At the same time that it confirmed marriage as one of the seven sacraments, the Council of Trent also confirmed marriage as a union of "two only" in "one flesh." On this point, the Council stood on relatively uncontroversial ground. Catholic, Protestant, and radical Protestant marriage theologies differed over issues including clerical access, impediments, divorce, separation, and jurisdiction, but most agreed that plural marriage lay squarely outside Christian bounds. Historically speaking, Christianities that have ventured outside these bounds have not survived to become prominent cultural or political forces. The Münster Rebellion (1534–35) offers a Reformation case in point. During his stint as leader of the rebellion, John of Leiden legalized polygyny—and, pace *Utopia*, common ownership of goods—but the failure of this rebellion fragmented and politically neutralized the Anabaptists. The Oneida Community of mid-nineteenth-century New York offers a more modern utopian example. Believing that Jesus had already returned to Earth and freed them from sin, all members of the Oneida Community considered themselves married to one another, with consensual sex permissible between all members. At their 1878 height, the community boasted 306 members—a body of believers large enough to attract state interest. Membership then went into freefall following the 1879 decision to abandon the practice of "complex marriage" under threat of prosecution.[18] In contrast, the Church of Latter-day Saints survived and, today, thrives in no small part because it banned plural marriage at the turn of the twentieth century. Small minorities of Mormons continue to practice polygyny, otherwise known as "the Principle," but these Mormons have been deemed heretics by the LDS Church, which recently devoted considerable resources to helping ensure that marriage remained a union between one man and one woman.[19]

The Council of Trent's confirmation of the union's restriction to a single male-female pair signaled its heightened sensitivity to the possibility that violations of canon law could, even if unwittingly, result in one's marriage to multiple partners. Certainly nothing in English Renaissance history illustrates this possibility more dramatically than Henry VIII's efforts to divorce Catherine of Aragon and marry Anne Boleyn. Despite Pope Julius II's dispensation, Henry claimed that his marriage to Catherine violated the impediment of affinity. (Catherine had previously been the wife of Henry's brother Arthur.) When the 1534 papal court upheld Henry's first marriage as valid, Thomas Cramner had already annulled Henry and Catherine's marriage and ratified Henry and Anne's. Political strong-arming aside, the theological questions in this case pivoted around the mechanisms for assuring that marriage remained a union of "two only." Impediments of affinity guarded against the union of two people who were already related, as well as against unions that would seal more than two. For those loyal to the pope, Henry's marriage to Anne was bigamous. For Henry's supporters, his marriage to Catherine was bigamous. Before his death in 1547, Henry would be joined as one flesh with still four more wives, his flesh arguably one with six women.[20]

The story of Thomas More's execution for refusing to take the Oath of Supremacy is as familiar as the story of Henry VIII's divorce from Catherine of Aragon. To put the matter simply, More died in defense of a church whose internal division he likely did not foresee when writing *Utopia*.[21] One early eruption of this threat was Martin Luther's blistering 1520 attack on the church's "captivity" of the sacraments, including marriage. Luther railed against the confusion of "sacrament" for "mystery" in the translation of Ephesians 5:32.[22] He railed, too, against the imposition of celibacy on clerics, like himself, without God's gift of continence.[23] Against Luther and William Tyndale, More defended the sacramentalization of marriage as a plain teaching of the church and turned the argument for licensing clerical marriage on its head, claiming that marriage "defyleth the preste more than dowble or treble horedome."[24] In 1516, More could imagine his preconverted Utopians allowing priests, both male and female, the right to marry. Presumably, this custom would fade away when the islanders joined the body of Christ.

As internal contests over how to interpret Ephesians 5 grew, however, More could only see in the desacramentalization of marriage and the legalization of clerical marriage the fracture of Christian civilization. What awaited the Reformed nations were wars that would leave the people "drunk with the blood of princes and reveling in the gore of the nobles," then "turn[ing] their hands against themselves and . . . run[ning] each other through."[25] Like many of today's most fervent evangelicals, fearing the civilization-destroying consequences of legalizing gay marriage, More feared that Christendom was poised on the edge of a slippery slope.[26] Today, the definition of marriage changes. Tomorrow, the members of the body of Christ begin to sever.

ACKNOWLEDGMENTS

I have no formal training as a biblical scholar. My first words of gratitude therefore go to Joseph Marchal, who early on in this project provided me with a reading list on queer Christian theology. Of course, all errors of biblical interpretation that appear in this book, from gross to trivial, are my own.

On the early modern side, I have enjoyed helpful exchanges with Jim Bromley, Drew Daniel, Fran Dolan, Ari Friedlander, D. Gilson, Erin Labbie, Ania Loomba, Julia Lupton, Tom Luxon, Carla Mazzio, Jeff Masten, Lee Morrissey, Vin Nardizzi, David Orvis, Elizabeth Rivlin, Melissa Sanchez, Allie Terry-Fritsch, Valerie Traub, and Dan Vitkus.

Andrew Barnaby and Mario DiGangi read this book for Fordham University Press, and this book is much better for their astute suggestions.

Thank you, finally, to the Fordham editorial and marketing team, including Eric Newman, Edward Batchelder, Katie Sweeney, and Richard Morrison.

This book is for Hunter Anderson-Stockton and Ricci Rader.

NOTES

INTRODUCTION: MARRIAGE AND THE BODY OF CHRIST

1. The principle poetic expression of this metaphor might be the last two lines of Edmund Spenser's Amoretti 68: "So let us love, deare love, lyke as we ought,/Love is the lesson which the Lord us taught." See *Edmund Spenser's Poetry*, 4th ed., ed. Anne Lake Prescott and Andrew D. Hadfield (New York: Norton, 2014), 644. On the structural relationship between *Amoretti* and Song of Songs, often read in the Renaissance as a metaphor for Christ's relationship with the church, see Theresa Krier, "Generations of Blazons: Psychoanalysis and the Song of Songs in the *Amoretti*," *Texas Studies in Literature and Language* 40, no. 3 (1998): 292–327.

2. John Booty, ed. *The Book of Common Prayer: 1559* (Charlottesville: University of Virginia Press, 1976), 290–91.

3. Augustine, to take just one example, describes marriage as the "seedbed" of the state in *The City of God against the Pagans*, ed. and trans. by R. W. Dyson (Cambridge: Cambridge University Press, 1998), 667. In *Of Domesticall Duties* (London: n.p., 1622), the first part of which expounds at length on the household codes of Ephesians, William Gouge depicts families in Augustinian terms as "excellent seminaries" for "both Church and Commonwealth" (sig. A2v). More commonly among English Renaissance Protestants, marriage was a "little commonwealth." See, for instance, Robert Cleaver, *A Godlie Forme of Householde Government* (London, 1598), 13.

4. See Thomas Becon's preface to Heinrich Bullinger, *The Christen State of Matrimony* (London: n.p., 1546), sig. A4v.

5. Eamon Duffy's revisionist history of the English Reformation is pivotal. See *The Stripping of the Altars: Traditional Religion in England, c. 1400–1580* (New Haven, Conn.: Yale University Press, 1992). For Duffy, the Reformation was more interruptive than welcome.

6. My summary of this legal story draws on multiple histories of marriage in Renaissance England and pre- and early modern Europe. The most valuable have been Martin Ingram, *Church Courts, Sex and Marriage in England, 1570–1640* (Cambridge: Cambridge University Press, 1987); Eric Joseph Carlson, *Marriage and the English Reformation* (Oxford, U.K.: Blackwell,

1994); and John Witte Jr., *From Sacrament to Contract: Marriage, Religion, and Law in the Western Tradition*, 2nd ed. (Louisville, Ky.: Westminster John Knox Press, 2012). The now indispensible study of Shakespeare and English marriage law is B. J. Sokol and Mary Sokol, *Shakespeare, Law, and Marriage* (Cambridge: Cambridge University Press, 2003).

7. Jennifer R. Rust, *The Body in Mystery: The Political Theology of the* Corpus Mysticum *in the Literature of Reformation England* (Evanston, Ill.: Northwestern University Press, 2014). Other recent studies attuned to the coexistence of Protestant and Catholic thought include James Kearney, *The Incarnate Text: Imagining the Book in Reformation England* (Philadelphia: University of Pennsylvania Press, 2009); Adrian Streete, *Protestantism and Drama in Early Modern England* (Cambridge: Cambridge University Press, 2009); and Alexandra Walsham, *The Reformation of the Landscape: Religion, Identity, and Memory in Early Modern Britain and Ireland* (Cambridge: Cambridge University Press, 2012).

8. Also obscuring the distinction between Protestant and Catholic positions on marriage is the fact that many reformers drew on Catholic humanists, including Juan Luis Vives, Desidarius Erasmus, and Thomas More, in defending the holy status of matrimony against alleged Catholic degradation. See Margo Todd, "Humanists, Puritans, and the Spiritualized Household," *Church History* 49, no. 1 (1980): 18–34. Meanwhile, as Amy Froide has shown in *Never Married: Singlewomen in Early Modern England* (Oxford: Oxford University Press, 2007), about twenty percent of the adult urban population never married. The disjunctions between official marriage discourse and actual marriage practice could be vast.

9. The term "evangelical" needs to be distinguished from "fundamentalist." Although evangelicals are often called fundamentalists, and sometimes even identify as such, I follow most religious studies scholars in distinguishing fundamentalists as separatists averse to political engagement with the secular world. For the sake of convenience, my use of the term "evangelical" also excludes the evangelical left. Stephen P Miller tracks the recent history of these distinctions in *The Age of Evangelicals: America's Born-Again Years* (Oxford: Oxford University Press, 2014).

10. For the early modernist, James Grantham Turner's *One Flesh: Paradisal Relations in the Age of Milton* (Oxford: Oxford University Press, 1993) provides a valuable exegetical history of these verses. See also Frances E. Dolan, *Marriage and Violence: The Early Modern Legacy* (Philadelphia: University of Pennsylvania Press, 2008), which offers an extended discussion of the one-flesh doctrine. I engage Dolan's work more extensively in Chapter 1.

11. As Daniel Boyarin writes in *A Radical Jew: Paul and the Politics of Identity* (Berkeley: University of California Press, 1994), the Pauline *flesh* "enters

into a rich metaphorical and metonymic semantic field bounded on the one hand by metaphorical usages already current in biblical parlance, and on the other hand by the dualism of flesh and spirit current in the milieu of Hellenistic—that is, first-century—Judaism" (68). At the same time, the flesh can denote both body *and* spirit. Ephesians 5:30 seems to describe a body of Christ in which all Christians, dead or alive, embodied or disembodied, participate, whether through faith, the sacraments, or both. As Jennifer Waldron has demonstrated in *Reforming the Body: Idolatry, Sacrifice, and Early Modern Theater* (New York: Palgrave Macmillan 2013), many Renaissance Protestants labored against the dualism of flesh and spirit exacerbated by reformed critiques of Catholic materialism. For Calvinists, especially, the physical body remained "an indispensible component of sacramental experience" (56) and a "kind of conduit between the supernatural and natural spheres" (57).

12. I share Anthony Dawson's perspective that the theater is "a secular, and secularizing, institution," structured as such through the 1559 ban on theatrical interference in "matters of religion." Of course, plays articulate religious ways of thinking. The theater also has church origins: See Sarah Beckwith, *Signifying God: Social Relation and Symbolic Act in the York Corpus Christi Plays* (Chicago: Chicago University Press, 2001). But whereas churches speak on religious matters with relative cultural authority—monologically—the discourse of Renaissance theater is heteroglossic; see Dawson, "The Secular Theater," *Shakespeare and Religious Change*, ed. Kenneth J. E. Graham and Philip Collington (New York: Palgrave Macmillan, 2009), 240. For the 1559 ban, see *Tudor Royal Proclamations, Volume II: The Later Tudors (1553–1587)*, ed. Paul H. Hughes and James F. Larkin (New Haven, Conn.: Yale University Press, 1969), 115–116.

13. For background, see Michael L. Satlow, *Jewish Marriage in Antiquity* (Princeton, N.J.: Princeton University Press, 2001); and David Instone-Brewer, *Divorce and Remarriage in the Bible: The Social and Literary Context* (Grand Rapids, Mich.: William B. Eerdmans Publishing Company, 2002).

14. Marc Shell, *The End of Kinship: "Measure for Measure," Incest, and the Ideal of Universal Siblinghood* (Stanford, Calif.: Stanford University Press, 1988).

15. *Oxford English Dictionary*, 3rd ed., 2014, s.v. "individual," accessed 7 September 2015, http://www.oed.com.libproxy.clemson.edu/view/Entry/94633?redirectedFrom=individual#eid.

16. On the rise of the individual, see Jacob Burckhardt, *The Civilization of the Renaissance in Italy*, trans. S. G. C. Middlemore (1878; New York: Penguin, 1990); Stephen Greenblatt, *Renaissance Self-Fashioning: From More to Shakespeare* (Chicago: University of Chicago Press, 1980); and John Jeffries Martin, *Myths of Renaissance Individualism* (New York: Palgrave Macmillan,

2006). On subjectivity, see Francis Barker, *The Tremulous Private Body* (New York: Methuen, 1984); Catherine Belsey, *The Subject of Tragedy: Identity and Difference in Renaissance Drama* (New York: Methuen, 1985); Katharine Eisaman Maus, *Inwardness and Theater in the English Renaissance* (Chicago: University of Chicago Press, 1995); Elizabeth Hanson, *Discovering the Subject in Renaissance England* (Cambridge: Cambridge University Press, 1998); Christopher Pye, *The Vanishing: Shakespeare, the Subject, and Early Modern Culture* (Durham, N.C.: Duke University Press, 2000).

17. Douglas Bruster, *Drama and the Market in the Age of Shakespeare* (Cambridge: Cambridge University Press, 2005); Ann Rosalind Jones and Peter Stallybrass, *Renaissance Clothing and the Materials of Memory* (Cambridge: Cambridge University Press, 2001); Michael Shapiro, *Gender in Play on the Shakespearean Stage: Boy Heroines and Female Pages* (Ann Arbor: University of Michigan Press, 1996); Laura Levine, *Men in Women's Clothing: Anti-theatricality and Effeminization, 1579–1642* (Cambridge: Cambridge University Press, 1994); Jean E. Howard, *The Stage and Social Struggle in Early Modern England* (New York: Routledge, 1993); Jean-Christophe Agnew, *Worlds Apart: The Market and Theater in Anglo-American Thought, 1550–1750* (Cambridge: Cambridge University Press, 1988).

18. Laurie Shannon, *Sovereign Amity: Figures of Friendship in Shakespearean Contexts* (Chicago: University of Chicago Press, 2002); and Thomas MacFoul, *Male Friendship in Shakespeare and His Contemporaries* (Cambridge: Cambridge University Press 2009). On friendships as group relationships, see John Garrison, *Friendship and Queer Theory in the Renaissance: Gender and Sexuality in Early Modern England* (New York: Routledge, 2014).

19. Daniel Juan Gil, *Shakespeare's Anti-Politics: Sovereign Power and the Life of the Flesh* (New York: Palgrave Macmillan, 2013); Gail Kern Paster, *Humoring the Body: Emotions and the Shakespearean Stage* (Chicago: University of Chicago, 2004); and Mary Floyd-Wilson, *English Ethnicity and Race in Early Modern Drama* (Cambridge: Cambridge University Press, 2003).

20. Graham Hammill and Julia Reinhard Lupton, introduction to *Political Theology and Early Modernity*, ed. Hammill and Lupton (Chicago: University of Chicago Press, 2012), 1.

21. Exemplary here is Susan Dwyer Amussen, *An Ordered Society: Gender and Class in Early Modern England* (New York: Columbia Un`iversity Press, 1988).

22. Ken Jackson and Arthur F. Marotti are frequently regarded as marking this turn in "The Turn to Religion in Early Modern English Studies," *Criticism* 46, no. 1 (2004): 167–190. See also their coedited volume *Shakespeare and Religion: Early Modern and Postmodern Perspectives* (South Bend, Ind.: University of Notre Dame Press, 2011). In *Citizen-Saints: Shakespeare and Political*

Theory (Chicago: University of Chicago Press, 2005), Julia Lupton likewise emphasizes marriage's place at the threshold of both secular and spiritual citizenship. Marriage, she reminds us, is an institution of the church or churches *and* part of the biopolitical machinery of a state.

23. On the many different models of marriage on offer in the Bible, see Joseph A. Marchal, "Who's Getting (Some) Biblical Marriage," *Feminist Studies in Religion*, 11 May 2012, http://www.fsrinc.org/blog/whos-getting-some-biblical-marriage/; and Jennifer Wright Knust, *Unprotected Texts: The Bible's Surprising Contradictions about Sex and Desire* (New York: HarperOne, 2011), 47–77.

24. On Jesus's anti-family-values campaign, see Dale Martin, "Familiar Idolatry and the Christian Case against Marriage," in *Sex and the Single Savior: Gender and Sexuality in Biblical Interpretation* (Louisville, Ky.: Westminster John Knox Press, 1996), 103–24. I set aside here all conspiracy theories regarding church cover-ups of Jesus's marriage. On the heterosexual agenda of these conspiracy theories' most popular articulation, Dan Brown's 2003 novel *The Da Vinci Code*, see Richard Rambuss, "The Straightest Story Ever Told," *GLQ: A Journal of Lesbian and Gay Studies* 17:4 (2011): 543–73.

25. Of course, this fact has not stopped countless Christian theologians from sourcing so much Jewish suffering to the practice of polygyny. See, for instance, Calvin's gloss on Lamech's marriage to two wives in Genesis 4:19: "We have here the origin of polygamy in a perverse and degenerate race; and the first author of it, a cruel man, destitute of all humanity. . . . For God had determined, that 'they two should be one flesh,' and that is the perpetual order of nature. Lamech, with brutal contempt of God, corrupts nature's laws. The Lord, therefore, willed that the corruption of lawful marriage should proceed from the house of Cain, and from the person of Lamech, in order that polygamists might be ashamed of the example" (*Commentaries on the First Book of Moses Called Genesis*, trans John King, in *Calvin's Commentaries*, vol. 1. [Grand Rapids, Mich.: Baker Book House, 1984], 217).

26. The extent to which David's love for Jonathan is or approximates erotic love or homosexual love is much debated. See, for starters, Anthony Heacock, *Jonathan Loved David: Manly Love in the Bible and the Hermeneutics of Sex* (Sheffield, U.K.: Sheffield Phoenix Press, 2011). The Geneva gloss leverages the ambiguity of the genitive to posit, however improbably, that David means the love of women "towarde their housbands, or their children."

27. Alice Odgen Bellis, *Helpmates, Harlots, and Heroes: Women's Stories in the Hebrew Bible*, 2nd ed. (Louisville, Ky.: Westminster John Knox Press, 2007), 184–90.

28. On the presence of different Pauls in Shakespeare (namely Catholic, Jewish, Protestant, and postmodern), see also Julia Reinhard Lupton, "Paul

Shakespeare," in *Thinking with Shakespeare: Essays on Politics and Life* (Chicago: University of Chicago Press, 2011), 219–46.

29. On this point I follow Travis DeCook and Alan Galey's call for "approaching Shakespeare's use of Scripture with an understanding of the unstable and contested nature of the Bible." See their Introduction: Scriptural Negotiations and Textual Afterlives, *Shakespeare, the Bible, and the Form of the Book: Contested Scriptures*, ed. De Cook and Galey (New York: Routledge, 2012), 11. The dually historicist and presentist aspirations of my work should otherwise be transparent. For an introduction to presentism, see Ewan Fernie, "Shakespeare and the Prospect of Presentism," *Shakespeare Survey* 58 (2005): 169–84. Dolan also adopts a dually historicist and presentist approach to marriage in *Marriage and Violence*.

30. For broader context on the marriage debate, see Melanie Heath, *One Nation under God: The Campaign to Promote Marriage in America* (New York: New York University Press, 2012); Ludger H. Viefhues-Bailey, *Between a Man and a Woman?: Why Conservatives Oppose Same-Sex Marriage* (New York: Columbia University Press, 2010); and Kathleen E. Hull, *Same-Sex Marriage: The Cultural Politics of Love and Law* (Cambridge: Cambridge University Press, 2006).

31. *Obergefell v. Hodges*, 135 S. Ct. 2584 (2015). In his dissent from the majority opinion, Chief Justice John Roberts claims that this expansion opens the legal door to plural marriage. See 135 S. Ct. at 2621 (Roberts, C. J., dissenting).

32. Queer histories of marriage include Mark D. Jordan, *Blessing Same-Sex Unions: The Perils of Queer Romance and the Confusions of Christian Marriage* (Chicago: University of Chicago Press, 2005); and John Boswell, *Same-Sex Unions in Premodern Europe* (Chicago: University of Chicago Press, 1995).

33. Popular Christian literature defending gay marriage includes Gene Robinson, *God Believes in Love: Straight Talk on Gay Marriage* (New York: Vintage, 2013); and David G. Myers and Letha Dawson Scanzoni, *What God Has Joined Together: The Christian Case for Gay Marriage* (New York: HarperOne, 2006). More critically, see many of the essays collected in Kathleen T. Talvacchia, Michael F. Pettinger, and Mark Larrimore, eds., *Queer Christianities: Lived Religion in Transgressive Forms* (New York: New York University Press, 2014).

34. According to US Census Bureau, the rate of marriage has fallen roughly twenty percent since 1950. It currently hovers around fifty percent. See "Families and Living Arrangements," The United States Census Bureau, https://www.census.gov/hhes/families/data/marital.html.

35. Michael Warner, *The Trouble with Normal: Sex, Politics, and the Ethics of Queer Life* (Cambridge, Mass.: Harvard University Press, 2000).

36. Lisa Duggan, "Beyond Marriage: Democracy, Equality, and Kinship for a New Century," *S&F Online* 10, no. 1–2 (Fall 2011/Spring 2012). See also Duggan's *Twilight of Equality: Neoliberalism, Cultural Politics, and the Attack on Democracy* (Boston: Beacon Press, 2003).

37. Judith Butler, "Is Kinship Always Already Heterosexual?" *differences: A Journal of Feminist Cultural Studies* 13, no. 1 (2002): 40. See also *Against Equality: Queer Critiques of Gay Marriage*, ed. Ryan Conrad (Lewiston, Maine: Against Equality Press, 2010); and Michael Cobb, *Single: Arguments for the Uncoupled* (New York: New York University Press, 2012). Dissenting from the majority holding in *Obergefell v. Hodges* that access to marriage and its attendant nurturing of "intimacy" and "spirituality" were unbridgeable freedoms, Justice Antonin Scalia unwittingly aligned himself with the queer left when he opined, "Freedom of intimacy is abridged rather than expanded by marriage." See *Obergefell v. Hodges*, 135 S. Ct. 2630 (Scalia, J., dissenting).

38. I largely take for granted the coexistence of homoeroticism with domestic heterosexuality in Shakespeare. On this coexistence, see Julie Crawford, "Shakespeare. Same Sex. Marriage," *The Oxford Handbook of Shakespeare and Embodiment: Gender, Sexuality, and Race*, ed. Valerie Traub (Oxford: Oxford University Press, 2016), 251–68; Crawford, "The Homoerotics of Shakespeare's Elizabethan Comedies," *A Companion to Shakespeare's Works, Vol. 3: The Comedies*, ed. Richard Dutton and Jean E. Howard (Malden, Mass.: Blackwell, 2003), 137–58; and Mario DiGangi, "Queering the Shakespearean Family," *Shakespeare Quarterly* 47, no. 3 (1996): 269–90. Several critics have also taken a cue from the present contests over gay marriage to theorize the queerness (qua homoeroticism) of Shakespearean marriages: See Arthur L. Little Jr., "The Rites of Queer Marriage in *The Merchant of Venice*," in *Shakesqueer: A Queer Companion to the Complete Works of Shakespeare*, ed. Madhavi Menon (Durham, N.C.: Duke University Press, 2011); Little Jr., "'A Local Habitation and a Name': Presence, Witnessing, and Queer Marriage in Shakespeare's Romantic Comedies," *Presentism, Gender, and Sexuality in Shakespeare*, ed. Evelyn Gajowski (New York: Palgrave Macmillan, 2009), 207–36; Linda Charnes, "Uncivil Unions," *Presentism, Gender, and Sexuality in Shakespeare*, ed. Gajowski, 195–206; and David L. Orvis, "Figuring Marital Queerness in Shakespeare's Sonnets," *Magic, Marriage, and Midwifery: Eroticism in the Middle Ages and the Renaissance*, ed. Ian Frederick Moulton (Amsterdam: Rodopi, 2015), 131–50.

39. Jonathan Dollimore, *Sexual Dissidence: Augustine to Wilde, Freud to Foucault* (Oxford: Oxford University Press, 1991), 121.

1. PAUL IN EPHESUS: SELF AND SEXUAL DIFFERENCE IN *THE COMEDY OF ERRORS*

1. Also relevant is Ephesians' description of Christ breaking "the stoppe of the partition wall" and "abrogating through his flesh . . . the Law . . . for to make of twaine one newe man in him self" (2:14–15). While no less keyed to salvation, this process is somewhat reversed at the end of *The Comedy of Errors*, as one pair of men, Antipholus and Dromio, become socially legible as two pairs: Antipholus of Ephesus and Antipholus of Syracuse, Dromio of Ephesus and Dromio of Syracuse.

2. The second edition of *The Norton Shakespeare* follows this emendation. The third edition, released in 2015, reverts to "nativity."

3. David Cressy, *Birth, Marriage and Death: Ritual, Religion, and the Life-Cycle in Tudor and Stuart England* (Oxford: Oxford University Press, 1997), 164–72. See also Richard Strier, *The Unrepentant Renaissance: From Petrarch to Shakespeare to Milton* (Chicago: University of Chicago Press, 2011), 184–85, about which I will have much more to say below.

4. Shakespeare chooses the number thirty-three despite the discrepancy it creates. Based on Egeon's claim that Antipholus of Syracuse left home at age eighteen (1.1.125), which was seven years ago (5.1.321), husband and wife have been separated for twenty-five years.

5. On the play's many apocalyptic references, see Patricia Parker, "The Bible and the Marketplace: *The Comedy of Errors*," in *Shakespeare from the Margins: Language, Culture, Context* (Chicago: University of Chicago Press, 1996), 56–82.

6. Lupton, *Citizen-Saints*, 46. Although Emilia's invitation extends only to the duke and her household, the stage directions, "*Exeunt omnes*," suggest that everyone becomes her guest. The Norton even includes "[into the priory]" for clarification.

7. See especially Ann C. Christensen, "'Because their business still lies out a' door': Resisting the Separation of the Spheres in Shakespeare's *The Comedy of Errors*," *Literature and History* 5 (1996): 19–37; and Laurie Maguire, "The Girls from Ephesus," *The Comedy of Errors: Critical Essays*, ed. Robert S. Miola (New York: Routledge, 1997), 355–91.

8. Strier, *The Unrepentant Renaissance*, 154. In a separate argument, Strier maintains that *The Comedy of Errors* critiques patience as a virtue that justifies ongoing hardship (42–48).

9. Strier, *The Unrepentant Renaissance*, 184.

10. Strier, *The Unrepentant Renaissance*, 186.

11. This obfuscation is ironic given Strier's previous critique of New Historicism's tendency toward totalization. See *Resistant Structures: Particularity,*

Radicalism, and Renaissance Texts (Berkeley: University of California Press, 1997).

12. Strier, *The Unrepentant Renaissance*, 181.

13. The scholar who has worked most on this figuration of Christ is, of course, Carolyn Walker Bynum, beginning with *Jesus as Mother: Studies in the Spirituality of the High Middle Ages* (Berkeley: University of California Press, 1984), and *Holy Feast and Holy Fast: The Religious Significance of Food to Medieval Woman* (Berkeley: University of California Press, 1988). On Shakespeare's medievalism generally, see Curtis Perry and John Watkins, eds. *Shakespeare and the Middle Ages* (Oxford: Oxford University Press, 2009); Ruth Morse, Helen Cooper, and Peter Holland, eds., *Medieval Shakespeare: Pasts and Presents* (Cambridge: Cambridge University Press, 2013); and Helen Cooper, *Shakespeare and the Medieval World* (New York: Bloomsbury, 2014).

14. Julian of Norwich, *The Shewings of Julian of Norwich*, ed. Georgia Ronan Crampton (Kalamazoo, Mich.: Medieval Institute Publications, 1994), 124.

15. Although Egeon states that only "by names" (1.1.52) could Dromio initially be distinguished from Dromio, the Dromios, like the Antipholus brothers, share the same name. In the Folio, names are even more confusing, as *E. Ant.* stands for Antipholus of Syracuse, initially designated *Ant. Errotis*. As Shankar Raman observes in "Marking Time: Memory and Market in *The Comedy of Errors*," *Shakespeare Quarterly* 56, no. 2 (2005), "the name intended to distinguish between the twins—*Ant. E*[*rrotis*]—becomes the very name that 'confounds' them—*Ant. E*[*phesus*]" (189).

16. See, especially, Barbara Freedman, "Reading Errantly: Misrecognition and the Uncanny," in *Staging the Gaze: Postmodernism, Psychoanalysis, and Shakespearean Comedy* (Ithaca, N.Y.: Cornell University Press, 1991), 78–113; and Lynn Enterline, *The Tears of Narcissus: Melancholia and Masculinity in Early Modern Writing* (Stanford, Calif.: Stanford University Press, 1995), 192–228. See also Lynne Huffer's Foucauldian rejection of Lacanian temptation in "In Praise of Error," in *Shakesqueer*, ed. Menon, 72–79.

17. Steve Mentz, *At the Bottom of Shakespeare's Ocean* (New York: Continuum, 2009), 41.

18. On Hamlet's lines, see Maus, *Inwardness and Theater*, 1–6.

19. With Antipholus of Syracuse's identical twin at this side, this "I am" is already spectacularly displaced. The utterance illustrates Barbara Freedman's claim that Shakespeare's comedies use the space of the stage to "enact the impossibility of self-presence" (*Staging the Gaze*, 110). If the sea promises, in Antipholus's original metaphor, to swallow all into one, the space of the stage at the end of the play spreads selves apart but confounds them

through surface-bouncing reflections. These reflections destabilize familial distinctions, turning the tide of error back to the sea's promise of universal incorporation and, in Egeon's opening account, the dissolution of the family. "Me thinks you are my glass," Dromio of Ephesus says to his brother, "*and not my brother*" (5.1.419, emphasis added).

20. Strier, *The Unrepentant Renaissance*, 176.

21. Strier, *The Unrepentant Renaissance*, 175–76.

22. On accident, see Michael Witmore, "The Avoidance of Ends in *The Comedy of Errors*," in *Culture of Accidents: Unexpected Knowledges in Early Modern England* (Stanford, Calif.: Stanford University Press, 2001), 62–81.

23. I borrow the term *heterotopia* from Michel Foucault, who defines it (loosely) as "a kind of effectively enacted utopia in which the real sites, all the other real sites that can be found within the culture, are simultaneously represented, contested, and inverted" ("Of Other Spaces," *Diacritics* 16, no. 1 [1986]: 24). Heterotopias are sites of spatio-temporal warping, where past and future sometimes converge in a single moment and are sometimes transversed outside the span of ordinary time. The theater is one of Foucault's examples. It ushers "onto the rectangle of the stage, one after the other, a whole series of places that are foreign to one another" (25). For more, see Joanne Tompkins, *Theater's Heterotopias: Performance and the Cultural Politics of Space* (New York: Palgrave Macmillan, 2014).

24. Curtis Perry, "Commerce, Community and Nostalgia in *The Comedy of Errors*," *Money and the Age of Shakespeare*, ed. Linda Woodbridge (New York: Palgrave Macmillan, 2003), 49. See also Raman, "Memory and Market"; and Douglas Lanier, "'Stigmatical in Making': The Material Culture of *The Comedy of Errors*," *English Literary History* 23 (1993): 81–112.

25. Elisabeth Schüssler Fiorenza, *But She Said: Feminist Practices of Biblical Interpretation* (Boston: Beacon Press, 1993), 7–8.

26. In *Rethinking the Turn to Religion in Early Modern English Literature: The Poetics of All Believers* (New York: Palgrave Macmillan, 2008), Gregory Kneidel cautions against the periodizing assumption that the Paul of the Renaissance is the Paul of inwardness while the Paul of universalism is the Paul of postmodernity. I claim only that *The Comedy of Errors* represents the universal body through a farcical rejection of inwardness.

27. Dromio of Ephesus is twice beaten for threatening his masters' headship. He is beaten for "flout[ing]" Antipholus of Syracuse "unto [his] *face*" (1.2.91, emphasis added). A scene later, Adriana beats him for flouting her second order to bring Antipholus home. She threatens to "break [his] pate across" (2.1.77), and Dromio quips that between her and her husband he "shall have a holy head" (2.1.79)—ironically, a head sacred for being full of

holes, like Christ's. On the tenuous lines between servants and masters in *The Comedy of Errors*, see Elizabeth Rivlin, *The Aesthetics of Service in Early Modern England* (Evanston, Ill.: Northwestern University Press, 2012), 30–35.

28. Jane Hwang Degenhardt, *Islamic Conversion and Christian Resistance on the Early Modern Stage* (Edinburgh: Edinburgh University Press, 2010), 46.

29. For discussions of the authorship of Ephesians, see Stephen Fowl, *Ephesians: Being a Christian at Home and in the Cosmos* (Sheffield, U.K.: Phoenix Sheffield Press, 2014), 17–32; Ernest Best, *A Critical and Exegetical Commentary on Ephesians* (London: T&T Clark, 1998), 6–36.

30. Desiderius Erasmus, *Paraphrases on the Epistles to the Corinthians, Ephesians, Philippians, Colossians, and Thessalonians*, Collected Works of Erasmus 43, ed. Robert D. Sider (Toronto: University of Toronto Press, 2009), 1524n12.

31. So lexically and theologically strange is this verse and the passage of which it is a part (11:2–16), however, that some scholars have argued it is a later interpolation. Raymond Collins provides a brief overview of these claims in *First Corinthians, Sacra Pagina* Series 7, ed. Raymond F. Collins (Collegeville, Minn.: The Liturgical Press, 1999), 393–94.

32. On the one-sex model of the body in Galatians 3:28, see especially Lone Fatum, "Images of God and the Glory of Man: Women in the Pauline Congregation," in *The Image of God: Gender Models in Judeo-Christian Tradition*, ed. Kari Elisabeth Børresen (Minneapolis, Minn.: Fortress Press, 1995), 50–133. For a history of the interpretations, see Dennis MacDonald, *There Is No Male or Female* (Philadelphia: Fortress Press, 1987); Judith Gundry-Volf, "Male and Female in Creation and New Creation: Interpretations of Galatians 3:28c in 1 Corinthians 7," in *To Tell the Mystery: Essays on New Testament Eschatology in Honor of Robert H. Gundry*, ed. Thomas E. Schmidt and Moises Silva (Sheffield, U.K.: Sheffield Academic Press, 1994), 95–121; and Dale Martin, "The Queer History of Galatians 3:28: 'No Male and Female,'" in *Sex and the Single Savior*, 77–90. Matthew Kueffler has further demonstrated that "the genderless ideal in earliest Christianity was understood mostly as a call for women to become men" (*The Manly Eunuch: Masculinity, Gender Ambiguity, and Christian Ideology in Late Antiquity* [Chicago: University of Chicago Press, 2001], 226). For early Christian efforts to locate the female in the body of Christ, see Benjamin Dunning, *Specters of Paul: Sexual Difference in Early Christian Thought* (Philadelphia: University of Pennsylvania Press, 2011). On the one-sex model of the body generally, see Thomas Laqueur, *Making Sex: Body and Gender from the Greeks to Freud* (Cambridge, Mass.: Harvard University Press, 1992).

33. Alain Badiou, *Saint Paul: The Foundations of Universalism*, trans. Ray Brassier (Stanford, Calif.: Stanford University Press, 2003), 9.

34. However clear this gloss's endorsement of the one-sex model of the body, the assumed dominance of this model in Renaissance England has been challenged. See Katharine Park, "The Rediscovery of the Clitoris: French Medicine and the Tribade, 1570–1620," *The Body in Parts: Fantasies of Corporeality in Early Modern Europe*, ed. Carla Mazzio and David Hillman (New York: Routledge, 1997), 171–93; and Janet Adelman, "Making Desire Perfection: Shakespeare and the One-Sex Model," *Enacting Gender on the English Renaissance Stage*, ed. Viviana Comensoli and Anne Russell (Urbana: University of Illinois Press, 1999), 23–52.

35. Ernest Best argues that the author of Ephesians—whom I have called Paul of Ephesus, and whom Best, serendipitously for my discussion of *The Comedy of Errors*, abbreviates as AE—most likely derived his theology of the body from 1 Corinthians (*A Critical and Exegetical Commentary on Ephesians*, 189–90).

36. Dale Martin, "Paul without Passion: On Paul's Rejection of Desire in Sex and Marriage," in *Sex and the Single Savior*, 65–76.

37. This distinction is based on a comparison of 1 Corinthians and Ephesians alone. For more discussion of Paul of Tarsus's eschatology and its relationship to Paul of Ephesus's, see Fowl, *Ephesians*, 27–29.

38. Dolan, *Marriage and Violence*, 50. Another aid to this expectation is the insistence of the author of 1 Peter that wives "be subject to their housbands" (3:1) while husbands give "honour unto the woman, as unto the weaker vessel" (3:7).

39. For this argument, see Jacob Taubes, *The Political Theology of Paul*, trans. Donna Hollander (Stanford, Calif.: Stanford University Press, 2003); and Kenneth Reinhard, "Paul and the Political Theology of the Neighbor," in *Paul among the Philosophers*, ed. Ward Blanton and Hent de Vries (New York: Fordham University Press, 2013), 449–65.

40. Best, *A Critical and Exegetical Commentary on Ephesians*, 548.

41. Kenneth Reinhard, "Toward a Political Theology of the Neighbor," in *The Neighbor: Three Inquires in Political Theology*, by Slavoj Žižek, Eric L. Santner, and Kenneth Reinhard (Chicago: University of Chicago Press, 2006), 18, 46.

42. Sigmund Freud, *Civilization and Its Discontents*, in *The Complete Psychological Works of Sigmund Freud*, ed. James Strachey (London: Hogarth Press, 1961), 21:109.

43. Jacques Lacan, *The Ethics of Psychoanalysis, 1959–1960: The Seminar of Jacques Lacan, Book VII*, ed. Jacques-Alain Miller, trans. Dennis Porter (New York: Norton, 1992), 186.

44. Žižek, *In Defense of Lost Causes* (New York: Verso, 2008), 16. See also

"Neighbors and Other Monsters: A Plea for Ethical Violence," in *The Neighbor*, 134–90.

45. Žižek, *In Defense of Lost Causes*, 16. This definition of the neighbor suggests a perverse reading of the parable of the Good Samaritan in Luke 10:29–37. Asked to identify the neighbor, Jesus responds with the story of a man beaten and robbed on his way from Jerusalem to Jericho. A priest and a Levite pass by the wounded man, but a Samaritan—traditionally an ethnic enemy of the Jews—shows compassion. The Samaritan bandages the Jew's wounds and takes him to an inn, paying the bill for the man's stay and promising to return and settle any outstanding debts. When Jesus asks his interlocutors to identify the neighbor among the three men who crossed paths with the wounded one, the answer seems obvious: the neighbor is the Samaritan, "He that showed mercie" (10:37). The parable thereby expands the category of "the neighbor" beyond one's fellow Jews, familiarizing what had been foreign and strange in keeping with the universalist aspirations of Luke's Christ. Yet the risk of posing a rhetorical question is that of receiving an answer one does not expect. What if Jesus and his interlocutors are wrong, and the real Neighbors are the two who left the man to die?

46. One source of inspiration for this chapter was Kent R. Lehnhof's discussion, in a 2013 Shakespeare Association of America paper for the seminar "Anti-Social Shakespeare," of the infrequent references to the second greatest commandment in the Book of Homilies. For Lehnhof, this silence registers a discomfort with the ethics of reciprocity. Portions of this paper, without the discussion of the Book of Homilies, were later published as "Relation and Responsibility: A Levinasian Reading of *King Lear*," *Modern Philology* 111, no. 3 (2014): 485–509.

47. *The Familie of Love* (London: n.p., 1608), C2v. For a history of the Family of Love, see Christopher Marsh, *The Family of Love in English Society, 1550–1630* (Oxford: Oxford University Press, 1994).

48. Henrie Smith, *A Preparative to Marriage* (London: n.p., 1591), 50–51. This formulation of the wife as the nearest neighbor also appears in Peter T. O'Brien, *The Letter to the Ephesians* (Grand Rapids, Mich.: William B. Eerdmans, 1999), 426.

49. It is possible to read Adriana as such a neighboring wife. Luciana chastises her sister for her show of "*head*strong liberty" (2.1.15, emphasis added). Antipholus of Ephesus claims that his "wife is shrewish when [he] keep[s] not hours" (3.1.2). And Emilia, for all the theological radicalism I attribute to her figuration of Christ as female, rebukes Adriana as if she were a basilisk: "The venom clamors of a jealous woman / Poisons more deadly than a mad dog's tooth" (5.1.69–70).

50. [John Jewel] "Of the State of Matrimonie," in *The Seconde Tome of Homilies* (London: n.p., 1563), Fol. 259v.

51. Dr. James Dobson and Shirley Dobson, *Night Light: A Devotional for Couples* (Sisters, Oreg.: Multnomah, 2000), 79.

52. Plautus, *Amphitryo*, in *The Rope and Other Plays*, trans. E. F. Watling (London: Penguin 1964), 258. Also quoted in Strier, *The Unrepentant Renaissance*, 172.

53. Strier, *The Unrepentant Renaissance*, 173.

54. Strier denies their sexual involvement as well, and rather weakly: "*Errors* seems to insist on Antipholus's lack of sexual involvement with the Courtesan" (*The Unrepentant Renaissance*, 163). Compare Laurie Maguire's argument about the "association between food and sex (the former a metaphor for the latter)," which Maguire imports from *Pericles* to raise questions about Antipholus of Ephesus dining with the Courtesan and Adriana dining with Antipholus of Syracuse ("The Girls from Ephesus," 367–68). I make a similar argument about the relationship between food and sex in "The Seduction of Milton's Lady: Rape, Psychoanalysis, and the Erotics of Consumption in *Comus*," in *Sex before Sex: Figuring the Act in Early Modern England*, ed. James Bromley and Will Stockton (Minneapolis: University of Minnesota Press, 2013), 233–62.

55. Again illustrating his difference from Paul of Ephesus, Paul of Tarsus contrasts this union of the flesh to that with the Lord as "one spirit" (1 Corinthians 6:17).

56. Thomas Luxon, *Single Imperfection: Milton, Marriage and Friendship* (Duquesne, Pa.: Duquesne University Press, 2005), 44.

57. Luxon, *Single Imperfection*, 44.

58. In Minucius Felix's *Octavius*, a late-second-century dialogic work of Christian apologetics, the pagan Caecilius Natalis reports, "Everywhere also there is mingled among them [Christians] a certain religion of lust, and they call one another promiscuously brothers and sisters, that even a not unusual debauchery [orgies] may by the intervention of that sacred name become incestuous." See Minucius Felix, *Octavius*, trans. R. E. Wallis, *The Ante-Nicene Fathers: Translations of the Writings of the Fathers down to A.D. 325*, ed. Alexander Roberts and James Donaldson, vol. 4. (Grand Rapids, Mich.: W. B. Eerdmans. 1965), 177. See also Robert Luis Wilken, *Christians as the Romans Saw Them* (1984; New Haven, Conn.: Yale University Press, 2003), 70; and Stephen Benko, *Pagan Rome and Early Christians* (Bloomington: Indiana University Press, 1984), 70.

59. John Ford, *'Tis Pity She's a Whore*, ed. Martin Wiggins (London: Bloomsbury, 2003), 1.1.34.

60. The phrase "romance of orthodoxy" belongs to the title of the eighth chapter of G. K. Chesterton's 1908 *Orthodoxy*, but I lean here on Žižek's

citation of Chesterton to describe libidinal attachment to the law. See Žižek's "The 'Thrilling Romance of Orthodoxy,'" in *The Puppet and the Dwarf: The Perverse Core of Christianity* (Cambridge, Mass.: The MIT Press, 2003), 34–57.

61. Patricia Parker, *Literary Fat Ladies: Rhetoric, Gender, Property* (Ithaca, N.Y.: Cornell University Press, 1987), 18.

62. On the transformation of human to animal in the play, see Holly Dugan, "Aping Rape: Animal Ravishment and Sexual Knowledge in Early Modern England," in *Sex before Sex*, ed. Bromley and Stockton, 216–23.

63. Brigitte Kahl notes that this figuration "doesn't fit any of the current clichés about Paul" (761). She then persuasively accounts for this oddity through a reading of Paul's replacement of biological with spiritual paternity in Galatians 3. For Paul at this moment in messianic history, the only father is God the Father. See "Galatians: On Discomfort about Gender and Other Problems of Otherness," trans. Everett R. Kalin, in *Feminist Biblical Interpretation: A Compendium of Critical Commentary on the Books of the Bible and Related Literature*, ed. Luise Schottroff and Marie-Theres Wacker (Grand Rapids, Mich.: William B. Eerdmans, 2012), 755–66.

2. PORTIA'S PAULINE PERVERSION: *THE MERCHANT OF VENICE* AND ROMANS 1

1. As Julia Lupton observes, the marriage between Lorenzo and Jessica takes on a sacramental cast through its conjunction with Jessica's conversion. Effected under the cover of darkness and without Shylock's knowledge, however, this marriage is also "*merely civil*, or *barely civil*, a libertine exercise at the limits of social norms" (*Citizen-Saints*, 85, emphasis in original). The Council of Trent upheld marriages made without parental approval, but it emphasized that both God and the church disapproved of them. See *Canons and Decrees of the Council of Trent*. trans. Henry Joseph Schroeder, O.P. (1941. Rockford, Ill.: Tan Books and Publishers, 1978), 183.

2. The Norton glosses Jessica's claim with reference to 1 Corinthians 7:14.

3. In *Shakespeare, Race, and Colonialism* (Oxford: Oxford University Press, 2002), Ania Loomba suggests that Jessica did not convert (158). See also Lara Bovilsky, *Barbarous Play: Race on the Renaissance Stage* (Minneapolis: University of Minnesota Press, 2008), 81–92; and Heather Anne Hirschfield, "'We all expect a gentle answer, Jew': *The Merchant of Venice* and the Psychotheology of Conversion," *ELH* 73, no. 1 (2006): 61–81. For a history of the controversy over Jewish convertibility, see Steven F. Kruger, *The Spectral Jew: Conversion and Embodiment in Medieval Europe* (Minneapolis: University of Minnesota Press, 2006).

4. On the gendering of Jews as feminine, see M. Lindsay Kaplan, "Jessica's Mother: Medieval Constructions of Jewish Race and Gender in *The Merchant of Venice*," *Shakespeare Quarterly* 58, no. 1 (2007): 1–30; Lisa Lampert, *Gender and Jewish Difference from Paul to Shakespeare* (Philadelphia: University of Pennsylvania Press, 2004); and Matthew Biberman, *Masculinity, Anti-Semitism and Early Modern English Literature: From the Satanic to the Effeminate Jew* (Aldershot, U.K.: Ashgate, 2004).

5. Allegorical readings include Barbara K. Lewalski, "Biblical Allusion and Allegory in *The Merchant of Venice*," *Shakespeare Quarterly* 13, no. 3 (1962): 327–43; Lisa Frienkel, "*The Merchant of Venice*: Modern Anti-Semitism and the Veil of Allegory," *Shakespeare and Modernity*, ed. Hugh Grady (New York: Routledge, 2000), 122–41; and Steven Marx, "'Dangerous Conceits' and 'Proofs of Holy Writ': Allusion in *The Merchant of Venice* and Paul's Letter to the Romans," in *Shakespeare and the Bible* (Oxford: Oxford UP, 2000), 103–24.

6. For modern biblical scholars, the conversation about Romans 1:16–27 centers in large part on the extent to which Paul's understanding of "homosexuality" differs from the understandings of modern evangelicals. Dale Martin speaks for the growing critical consensus when he argues that "Romans 1 offers no etiology of homosexual desire or orientation; its etiology of homosexual sex is one no modern scholar has advocated as factual; and its assumptions about 'nature' and sex are not those generally held by modern apologists for heterosexism" (*Sex and the Single Savior*, 60). For more on these verses, see Kyle Harper, *From Shame to Sin: The Christian Transformation of Sexual Morality in Late Antiquity* (Cambridge, Mass.: Harvard University Press, 2013), 93–99; Diana M. Swancutt, "'The Disease of Effemination': The Charge of Effeminacy and the Verdict of God (Romans 1:18–2:16)," in *New Testament Masculinities*, ed. Stephen D. Moore and Janice Capel Anderson (Atlanta: Society of Biblical Literature, 2003), 193–233; Stephen D. Moore, "Sex and the Single Apostle," in *God's Beauty Parlor: And Other Queer Spaces In and Around the Bible* (Stanford, Calif.: Stanford University Press, 2001), 133–72; Bernadette J. Brooten, *Love between Women: Early Christian Responses to Female Homoeroticism* (Chicago: University of Chicago Press, 1996), 29–58; and Martti Nissinen, *Homoeroticism in the Biblical World: A Historical Perspective* (Minneapolis, Minn.: Fortress Press, 1998), 103–13. Richard Halpern is one of the few Renaissance scholars to have discussed Shakespeare's handling of these verses, although he treats the Sonnets rather than *The Merchant of Venice*; see *Shakespeare's Perfume: Sodomy and Sublimity in the Sonnets, Wilde, Freud, and Lacan* (Philadelphia: University of Pennsylvania Press, 2002), 23–24.

7. Michel Foucault, *The History of Sexuality, Volume I: An Introduction*, trans. Robert Hurley (New York: Vintage, 1990), 101. On sodomy's theo-

logical history, see Mark Jordan, *The Invention of Sodomy in Christian Theology* (Chicago: University of Chicago, 1997).

8. Martin Luther, *Lectures on Romans*, in *Luther's Works*, ed. Hilton C. Oswald (St. Louis, Mo.: Concordia Publishing House, 1972), 25:12–13.

9. *Annotations upon All the Books of the Old and New Testament* (London: n.p., 1645), sig. AA1v.

10. Andrew Willet, *Hexapla: That Is, a Six-fold Commentarie upon the Most Divine Epistle of the Holy Apostle S. Paul to the Romanes* (Cambridge: n.p., 1611), sig. G3r.

11. Willet, *Hexapla*, sig G3r.

12. Brooten, *Love between Women*, 29–58.

13. Willet, *Hexapla*, sig G3r.

14. Sometimes the destruction is understood as the result of a generalized wickedness (Matthew 10:15, Amos 4:6), sometimes idolatry (Deuteronomy 29:17–23), and sometimes selfishness (Isaiah 1:10ff, Ezekiel 16:49–50). For the authors of Jude and 2 Peter, the Sodomites are guilty of wanting to have sex with angels (Jude 6–7, 2 Peter 2:4–10). Most biblical scholars now agree that Sodom and Gomorrah were destroyed for the sin of inhospitality. See Knust, *Unprotected Texts*, 164–73.

15. Thomas Wilson, *A Commentary upon the Most Divine Epistle of S. Paul to the Romans* (London: n.p., 1614), 45.

16. Martin, *Sex and the Single Savior*, 59.

17. Jean E. Howard, *The Stage and Social Struggle*, 112.

18. Will Fisher, "Queer Money," *ELH* 66, no. 1 (1999): 1–23. On Shylock's sexually suspicious financial dealings, see also A. W. Barnes, *Post-Closet Masculinities in Early Modern England* (Lewisburg, Pa.: Bucknell University Press, 2009), 90–101.

19. Thomas Pie, *Usuries Spright Conjured: Or a Scholasticall Determination of Usury*. (London: n.p., 1604), 19.

20. As David Hawkes observes, "the unnatural reproduction which is usury is employed as an ironic figure for the natural reproduction which springs from heterosexual love." At the same time, it is possible to read the speaker as a usurer who lends the young man's "use" to women and receives interest in return. See "Sodomy, Usury, and the Narrative of Shakespeare's Sonnets," *Renaissance Studies* 14, no. 3 (2000): 354.

21. Hence Joseph Pequigney's claim in "The Two Antonios and Same-Sex Love in *Twelfth Night* and *The Merchant of Venice*," *English Literary Renaissance* 22, no. 2 (1992), that Antonio can't be a homosexual because he is a Christian (215).

22. Little Jr., "The Rites of Queer Marriage," 221. Amy Greenstadt makes a similar argument in "The Kindest Cut: Circumcision and Queer

Kinship in *The Merchant of Venice*," *ELH* 80, no. 4 (2013): 945–80: Antonio's "fantasy points to a parallel between the rituals of marital consummation and circumcision, both of which establish covenants through the permanent sacrifice of a piece of genitalia—the hymen or the foreskin. In deciding to offer up his flesh, Antonio appropriates and merges elements of both rituals to enforce his love for Bassanio" (953). Compare the contest to the official rites of marriage offered by Sonnet 116, where marriage is not a union of flesh but rather of minds. If read as a poem about homoerotic love, the poem's disembodiment of the lovers may be understood as a way of overcoming the impediment of sex (Orvis, "Figuring Marital Queerness"). I would note, too, that nothing in Sonnet 116 restricts a reading of its imagined marriage to a monogamous union of two.

23. Little Jr., "The Rites of Queer Marriage," 216. See also Steve Patterson, "The Bankruptcy of Homoerotic Amity in Shakespeare's *Merchant of Venice*," *Shakespeare Quarterly* 50, no. 1 (1999): 9–32. Histories of this encroachment include Alan Bray, *The Friend* (Chicago: University of Chicago Press, 2006); and Valerie Traub, *The Renaissance of Lesbianism in Early Modern England* (Cambridge: Cambridge University Press, 2002), 229–325.

24. Natasha Korda incisively reads Portia as a usurer who "maneuvers within the legal system to protect her 'bond' and hedge against risk." See "Dame Usury: Gender, Credit, and (Ac)counting in the Sonnets and *The Merchant of Venice*," *Shakespeare Quarterly* 60, no. 2 (2009): 142–43 See also Lars Engle, "Money and Moral Luck in *The Merchant of Venice*," in *Shakespearean Pragmatism: Market of His Time* (Chicago: University of Chicago Press, 1993), 77–106. For a more textured account of the materiality of love than the one offered in my strategically moralizing account here, see Katharine Eisaman Maus, "The Properties of Friendship in *The Merchant of Venice*," in *Being and Having in Shakespeare* (Oxford: Oxford University Press, 2013), 75–97.

25. Martin, *Sex and the Single Savior*, 54. As Jennifer Wright Knust argues in *Abandoned to Lust: Sexual Slander and Ancient Christianity* (New York: Columbia University Press, 2005), this association of idolatry with sexual sin is also a rhetorical commonplace in the Hebrew Bible, deployed by Jews to separate themselves from other tribes (54–55).

26. Willet, *Hexapla*, sig. F6v.

27. I quote the verses from the Geneva Bible. The authors of the *Annotations* actually write that Asá took "away both the Idols, and male stews" (sig. AA1v).

28. Thomas H. Luxon, "A Second Daniel: The Jew and the 'True Jew' in *The Merchant of Venice*," *Early Modern Literary Studies* 4, no. 3 (1999): 22.

29. James O'Rourke, *Retheorizing Shakespeare through Presentist Readings* (New York: Routledge, 2011), 375–76.

30. Janet Adelman, *Blood Relations: Christian and Jew in* The Merchant of Venice (Chicago: University of Chicago Press, 2008), 133.

31. Adelman, *Blood Relations*, 133.

32. Eric S. Mallin, *Godless Shakespeare* (London: Continuum, 2007), 44. In his chapter on the play in *The Melancholy Assemblage: Affect and Epistemology in the English Renaissance* (New York: Fordham University, 2013), Drew Daniel reads Antonio's masochistic fantasy as "the political and ethical fantasy of subjection at the heart of the social assemblage that surround him" (95). Also relevant here is Harry Berger Jr.'s reading of Portia's "mercifixion," a form of "negative usury" that "sinks[s] hooks of gratitude and obligation deep into the beneficiary's bowels" ("Marriage and Mercifixion in *The Merchant of Venice*: The Casket Scene Revisited," *Shakespeare Quarterly* 32, no. 2 [1981]: 161).

33. Moore, *God's Beauty* Parlor, 162. See also Knust, *Abandoned to Lust*, 67–70; and Kent L. Brinthall, *Ecce Homo: The Male-Body-in-Pain as Redemptive Figure* (Chicago: University of Chicago Press, 2011). On Renaissance Protestant efforts to perform the same regendering, see Debora Keller Shuger, *The Renaissance Bible: Scholarship, Sacrifice, and Subjectivity* (Berkeley: University of California Press, 1994), 112–17.

34. Cressy, *Birth, Marriage and Death*, 344.

35. Willet, *Hexapla*, sig. G3r.

36. I am grateful to Mario DiGangi for this suggestion. Willet cites David Pareus (a German Protestant theologian and Willet's contemporary) and Chrysostom as authorities on this point, but I could not locate Pareus's commentary, and Chrysostom's homily on Romans 1:26–27 does not exactly clear up Willet's math. For Chrysostom, verse 26 refers to a violation of the union of man and woman as one flesh. The devil "sundered the sexes from one another, and made the one to become two parts in opposition to the law of God." The result is "war": "women again abused women, and not men only," and "men stood against one another, and against the female sex." See "Homily IV: Romans I: 26, 27," *A Select Library of the Nicene and Post-Nicene Fathers of the Christian Church*, vol. 11, ed. Philip Schaff (New York: The Christian Literature Company, 1889), 354.

37. Little Jr., "The Rites of Queer Marriage," 222. See similarly Bruce R. Smith, *Homosexual Desire in Shakespeare's England: A Cultural Poetics* (Chicago: University of Chicago Press, 1994), 67; and Richard Levin, "Odd Man Out in Venice," in *Love and Society in Shakespearean Comedy* (Newark: University of Delaware Press, 1985), 30–52. Even a critic as dedicated to reading against the grain as Alan Sinfield more or less agrees with this consensus.

Contrasting *The Merchant of Venice* with the ostensibly more queer-friendly ending of *Twelfth Night*, Sinfield leans on performance, rather than the text, to suggest that, at best, Antonio might be "delighted with his boyfriend's lucky break" ("How to Read *The Merchant of Venice* without Being Heterosexist," in *Shakespeare, Authority, Sexuality: Unfinished Business in Cultural Materialism* [New York: Routledge, 2006], 66). Contrast Pequigney, who argues for Antonio's "incorporation in the marriage" ("The Two Antonios," 218), and this despite his rather essentialist approach to sexual and religious identity.

38. Shannon, "Likenings," 19. Shannon proceeds to read the curious ring exchange in masculine terms: "Portia's husbandries of gender, friendship, and the ring rewrite the ring to signify a kind of male marriage, a marriage of likes" (20). For readings that also entertain the anal significance of the ring, see Orgel, *Impersonations*, 75–77; Edward J. Geiseidt, "Antonio's Claim: Triangulated Desire and Queer Kinship in Shakespeare's *The Merchant of Venice*," *Shakespeare* 5, no. 4 (2009): 338–54; and Joan Hutton Landis, "'By two-headed Janus': Double Discourse in *The Merchant of Venice*," *Upstart Crow* 16 (1996): 13–30.

39. On gynosodomy, see Celia R. Daileader, "Back-Door Sex: Renaissance Gynosodomy, Aretino, and the Exotic," *ELH* 69, no. 2 (2002): 303–34; and, although he does not use this particularly phrase, Mario DiGangi, *The Homoerotics of Early Modern Drama* (Cambridge: Cambridge University Press, 1996). On the anal deconstruction of sexual difference, see also Jonathan Goldberg, "*Romeo and Juliet*'s Open Rs," *Queering the Renaissance*, ed. Jonathan Goldberg (Durham, N.C.: Duke University Press, 1994), 218–35.

40. Will Stockton, *Playing Dirty: Sexuality and Waste in Early Modern Comedy* (Minneapolis: University of Minnesota, 2011). I discuss Graziano's joke briefly in Chapter 3's reading of *All's Well That Ends Well* (60).

41. In *Renaissance Literature before Heterosexuality* (New York: Palgrave Macmillan 2007), Rebecca Ann Bach argues that the period's pervasive misogyny renders anachronistic descriptions of male-female relations as heterosexual.

42. Without focusing on orifices, this queer reading of Galatians 3:28—a reading in which sex is fluid and inclusive rather than dichotomous—is the one Dale Martin advocates ("The Queer History," 100–102).

43. On the anality of Shylock's name, see David Hillman, "Freud's Shylock," *American Imago* 70, no. 1 (2013): 16; and Berger Jr., "Marriage and Mercifixion," 156. This discussion of Judaism and anality obliquely develops similar arguments I previously made in a reading of Thomas Nashe's *The Unfortunate Traveller* (*Playing Dirty*, 67–96).

44. Adelman, *Blood Relations*, 73.

45. Luxon, "A Second Daniel," 15.

46. Jonathan Walters, "'No More Than a Boy': The Shifting Construction of Masculinity from Ancient Greece to the Middle Ages," *Gender & History* 5 (1991): 29.

47. In "The Renaissance Beard: Masculinity in Early Modern England and Europe," *Renaissance Quarterly* 54, no. 1 (2001), 155–87, Will Fisher argues that the boy constitutes a kind of third gender.

48. Kathryn M. Ringrose, "Making Sense of Tradition: Regendering Legendary Narratives," in *Perfect Servant: Eunuchs and the Social Construction of Gender in Byzantium* (Chicago: University of Chicago Press, 2003), 87–107.

49. *Annotations* (1645), sig. VVVV1r.

50. *Annotations upon All the Books of the Old and New Testament* (London: n.p., 1651), sig. ZZ3r.

51. On early Christian interpretations of this verse, see Matthew Kueffler, "'Eunuchs for the Sake of the Kingdom of Heaven': Castration and Christian Manliness," in *The Manly Eunuch*, 245–82.

52. Richard Rambuss, *Closet Devotions* (Durham, N.C.: Duke University Press, 1998), 38; Moore, *God's Beauty Parlor*, 170.

53. Moore, *God's Beauty Parlor*, 170.

3. CHASTE IMPOSSIBILITIES: ADULTERY AND INDIVIDUATION IN *OTHELLO*

1. "Judean" appears in the Folio. The Quarto reads "Indian."

2. Robert N. Watson, "*Othello* as Protestant Propaganda," in *Religion and Culture in Early Modern England*, ed. Claire McEachern and Debora Shuger (Cambridge: Cambridge University Press, 1997), 234–57. Compare Maurice Hunt's argument in "Predestination and the Heresy of Merit in *Othello*," *Comparative Drama* 30, no. 3 (1996): 346–76, for the play's engagement with the Calvinist doctrine of double predestination. If, as Cassio says, "there be souls must be saved, and there be souls must not be saved" (2.3.89–90), marriage is irrelevant to salvation, and the play's marriage drama becomes the mere background against which Othello evinces his lack of grace.

3. Huston Diehl, *Staging Reform, Reforming the Stage: Protestantism and the Popular Theater in Early Modern England* (Ithaca, N.Y.: Cornell University Press, 1997), 128–37.

4. Degenhardt, *Islamic Conversion and Christian Resistance on the Early Modern Stage*, 49–70.

5. Throughout *Othello*, the rhetoric of sexual purity intertwines with the rhetoric of racial purity. Illustrative is the textual crux of 3.3.391–93, the interchangeable pronouns of which also bespeak the marital union of husband and wife as one flesh: "My ['Her' in Q2] name, that was as fresh / As Dian's visage, is now begrimed and black / As mine own face." Similarly illustrative is

Iago's even more famous debasement of human to animal: "Even now, now, very now, an old black ram / Is tupping your white ewe" (1.1.88–89). For an exceptional materialist analysis of Iago's associations of miscegenation with bodily impurity, see Ben Saunders, "Iago's Clyster: Purgation, Anality, and the Civilizing Process," *Shakespeare Quarterly* 55, no. 2 (2004): 148–76. As Sara Moslener has demonstrated in *Virgin Nation: Sexual Purity and American Adolescence* (Oxford: Oxford University Press, 2015), American evangelical preoccupations with adolescent sexual hygiene have also frequently accompanied fears of racial and national deterioration. In the nineteenth and early twentieth centuries, this racism was often overt, with purity advocates predicating their campaigns on the defense of white superiority. In more recent history, this racism tends to be subtler, as sexual purity campaigns align themselves with largely white middle-class economic and national values, sometimes citing the deterioration of black family as a consequence of sexual impurity. The long arm of the sacramental construction of marriage is especially apparent in these ongoing, often apocalyptic arguments that saving the race, nation, and civilization depends on remaining sexually pure.

6. On these many questions, see Ania Loomba, "*Othello* and the Racial Question," in *Shakespeare, Race, and Colonialism*, 91–111; Daniel Vitkus, "Othello Turns Turk," in *Turning Turk: The English Theater and the Multicultural Mediterranean* (New York: Palgrave Macmillan, 2002); Julia Reinhard Lupton, "Othello Circumcised," in *Citizen-Saints*, 103–23; Emily Bartels, "The 'stranger of here and everywhere': *Othello* and the Moor of Venice," in *Speaking of the Moor: From* Alcazar *to* Othello (Philadelphia: University of Pennsylvania Press, 2009), 155–90; Daniel Boyarin, "Othello's Penis: Or, Islam in the Closet," in *Shakesqueer*, ed. Menon, 254–62; and Dennis Austin Britton, "Transformative and Restorative Romance: Re-'turning' *Othello* and the Location of Christian Identity," in *Becoming Christian: Race, Reformation, and Early Modern English Romance* (New York: Fordham University Press, 2014), 112–41.

7. I am concerned here with the impossibility of this relinquishment, but as Kathryn Schwarz has demonstrated in *What You Will: Gender, Contract, and Shakespearean Social Space* (Philadelphia: University of Pennsylvania Press, 2011), women's attempts to enact it can also menace patriarchal structures.

8. The speculative reading belongs to Wayne Holmes, "Othello: Is't Possible?," *The Upstart Crow* 1 (1978): 1–23. For a parallel summary of this critical history, see Philip C. Kolin, "Blackness Made Visible: A Survey of *Othello* in Criticism, on Stage, and on Screen," in *Othello: New Critical Essays*, ed. Philip C. Kolin (New York: Routledge, 2002), 16–24.

9. Thomas Rymer, *A Short View of Tragedy* (London: n.p., 1693), 94–95.

10. John Quincy Adams, "Misconceptions of Shakespeare upon the Stage," *New England Magazine* 9 (1835): 438. See also Adams, "The Character of Desdemona," *American Monthly Magazine* 7 (1836): 209–17.

11. W. H. Auden, "The Joker in the Pack," in *The Dyer's Hand and Other Essays* (New York: Random House, 1962), 269.

12. Jan Kott, *Shakespeare Our Contemporary* (New York: Norton, 1974), 118.

13. Robert B. Heilman, *Magic in the Web: Action and Language in* Othello (Lexington: University of Kentucky Press, 1953), 214.

14. Robert G. Hunter, *Shakespeare and the Mystery of God's Judgment* (Athens, Ga.: University of Georgia Press, 1976), 136 (emphasis added).

15. A. C. Bradley, *Shakespearean Tragedy: Lectures on* Hamlet, Othello, King Lear, *and* Macbeth, 2nd ed. (London: Macmillan, 1905), 201–202.

16. S. N. Garner, "Shakespeare's Desdemona," *Shakespeare Studies* 9 (1976): 235.

17. Garner, "Shakespeare's Desdemona," 247.

18. Ann Jennalie Cook, "The Design of Desdemona: Doubts Raised and Resolved," *Shakespeare Studies* 13 (1980): 194.

19. Edward Snow, "Sexual Anxiety and the Male Order of Things in *Othello*," *English Literary Renaissance* 10 (1980): 388.

20. Stephen Greenblatt, "The Improvisation of Power," in *Renaissance Self-Fashioning: From More to Shakespeare* (Chicago: University of Chicago Press, 1980), 232–52.

21. Stanley Cavell, *Disowning Knowledge in Six Plays of Shakespeare* (Cambridge: Cambridge University Press, 1987), 125. Cavell's chapter, "Othello and the Stake of the Other" (125–42), first appeared as "Epistemology and Tragedy: A Reading of *Othello*," *Daedalus* 108, no. 3 (1979): 27–43.

22. Both *Renaissance Self-Fashioning* and *Disowning Knowledge* have been criticized for failing to engage feminism. See, for example, Marguerite Waller's discussion of the former in "Academic Tootsie: The Denial of Difference and the Difference it Makes," *Diacritics* 17, no. 1 (1987): 2–20; and Timothy Murray's review of the latter in *MLN* 105, no. 5 (1990): 1080–85.

23. W. D. Adamson, "Unpinned or Undone?: Desdemona's Critics and the Problem of Sexual Innocence," *Shakespeare Survey* 13 (1980): 179–80.

24. Adamson, "Unpinned or Undone?," 173–74 (emphasis added).

25. This assumption offers a stark example of what Gayle Rubin calls the "fallacy of misplaced scale," wherein "sexual acts are burdened with an excess of significance." See "Thinking Sex: Notes for a Radical Theory of the Politics of Sexuality," in *Deviations: A Gayle Rubin Reader* (Durham, N.C.: Duke University Press, 2011), 149.

26. Carol Thomas Neely, *Broken Nuptials in Shakespeare's Plays* (New Haven, Conn.: Yale University Press, 1985), 112.

27. Neely, *Broken Nuptials*, 113, 116.

28. Janet Adelman, *Suffocating Mothers: Fantasies of Maternal Origin in Shakespeare's Plays:* Hamlet *to* The Tempest (New York: Routledge, 1992), 64.

29. Loomba, *Shakespeare, Race, and Colonialism*, 99–100. In a rewriting of *Othello* as a short play called *Desdemona: A Play about a Handkerchief* (New York: Dramatists Play Service, 1994), Paula Vogel implicitly calls Loomba's bluff. Claiming a lack of interest in presenting "positive" depictions of women, Desdemona features Bianca as the mistress of a brothel in which Desdemona enjoys a Tuesday-night residency. Vogel aligns her feminist sympathies with Othello: "I empathize with Othello more than Desdemona. I am crying for a man who killed his wife because he believes he was cuckolded." Quoted in Jennifer Flaherty, "How Desdemona Learned to Die: Resistance in Paula Vogel's *Desdemona*," *Gender Forum: An Internet Journal for Gender Studies* 49 (2014), 5.

30. Michael Neill, introduction to *Othello*, by William Shakespeare (Oxford: Oxford University Press, 2006), 143.

31. Karen Newman, *Fashioning Femininity and English Renaissance Drama* (Chicago: University of Chicago Press, 1991), 86. The essay, "'And wash the Ethiop white': Femininity and the Monstrous in *Othello*," first appeared in *Shakespeare Reproduced: The Text in History and Ideology*, ed. Jean Howard and Marion F. O'Connor (New York: Methuen, 1987), 143–62. See also Valerie Traub on Othello's racialized distrust of Desdemona in *Desire and Anxiety: Circulations of Sexuality in Shakespearean Drama* (New York: Routledge, 1992), 35–36.

32. Parker, *Shakespeare from the Margins*, 235.

33. Neill, introduction, 135.

34. Laura Gowing, *Common Bodies: Women, Touch, and Power in Seventeenth-Century England* (New Haven, Conn.: Yale University Press, 2003), 32. In "Death and Theory: Or, the Problem of Counterfactual Sex," in *Sex before Sex*, ed. Bromley and Stockton, Kathryn Schwarz likewise reminds us that the "virginal body is one of early modernity's great escape artists, receding ever farther from proof as technologies of verification advance" (54). See further Kathleen Coyne Kelly, *Performing Virginity and Testing Chastity in the Middle Ages* (New York: Routledge, 2000); and Marie H. Loughlin, *Hymeneutics: Interpreting Virginity on the Early Modern Stage* (Lewisburg, Pa.: Bucknell University Press, 1997).

35. Theodora A. Jankowski, *Pure Resistance: Queer Virginity in Early Modern English Drama* (Philadelphia: University of Pennsylvania Press, 2000), 99.

36. Thomas Middleton and William Rowley, *The Changeling*, ed. Michael Neill (London: Methuen, 2006).

37. On adultery plots and the technology of theater, see Katherine Eisaman Maus, "Horns of Dilemma: Jealousy, Gender and Spectatorship in English Renaissance Drama," *ELH* 54, no. 3 (1987): 561–83.

38. Maus, *Inwardness and Theater*, 120.

39. Michael Neill, "Unproper Beds: Race, Adultery, and the Hideous in *Othello*," *Shakespeare Quarterly* 40, no. 1 (1989): 407–411; Bovilsky, "Desdemona's Blackness," in *Barbarous Play*, 37–65.

40. Neill, "Unproper Beds," 400 (emphasis added).

41. This construction, as well as its accompanying jurisprudence, is not the only one in early modern world, of course. The jurisprudence of defamation provides a relevant alternative in which the accused are sometimes vindicated after challenging their accusers. Lisa Jardine pursues this alternative in "'Why Should He Call Her a Whore?': Defamation and Desdemona's Case," in *Reading Shakespeare Historically* (New York: Routledge, 1996), 18–33.

42. Edmund Spenser, "Epithalamion," in *Edmund Spenser's Poetry*, ed. Prescott and Hadfield, 655–67.

43. For a fuller survey, see Jankowski, *Pure Resistance*, 75–110.

44. Juan Luis Vives, *The Education of a Christian Woman: A Sixteenth-Century Manual*, ed. and trans. Charles Fantazzi (Chicago: University of Chicago Press, 2000), 80 (emphasis added).

45. Vives, *Education*, 81.

46. Vives, *Education*, 177 (emphasis added).

47. In a discussion of how wives should behave on those hopefully few occasions when they appear in public, Vives justifies his instructions with a claim that evokes *Othello*'s preoccupation with reputation: "When she was unmarried, she could have the excuse of ignorance if she heard or said anything obscene without blushing. Now, as a married woman with carnal experience of a man, she will not be exempt from the charge of licentiousness and disgrace if that sort of thing should arise" (*Education*, 249). Unlike critics of *Othello*, Vives shows no concern with the truth behind the charge. What matters, as he makes plain in a chapter titled "On Jealousy," is the existence of the charge itself: "I warn women often, not to be deceived into thinking that it does not matter whether you actually do something or seem to do something" (231). In Vives's court of chastity, seeming is being, and the accusation of licentiousness carries the force of a speech act. A wife thus loses her (reputation for) chastity with merely a blush someone reads the "wrong" way; the blush signifies a knowledge whose possession registers as illicit regardless as to how rightfully it was obtained.

48. On the play's gendered construction of race, see Dympna Callaghan, "Re-reading Elizabeth Carey's *The Tragedie of Mariam, Faire Queene of Jewry*," *Women, 'Race,' and Writing in the Early Modern Period*, ed. Margo

Hendricks and Patricia Parker (New York: Routledge, 1994): 163–77; and Kimberly Woosley Poitevin, "'Counterfeit Colour': Making Up Race in Elizabeth Carey's 'The Tragedy of Mariam,'" *Tulsa Studies in Women's Literature* 24, no. 1 (2005): 13–34.

49. Parenthetical citations refer to Elizabeth Carey, *The Tragedy of Mariam*, ed. Karen Britland (London: Methuen, 2010).

50. Alexander Niccholes, *A Discourse, of Marriage and Wiving* (London: n.p., 1615), sig. H.

51. D[aniel] R[ogers], *Matrimoniall Honour: or, The Mutuall Crowne and Comforte of Godly, Loyall, and Chaste Marriage* (London: n.p., 1642), sig. Z2v. Claims about a slippery slope from mental to bodily pollution persist today in evangelical discourse. For instance, writing for Boundless, a ministry of Focus on the Family, Juli Slattery unwittingly echoes Rogers when attempting to debunk the "lie" that "sexual purity is about whether or not you have sex." Slattery claims, "Engaging with sexually stimulating movies, websites, romance novels and television shows is like willingly giving Satan a piece of your mind and your heart. It may seem 'harmless' but will lead you down a path that may ultimately compromise the potential of a pure sexual relationship in the future." See Juli Slattery, "Five Lies That Make Sexual Purity More Difficult," *Boundless*, 14 May 2014.

52. See M. R. Ridley's note to 2.1.109–66 in his edition of *Othello* (London: Methuen, 1958). In "Historical Differences: Misogyny and *Othello*," in *The Matter of Difference: Materialist Feminist Criticism of Shakespeare*, ed. Valerie Wayne (Ithaca, N.Y.: Cornell University Press, 1991), Valerie Wayne offers a more sophisticated version of my imagined evangelical gloss when she foregrounds this scene, and Ridley's distaste for it, to argue for the collusion of Desdemona's speech in the patriarchal project of writing women.

53. A. J. Honigmann, introduction to *Othello*, by William Shakespeare (Walton-on-Thames, U.K.: Thomas Nelson, 1997), 42.

54. Honigmann, introduction, 43 (emphasis added).

55. Honigmann, introduction, 43.

56. Edward Pechter, Othello *and Interpretive Traditions* (Iowa City: University of Iowa Press, 1999), 72.

57. Pechter, Othello, 71.

58. Rymer, *A Short View of Tragedy*, 88.

59. See Joel Altman, "'Preposterous Conclusions': Eros, *Enargeia*, and Composition in *Othello*," in *The Improbability of* Othello: *Rhetorical Anthropology and Shakespearean Selfhood* (Chicago: University of Chicago Press, 2010), 183–205; Parker, *Shakespeare from the Margins*, 51; and Jonathan Gil Harris, *Untimely Matter in the Time of Shakespeare* (Philadelphia: University of Pennsylvania Press, 2011), 182–87.

60. See Shell, "Individual Act and Intent," in *The End of Kinship*, 79–93, for an incisive analysis of how *Measure for Measure* exercises this logic and a more merciful alternative: condemning Angelo to death for intending to sleep with Isabella, and then pardoning him because his attempt failed.

61. Cavell, *Disowning Knowledge*, 138.

62. Cavell, *Disowning Knowledge*, 136.

63. Lena Cowen Orlin, "Desdemona's Disposition," *Shakespearean Tragedy and Gender*, ed. Shirley Nelson Garner and Madelon Sprengnether (Bloomington: Indiana University Press, 1996), 187 (emphasis added).

64. My coedited volume with James Bromley, *Sex before Sex: Figuring the Act in Early Modern England*, more fully develops this line of inquiry into the definition of sex. See also Valerie Traub, *Thinking Sex with the Early Moderns* (Philadelphia: University of Pennsylvania Press, 2015), especially chapter five, "The Joys of Martha Joyless: Queer Pedagogy and the (Early Modern) Production of Sexual Knowledge," 103–24.

65. Greenblatt, *Renaissance Self-Fashioning*, 246.

66. "To lie" is the same verb that the Clown manipulates in his exchange with Desdemona about the location of Cassio's residence (3.4.1–12). In "Charivari and the Comedy of Abjection in *Othello*," *Renaissance Drama* 21 (1990), Michael D. Bristol describes *Othello*'s transition from comedy to tragedy after Act 1 as a "rite of 'unmarrying'" (3). Juxtaposing 3.4 and 4.1, I would add that this transition turns comic wordplay with the facts of sex into a deadly game.

67. Maus, *Inwardness and Theater*, 118.

68. I use the phrase "primal scene" with a nod to Arthur Little's superb discussion of fugitive blackness in "'An essense that's not seen': The Primal Scene of Racism in *Othello*," *Shakespeare Quarterly* 44, no. 3 (1993), 304–24.

69. On *Othello* as pornography, see Lynda E. Boose, "'Let it be hid': The Pornographic Aesthetic of Shakespeare's *Othello*," in Othello*: Contemporary Critical Essays*, ed. Lena Cowen Orlin (New York: Palgrave Macmillan, 2003), 21–48.

70. Diane Fuss, *Dying Modern: A Meditation on Elegy* (Durham, N.C.: Duke University Press, 2013), 22.

71. Neely, *Broken Nuptials*, 125.

72. Joyce Green MacDonald, "Black Ram, White Ewe: Shakespeare, Race, and Women," *A Feminist Companion to Shakespeare*, ed. Dympna Callaghan (Malden, Mass.: Blackwell, 2000), 197.

73. Eamon Grennan, "The Women's Voices in *Othello*: Speech, Song, Silence," *Shakespeare Quarterly* 38, no. 3 (1987): 290.

74. Harry Berger Jr., *Fury in the Words: Love and Embarrassment in Shakespeare's Venice* (New York: Fordham University Press, 2013), 169.

75. Altman, *The Improbability of* Othello, 283.

76. Kaara Peterson, "Shakespeare Revivifications," *Shakespeare Studies* 32 (2004): 258.

77. For a more extensive discussion, see Edward Pechter, "Why Should We Call Her a Whore?: Bianca in *Othello*," in *Shakespeare and the Twentieth Century*, ed. Jonathan Bate, Jill Levenson, and Dieter Mehl (Newark: University of Delaware Press, 1998), 364–77.

78. Marianne Novy, *Shakespeare and Outsiders* (Oxford: Oxford University Press, 2013), 108.

4. THE ECOLOGY OF ADULTERY: FLESH, BLOOD, AND STONE IN *THE WINTER'S TALE*

1. Jennifer Waldron, "Of Stones and Stony Hearts: Desdemona, Hermione, and Post-Reformation Theater," in *The Indistinct Human in Renaissance Literature*, ed. Jean E. Feerick and Vin Nardizzi (New York: Palgrave Macmillan, 2012), 207. This essay reworks for ecocritical purpose many of the claims Waldron makes in *Reformations of the Body*, 78–83.

2. Waldron, "Of Stones and Stony Hearts," 215.

3. Tiffany Jo Werth, "A Heart of Stone: The Ungodly in Early Modern England," in *The Indistinct Human in Renaissance Literature*, ed. Feerick and Nardizzi, 193. On the life of stone, see also Jeffrey Jerome Cohen, *Stone: An Ecology of the Inhuman* (Minneapolis: University of Minnesota Press, 2015).

4. Howard Felperin, "'Tongue-tied our queen?': The Deconstruction of Presence in *The Winter's Tale*," *Shakespeare and the Question of Theory*, ed. Geoffrey H. Hartman and Patricia Parker (New York: Routledge, 1985), 8. See also Michelle Ephraim, "Hermione's Suspicious Body: Adultery and Superfetation in *The Winter's Tale*," *Performing Maternity in Early Modern England*, ed. Kathryn M. Moncrief and Kathryn Read McPherson (Burlington, Vt.: Ashgate, 2007), 45–58.

5. Work on this bear and its significance in this "human" drama includes Andrew Gurr, "The Bear, the Statue, and Hysteria in *The Winter's Tale*," *Shakespeare Quarterly* 34, no. 4 (1983): 420–25; and Michael Bristol, "Spatiotemporal Form and the Heterogeneity of Economies in *The Winter's Tale*," *Shakespeare Quarterly* 42, no. 2 (1991): 145–67.

6. Hannibal Hamlin, *The Bible in Shakespeare* (Oxford: Oxford University Press, 2013), 171. See also Catherine Belsey, "Parenthood: Hermione's Statue," in *Shakespeare and the Loss of Eden*, 85–127.

7. Paul of Tarsus makes draws the same connection between Adam and Christ in Romans 5:12–20. I focus on the connection in 1 Corinthians only because I am otherwise concerned with *The Winter's Tale*'s references to that epistle. Randall Martin, too, argues for the play's feminist engagement with

1 Corinthians in "Revisioning Pauline Ideology in *The Winter's Tale*," *Shakespeare, the Bible, and the Form of the Book: Contested Scriptures*, ed. DeCook and Galey, 55–76. I discuss Martin's argument briefly at the conclusion of this chapter.

8. Theodore Hieber, *The Yahwist's Landscape: Nature and Religion in Early Israel* (Oxford: Oxford University Press, 1996), 34–38. See also Wayne Meeks, "The Image of the Androgyne: Some Uses of a Symbol in Early Christianity," *History of Religions* 13, no. 3 (1974): 185–89; and Dennis Ronald MacDonald, "Corinthian Veils and Gnostic Androgynes," in *Images of the Feminine in Gnosticism*, ed. Karen L. King (Philadelphia: Fortress Press, 1988), 276–92.

9. Citations of "The Garden" refer to Andrew Marvell, *The Complete Poems*, ed. George de Forest Lord (New York: Knopf, 1984). Numerous epithalamia and country house poems also negotiate the Genesis stories. See Heather Dubrow, *A Happier Eden: The Politics of Marriage in the Stuart Epithalamium* (Ithaca, N.Y.: Cornell University Press, 1990), 124–26.

10. Laurie Shannon, *The Accommodated Animal: Cosmopolity in Shakespearean Locales* (Chicago: Chicago University Press, 2013), 40–42.

11. As Stephen Guy-Bray has argued, the speaker plainly articulates a sexual preference for plants: "Animal, Vegetable, Sexual: Metaphor in John Donne's 'Sappho to Philaenis' and Andrew Marvell's 'The Garden,'" in *Sex before Sex*, ed. Bromley and Stockton, 205–9.

12. See Ken Hiltner, *Milton and Ecology* (Cambridge: Cambridge University Press, 2010), 30–54; Diane Kelsey McColley, "Beneficent Hierarchies: Reading Milton Greenly," in *Spokesperson Milton*, ed. Charles W. Durham and Kristin Pruitt (Selinsgrove, Pa.: Susquehanna University Press, 1994), 231–48; and McColley, *Milton's Eve* (Urbana: University of Illinois Press, 1983).

13. All quotations from *Paradise Lost* reference John Milton, *The Riverside Milton*, ed. Roy Flannagan (New York: Houghton Mifflin, 1998).

14. On Milton's efforts to reconcile the creation accounts of Genesis 1 and 2, see Mary Nyquist, "The Genesis of Gendered Subjectivity in the Divorce Tracts and *Paradise Lost*," *Critical Essays on John Milton*, ed. Christopher Kendrick (New York: G. K. Hall, 1995), 165–93.

15. Will Stockton, "An Introduction Justifying Queer Ways," *Early Modern Culture* 10 (2014). See also Gregory Chaplin, "'One Flesh, One Heart, One Soul': Renaissance Friendship and Miltonic Marriage," *Modern Philology* 99 (2001): 266–92; and Luxon, *Single Imperfection*.

16. Adelman, *Suffocating Mothers*, 221. See also Gail Kern Paster, *The Body Embarrassed: Drama and the Disciplines of Shame in Early Modern England* (Ithaca, N.Y.: Cornell University Press, 1993), 260–80.

17. Orgel, *Impersonations*, 15.

18. Walter S. H. Lim, "Knowledge and Belief in *The Winter's Tale*," *SEL: Studies in English Literature, 1500–1900* 41, no. 2 (2001): 325.

19. For a more extensive account of the play's Christian treatment of lambs, including the sheep-sheering festival, see Paul Yachnin, "Sheepishness in *The Winter's Tale*," in *How to Do Things with Shakespeare: New Approaches, New Essays*, ed. Laurie Maguire (New York: Bloomsbury, 2008), 210–30.

20. See Laurie Shannon's discussion of the fantasy as one of prepolitical privacy in *Sovereign Amity*, 185–87.

21. MacDonald, "Corinthian Veils," 235. See also Boyarin, *A Radical Jew*, 19–22.

22. My deletions make it easier to hear that Leontes borrows the verbal pattern of 1 Corinthians 2:9 to make his wife's slippage as obvious as Paul of Tarsus makes wondrous God's reward for believers: "But as it is written, The things which eye hathe not seen, nether eare hathe heard, nether came into mans heart, are, which God hathe prepared for them that love him."

23. Indeed, it does not matter in Leontes's analysis whether Hermione has actually had sex (whatever that would mean) with Polixenes or with anyone other than her husband. By definition, a heifer has never given birth; to pick up on yet another of Leontes's puns, a heifer is likely a virgin. Both father and son have become cattle because both share in the sin of the mother, the sin of the flesh, the sin of being human.

24. Orgel, *Impersonations*, 16. We might interpret Leontes's paranoia as a simultaneous refusal and acceptance of Lavatch's reasoning about friends and spouses in *All's Well That Ends Well*: "He that comforts my wife is the cherisher of my flesh and blood; he that cherishes my flesh and blood loves my flesh and blood; he that loves my flesh and blood is my friend; *ergo*, he that kisses my wife is my friend. If men could be contented to be what they are [i.e., cuckolds], there were no fear in marriage" (1.3.40–45).

25. John Donne will later play off these twinned associations in his poem "The Flea," whose speaker trivializes sex by likening it to a bug bite. How sinful could "two bloods mingled be" (4) be when preformed by a mere flea? See John Donne, "The Flea," *John Donne's Poetry*, 2nd ed., ed. Arthur L Clements (New York: W. W. Norton, 1992), 25.

26. To "mingle" without blood would be to mingle as Milton's Raphael says angels do, in a "Union of Pure with Pure desiring," without "restrain'd conveyance need/As Flesh to mix with Flesh, or Soul with Soul" (8.627–29). For Milton, the purity of angelic mingling depends on the absence of bodies, of flesh and blood. Humans are not so unrestrained. I avoid here any discussion of whether or to what extent Milton's Adam and Eve have sex before the fall, a

subject that Kent R. Lehnhof treats brilliantly in "'Nor turnd I weene': *Paradise Lost* and Prelapsarian Sexuality," *Milton Quarterly* 34, no. 3 (2007): 67–83.

27. In a note in Chapter 1, I suggested that the Neighbor of Jesus's parable might be the priest and the Levite who leave the beaten man to die. *The Winter's Tale* even more perversely reworks this parable when Autolycus pretends to have been beaten and robbed so as to pick the Clown's pocket (4.3.46ff). In *The Winter's Tale*, the Neighbor is the man who feigns his injuries—a description that could easily apply to Leontes.

28. Rebecca Bushnell notes the Edenic aspirations of many early modern gardens in *Green Desire: Imagining Early Modern English Gardens* (Ithaca, N.Y.: Cornell University Press, 2003), 101.

29. Amy L. Tigner, "*The Winter's Tale*: Gardens and the Marvels of Transformation," *English Literary Renaissance* 36, no. 1 (2006): 125.

30. Tigner, "*The Winter's Tale*," 126. See also Ruth Vanita, "Mariological Memory in *The Winter's Tale* and *Henry VIII*," *Studies in English Literature, 1500–1900* 40, no. 2 (2000): 311–37. On the Christian origins of the typological conjunction of Eve and Mary, see Dunning, *Specters of Paul*, especially Chapters 4 ("Virgin Earth, Virgin Birth: Irenaeus of Lyons and the Predicaments of Recapitulation," 97–123) and 5 ("The Contrary Operation: Resignifying the Unpenetrated Body in Tertullian of Carthage," 124–50).

31. Autolycus will later hawk a ballad by a woman who "was turned into a cold fish for she would not exchange flesh with one that loved her" (4.4.268–70). Like Leontes's depiction of his wife as a hot fish, Autolycus's ballad is standard misogynistic fare, an instance of the routine dehumanization of women both abstinent and adulterous.

32. When God (the Priestly Writer's *Elohim*) tells Noah that "An end of all flesh is come before me" (Genesis 6:13), the divine judge means "all except two." He intends a reduction of every kind to its primary hetero-pair unit: "two of everie sorte [of animal] . . . male and female" (6:19). (The Yahwist's God works by a different set of numbers. The clean beasts come aboard in groups of seven, the unclean beasts in groups of two [Genesis 7:4].) Noah and his human family are also saved, but only as set of male-female couples: "thou, and thy sonnes, and thy wife, and thy sonnes wives with thee" (6:18). God gestures toward the restoration of what he previously dubbed "good" through this reduction in number to creaturely unions of two. As we have seen, this numerical logic governs Polixenes's prelapsarian fantasy of himself and Leontes as sexually undifferentiated, twinned lambs. This logic also underwrites Leontes's effort to kill the third person in his marriage—to eliminate the neighbor who has adulterated the marital body. But the effort at restoration fails in both Genesis and *The Winter's Tale*. Postdiluvian man

falls again when Noah's son Ham sees "the nakednes of his father" (9:22)—an enigmatic construction that, no less evocatively for this discussion of *The Winter's Tale*, seems to suggest incest, either between father and son or son and mother. Carol Thomas Neely reads Leontes's attachments to Mamillius and Polixenes as incestuous in "Incest and Issue in *The Winter's Tale*," in *Broken Nuptials in Shakespeare's Plays*, 166–209. On Genesis 9:22, see John Sietze Bergsma and Scott Walker Hahn, "Noah's Nakedness and the Curse on Canaan (Genesis 9:20–27)," *Journal of Biblical Literature* 121.1 (2005): 25–40.

33. Gabriel Egan, *Green Shakespeare: From Ecopolitics to Ecocriticism* (New York: Routledge, 2006), 106. See also Jennifer Munroe, "It's All About the Gillyvors: Engendering Art and Nature in *The Winter's Tale*," *Ecocritical Shakespeare*, ed. Lynne Bruckner and Dan Brayton (Farnham, U.K.: Ashgate, 2011), 139–54; and Tigner, "*The Winter's Tale*," 118–26.

34. As Cohen points out, medieval and early modern people commonly viewed fossils as evidence of the deluge (*Stone*, 83). Fossils served as reminders of God's punishment of the flesh. I will argue, however, that the transformation of stone to flesh in *The Winter's Tale* allows for the miraculous revivification of fantasies of fleshly innocence.

35. Gail Kern Paster, *The Body Embarrassed: Drama and the Disciplines of Shame in Early Modern England* (Ithaca, N.Y.: Cornell University Press, 1993), 279.

36. Tigner, "*The Winter's Tale*," 130.

37. Julia Reinhard Lupton, *Afterlives of the Saints: Hagiography, Topology, and Renaissance Literature* (Stanford, Calif.: Stanford University Press, 1996), 217–18. See also, more recently, Lupton's reading of the scene as entertainment in *Thinking with Shakespeare*, 180.

38. Michael O'Connell, *The Idolatrous Eye: Iconoclasm and Theater in Early-Modern England* (Oxford: Oxford University Press, 2000), 141, 142. On the play's Catholicism, see also Francis Dolan, "Hermione's Ghost: Catholicism, the Feminine, and the Undead," *The Impact of Feminism*, ed. Dympna Callaghan (New York: Palgrave Macmillan, 2007), 213–237; and Phebe Jensen, "Singing Psalms to Horn-Pipes: Festivity, Iconoclasm, and Catholicism in *The Winter's Tale*," *Shakespeare Quarterly* 55, no. 3 (2004): 279–304.

39. Waldron, *Reformations of the Body*, 78–83.

40. Martin, *The Corinthian Body*, 188. My contrast between the positions in 1 Corinthians 8 and 10 derives in large part from Martin as well.

41. Martin, *The Corinthian Body*, 243. See also Knust, *Unprotected Texts*, 159–60. Paul's insistence that women cover their heads arguably serves as a corrective to the view of the apostle as a gender egalitarian. Head covering serves to distinguish the sexes hierarchically: "For a man ought not to cover his head: for asmuche as he is the image and glorie of God; but the woman

is the glorie of the man" (1 Corinthians 11:7). In "Women Holy in Body and Spirit: The Social Setting of 1 Corinthians 7," *New Testament Studies* 36, no. 2 (1990): 161–81, Margaret MacDonald argues that Paul directs his comments against female celibates who, according to the baptismal formula of Galatians 3:28, misunderstood themselves to be equal with men. See also Gundry-Volf, "Male and Female in Creation and New Creation."

42. Paul would seem to proffer this thesis, too, when earlier he distinguishes between legality and profitability: "All things are lawful unto me: but all things are not profitable" (1 Corinthians 6:12).

43. Leontes signals his weak stance on first seeing the statue and attributing to it a "magic" that "has/[his] evils conjured to remembrance, and/From thy admiring daughter took the spirits,/Standing like stone with thee" (5.339–72). It is not clear that Leontes understands this magic to be godly. Perdita shares this weakness: she asks her father's "leave, and do not say 'tis superstition, that/I kneel and then implore her blessing" (5.3.42–44). Perdita may sound a Catholic rebuke to the Protestant critique of idolatry here, but she also sounds like one of the weak Corinthians who believes in the animation of idols. What I am calling Corinthian weakness, other critics have explored under the rubrics of skepticism and wonder. See, for example, James Kuzner, "*The Winter's Tale*: Faith in Law and the Law of Faith," *Exemplaria* 24, no. 3 (2012): 271–76; Anita Gilman Sherman, *Skepticism and Memory in Shakespeare and Donne* (New York: Palgrave Macmillan, 2007), 80–85; David Hillman, "'No Barricado for a Belly': *The Winter's Tale*," in *Shakespeare's Entrails: Belief, Skepticism and the Interior of the Body* (New York: Palgrave Macmillan, 2007), 153–72; Kenneth Gross, *Dream of a Moving Statue* (1992; University Park: Pennsylvania State University Press, 2006), 100–09; Lim, "Knowledge and Belief"; and T. G. Bishop, *Shakespeare and the Theatre of Wonder* (Cambridge: Cambridge University Press, 1996), 161–75.

44. In 2.1, Leontes figures his knowledge as polluted by a venomous spider: "There may be in the cup/A spider steeped, and one may drink, depart,/And yet partake no venom, for his knowledge is not infected; but if one present/The 'abhorred ingredient to his eye, make known/How he hath drunk, he cracks his gorge, his sides,/With violent hefts. I have drunk and seen the spider" (2.1.41–47). In this metaphor, the fall from innocence, or "lesser knowledge" (2.1.40), is consonant with conscious consumption of an inhuman adulterating agent.

45. Oxford English Dictionary, 3rd ed., 2014, s.v. "art," accessed 5 August 2015, http://www.oed.com.libproxy.clemson.edu/view/Entry/11125?rskey=FvPYsp&result=1&isAdvanced=false#eid.

46. This sense is more or less the one Robert Applebaum deduces: "It does not seem to be the case that Leontes thinks of eating as an art, or even

as a form of regulated behavior, but that he thinks of something artless that goes without saying—at once authentic, necessary and un-disallowable"—like the eating of Antigonus by the bear. See "'Lawful as Eating': Art, Life, and Magic in *The Winter's Tale*," *Shakespeare Studies* 42 (2014): 37.

47. As far as I know, Stanley Cavell was the first to note the resemblance between Paulina's resurrection of Hermione and a marriage ceremony. In his analysis, this ceremony banishes the specter of incest—Leontes marrying a new Hermione, so much like the old Hermione—through its own enactment. Like grafting according to Polixenes in his famous speech to Perdita (4.4.88–97), marriage "gives birth to legitimacy, lawfulness" (*Disowning Knowledge*, 217). Lupton also accounts the scene a remarriage (*Thinking with Shakespeare*, 179).

48. One may read Leontes's marriage of Paulina to Camillo as an aggressive rejoinder to Paulina's sixteen-year play at being Hermione's wife. See Theodora Jankowski, " . . . in the Lesbian Void: Woman-Woman Eroticism in Shakespeare's Plays," in *A Feminist Companion to Shakespeare*, ed. Dympna Callaghan (Malden, Mass.: Blackwell, 2000), 302–07. In *Sexual Types: Embodiment, Agency, and Dramatic Character from Shakespeare to Shirley* (Philadelphia: University of Pennsylvania Press, 2011), Mario DiGangi argues for Paulina's legibility as a tribade (84–87). I would add that the scene's concerns with idolatry—the exchange of Creator for creator on which Paul predicates same-sex activity—only enhance this legibility.

49. Raymond F. Collins, *First Corinthians, Sacra Pagina Series*, vol. 7, ed. Daniel J. Harrington (Collegeville, Minn.: The Liturgical Press, 1999), 267. See also Richard A Horsley, *1 Corinthians* (Nashville, Tenn.: Abingdon Press, 1998), 99–100; and Craig S. Keener, *1–2 Corinthians* (Cambridge: Cambridge University Press, 2005), 64–65.

50. Augustine, "On the Merits and Forgiveness of Sins, and on the Baptism of Infants," *The Nicene and Post-Nicene Fathers: First Series*, ed. Philip Schaff, vol. 5 (New York: The Christian Literature Company, 1897), 77–78.

51. Augustine, "On the Merits and Forgiveness of Sins," 77.

52. Augustine, "On the Merits and Forgiveness of Sins," 78.

53. John Calvin, *Commentary on the Epistles of Paul the Apostle to the Corinthians*, ed. and trans. Rev. John Pringle, vol. 1 (Grand Rapids, Mich.: Baker Book House, 1998), 241–42.

54. Kuzner, "*The Winter's Tale*," 263. I quibble with this Badiouian proposition because faith *is* a matter of factual propositions for Paul of Tarsus. "And if Christ be not risen," he tells the Corinthians, "then is our preaching vaine, and your faith is also vaine" (1 Corinthians 15:14). Contra Badiou, Paul of Tarsus is hardly uninterested in the question of whether the resurrection actually happened.

55. Sarah Beckwith, *Shakespeare and the Grammar of Forgiveness* (Ithaca, N.Y.: Cornell University Press, 2011), 144.

56. Richard C. McCoy, *Faith in Shakespeare* (Oxford: Oxford University Press, 2013), 141.

57. I agree with Walter S. Lim that *The Winter's Tale* "facilitate[s] consideration of the distinction, *if any*, between knowledge and opinion, faith and gullibility. The play refuses to grant to faith a privileged position in the apprehension and interpretation of experiential reality" ("Knowledge and Belief," 329–30, emphasis added).

58. Beckwith, *Shakespeare and the Grammar of Forgiveness*, 145.

59. Huston Diehl, "'Does not the stone rebuke me?': The Pauline Rebuke and Paulina's Lawful Magic in *The Winter's Tale*," in *Shakespeare and the Cultures of Performance*, ed. Paul Yachnin and Patricia Badir (Aldershot, U.K.: Ashgate, 2008), 76.

60. Martin, "Revisioning Pauline Ideology in *The Winter's Tale*," 70.

EPILOGUE: WHY (AGAIN) ARE THE UTOPIANS MONOGAMOUS?

1. All parenthetical citations to *Utopia*, *New Atlantis*, and *The Isle of Pines* refer to Thomas More, Francis Bacon, and Henry Neville, *Three Early Modern Utopias*, ed. Susan Bruce (Oxford: Oxford University Press, 1999).

2. Contrast Plato's *Republic*, one of the texts to which More responds. Alongside the abolition of private property, Socrates proposes that the Guardians practice the common ownership of wives and children. See *The Republic of Plato*, 2nd ed, ed. Allan Bloom (New York: Basic Books, 1991), 136.

3. Janel Mueller, "'The Whole Island Like a Single Family': Positioning Women in Utopian Patriarchy," *Rethinking the Henrican Era: Essays on Early Tudor Texts and Contexts*, ed. Peter C. Herman (Urbana: University of Illinois Press, 1994), 99.

4. Mueller, "'The Whole Island Like a Single Family,'" 100.

5. The role Judaism plays in *New Atlantis* is otherwise far more complicated. Travis DeCook has argued persuasively, for example, that the Bensalemite Jews serve the purpose of distinguishing millenarianism from Bacon's apocalyptic Instauration. See "Francis Bacon's 'Jewish Dreams': The Specter of the Millennium in *New Atlantis*," *Studies in Philology* 110, no. 1 (2013): 115–31.

6. I bracket here the biblical-racial politics of *The Isle of Pines*, richly explored by Amy Boesky in "Nation, Miscegenation: Membering Utopia in Henry Neville's *Isle of Pines*," *Texas Studies in Literature and Language* 37, no. 2 (1995): 165–84.

7. I make this claim with a nod to Linda Charnes's theory of textual wormholes: "Future ideas must in some way be 'embedded' in the texts of the

past in order for us to discern their emergence from the position of hindsight." See "Anticipating Nostalgia: Finding Temporal Logic in a Textual Anomaly," *Textual Cultures: Texts, Contexts, Interpretation* 4, no. 1 (2009): 76.

8. Greenblatt, *Renaissance Self-Fashioning*, 44.

9. Greenblatt, *Renaissance Self-Fashioning*, 64.

10. Greenblatt, *Renaissance Self-Fashioning*, 64.

11. Consider in this respect the possible significance of monogamy in Christopher Columbus's 1493 account of the native Americans: "En todas estas islas me parece que todos los [h]ombres sean contentos con una mujer, y a su mayoral o Rey dan hasta veinte" (224). ["In all these islands it seems to me that the men are content with one wife, although they give their chief or king up to twenty wives."] Columbus then concludes his letter by invoking the glory, for Spain and Christendom, of all the potential converts: "el tanto ensalzamiento que habrán en tornándose tantos pueblos a nuesta santa fe" [the high praise that will come from turning so many people to our holy faith]. See Cristóbal Colón, "Carta a Luis Santángel," in *Textos ys Documentos Completos*, 3rd ed., ed. Consuelo Varela (Madrid: Alianza, 2003), 219–26 (translation mine). Greenblatt compares More's fantasy of easy Utopian conversion to Columbus's (*Renaissance Self-Fashioning*, 64). Yet consider, too, the counterexample of Aphra Behn's *Oroonoko* (1688). The African prince is unusually monogamous. "[C]ontrary to the Custom of his Country," Oroonoko promises Imoinda that "she shou'd be the only woman he wou'd possess while he lived" (15). This usual "virtue" accords with his uniquely European (French) education; although black, he is fit to be Behn's aristocratic romance hero. But Oroonoko finds the Christian doctrine of the Trinity quite silly: "it was a Riddle, he said, wou'd turn his Brain to ceonceive, and one cou'd not make him understand what faith was" (15). See Behn, *Oroonoko*, ed. Joanna Lipking (New York: Norton, 1997).

12. *Canons and Decrees of the Council of Trent*, trans. Henry Joseph Schroeder, O.P. (1941; Rockford, Ill.: Tan Books and Publishers, 1978), 180.

13. Pope Innocent III issued this mandate to the Waldensians in 1208, as did the Second Council of Lyons to Palaeologus in 1274. See Francis Schuüssler Fiorenza, *Systematic Theology: Roman Catholic Perspectives*, vol. 2 (Minneapolis, Minn.: Fortress Press, 1991), 320.

14. Peter Brown, *The Body and Society: Men, Women, and Sexual Renunciation in Early Christianity*, 2nd ed. (New York: Columbia University Press, 2008).

15. St. Augustine, "On Marriage and Concupiscence," *The Nicene and Post-Nicene Fathers: First Series*, vol. 5, ed. Philip Schaff (New York: The Christian Literature Company, 1887), 268.

16. Gratian, *Corpus iuris canonici*, vol. 1, ed. Aemilius Friedberg (Union, N.J.: The Lawbook Exchange, 2000), Causa 27, Quest 2, C2, C29, and C45; John Duns Scotus, *Quaestiones in IV libros Senteniarum*, in *Opera omnia*, vol. 19 (Farnbough, U.K.: Gregg, 1969), 168. Gratian's view about marital sex persists in modern evangelical circles. According to Juli Slattery, "Ephesians 5:31–32 alludes to the fact that sex within marriage is a holy metaphor that points to the spiritual mystery of God's covenant love for us. Throughout Scripture, sex is used to express aspects of God's covenant and the degree of intimacy He has with His people. This means that married men and women should be learning mysteries of God as they experience sex together" ("Five Lies").

17. Saint Thomas Aquinas, *Summa contra Gentiles*, trans. Vernon J. Bourke, vol. 4 (Notre Dame, Ind.: University of Notre Dame Press, 1975), 78.

18. Lawrence Foster, "Free Love and Community: John Humphrey Noyes and the Oneida Perfectionists," *American Communal Utopias*, ed. Donald E. Pitzer (Chapel Hill: University of North Carolina Press, 2010), 253–78.

19. On Mormon polygyny and its American legacy, see Sarah Barringer Gordon, *The Mormon Question: Polygamy and Constitutional Conflict in Nineteenth-Century America* (Chapel Hill: University of North Carolina Press, 2002); and Cardell Jacobson and Lara Burton, eds., *Modern Polygamy in the United States: Historical, Cultural, and Legal Issues* (Oxford: Oxford University Press, 2011).

20. Henry's divorce and marriage emboldened the prominent reformer Landgrave Philip of Hesse, who in 1540 scandalously married a second wife without divorcing his first. He did so, somewhat dubiously, on the advice of Martin Luther, Martin Bucer, and Philipp Melanchthon, who had privately conceded to the distraught Hesse that bigamy was preferable to ongoing adultery (Witte, *From Sacrament to Contract* 129–130).

21. For Greenblatt, again, the ease of Utopian conversion to Christianity points to More's "faith in a single, unchangeable religious consensus," the monolithic rightness of (Catholic) Christianity and its consequent ability to absorb other faiths (*Renaissance Self-Fashioning*, 64) At no point in his work does More allow that "there could be a counterconsensus on religion" (64).

22. Martin Luther, *The Babylonian Captivity of the Church*, trans A. T. W. Steinhäuser, ed. Abdel Ross Wentz, in *Luther's Works*, ed. Helmut T. Lehmann (Philadelphia: Fortress Press, 1959), 36:92–96.

23. Clerical celibacy, Luther charged, made no sense if marriage was a sacrament. Why would clergy be denied a sacrament? Indeed, the prohibition

only "increased fornication and sodomy and filled the world with these sins." See Martin Luther, *The Misuse of the Mass*, trans Frederick C. Ahrens, ed. Abdel Ross Wentz, in *Luther's Works*, ed. Lehmann, 36:206.

24. Thomas More, *The Confutation of Tyndale's Answer*, ed. Louis A Schuster, Richard C. Marius, James P. Lusardi, and Richard J. Schoeck, in *The Complete Works of St. Thomas More*, vol. 8, part 1 (New Haven, Conn.: Yale University Press, 1973), 307.

25. Thomas More, *Responsio ad Luthrum*, ed. John M. Headley, trans. Sister Scholastica Mandeville, in *The Complete Works of St. Thomas More*, vol. 5, part 1, 692. More also reasoned that God showed his hatred of Lutheranism by "not allow[ing] the priests who take wives to be joined to any other than public strumpets." Luther's own wife, the former Katharina von Bora, was a strumpet by More's own self-serving definition, as she violated her sacred vows (692).

26. To take one example of many, consider the (somewhat inarticulate) claim of The Family Research Council: "No society has ceased to regulate sexuality within marriage as defined as the union of a man and a woman, and survived." See Timothy J. Dailey, *The Slippery Slope of Same-Sex Marriage* (Washington DC, Family Research Council, 2004).

BIBLIOGRAPHY

Adams, John Quincy. "The Character of Desdemona." *American Monthly Magazine* 7 (1836): 209–17.

———. "Misconceptions of Shakespeare upon the Stage." *New England Magazine* 9 (1835): 435–40.

Adamson, W. D. "Unpinned or Undone? Desdemona's Critics and the Problem of Sexual Innocence." *Shakespeare Survey* 13 (1980): 169–86.

Adelman, Janet. *Blood Relations: Christian and Jew in* The Merchant of Venice. Chicago: University of Chicago Press, 2008.

———. "Making Desire Perfection: Shakespeare and the One-Sex Model." In *Enacting Gender on the English Renaissance Stage*, edited by Viviana Comensoli and Anne Russell, 23–52. Urbana: University of Illinois Press, 1999.

———. *Suffocating Mothers: Fantasies of Maternal Origin in Shakespeare's Plays:* Hamlet *to* The Tempest. New York: Routledge, 1992.

Agamben, Giorgio. *The Time That Remains: A Commentary on the Letter to the Romans*. Translated by Patricia Dailey. Stanford, Calif.: Stanford University Press, 2005.

Agnew, Jean-Christophe. *Worlds Apart: The Market and Theater in Anglo-American Thought, 1550–1750*. Cambridge: Cambridge University Press 1988.

Altman, Joel B. *The Improbability of* Othello: *Rhetorical Anthropology and Shakespearean Selfhood*. Chicago: University of Chicago Press, 2010.

Amussen, Susan Dwyer. *An Ordered Society: Gender and Class in Early Modern England*. New York: Columbia University Press, 1988.

Annotations upon All the Books of the Old and New Testament. London: n.p., 1645.

Annotations upon All the Books of the Old and New Testament. London: n.p., 1651.

Applebaum, Robert. "'Lawful as Eating': Art, Life, and Magic in *The Winter's Tale*." *Shakespeare Studies* 42 (2014): 32–41.

Aquinas, Saint Thomas. *Summa contra Gentiles*. Translated by Vernon J. Bourke. Vol. 4. Notre Dame, Ind.: University of Notre Dame Press, 1975.

Auden, W. H. *The Dyer's Hand and Other Essays*. New York: Random House, 1962.

Augustine. *The City of God against the Pagans*. Edited and translated by R. W. Dyson. Cambridge: Cambridge University Press, 1998.

———. "On Marriage and Concupiscence." In *The Nicene and Post-Nicene Fathers*, edited by Schaff, 5:263–308.

———. "On the Merits and Forgiveness of Sins, and on the Baptism of Infants." In *The Nicene and Post-Nicene Fathers*, edited by Schaff, 5:11–78.

Bach, Rebecca Ann. *Renaissance Literature before Heterosexuality*. New York: Palgrave Macmillan, 2007.

Badiou, Alain. *Saint Paul: The Foundations of Universalism*. Translated by Ray Brassier. Stanford, Calif.: Stanford University Press, 2003.

Barker, Francis. *The Tremulous Private Body*. New York: Methuen, 1984.

Barnes, A. W. *Post-Closet Masculinities in Early Modern England*. Lewisburg, Pa.: Bucknell University Press, 2009.

Bartels, Emily. *Speaking of the Moor: From* Alcazar *to* Othello. Philadelphia: University of Pennsylvania Press, 2009.

Becon, Thomas. Preface to *The Christen State of Matrimony*, by Heinrich Bullinger. London: n.p., 1546. Sig. A2–B4v.

Beckwith, Sarah. *Shakespeare and the Grammar of Forgiveness*. Ithaca, N.Y.: Cornell University Press, 2011.

———. *Signifying God: Social Relation and Symbolic Act in the York Corpus Christi Plays*. Chicago: Chicago University Press, 2001.

Behn, Aphra. *Oroonoko*. Ed. Joanna Lipking. New York: Norton, 2007.

Bellis, Alice Odgen. *Helpmates, Harlots, and Heroes: Women's Stories in the Hebrew Bible*. 2nd ed. Louisville, Ky.: Westminster John Knox Press, 2007.

Belsey, Catherine. *Shakespeare and the Loss of Eden: The Construction of Family Values in Early Modern Culture*. Basingstoke, U.K.: Macmillan, 1999.

———. *The Subject of Tragedy: Identity and Difference in Renaissance Drama*. New York: Methuen, 1985.

Benko, Stephen. *Pagan Rome and the Early Christians*. Bloomington: Indiana University Press, 1984.

Berger, Harry, Jr. *Fury in the Words: Love and Embarrassment in Shakespeare's Venice*. New York: Fordham University Press, 2013.

———. "Marriage and Mercifixion in *The Merchant of Venice*: The Casket Scene Revisited." *Shakespeare Quarterly* 32, no. 2 (1981): 155–62.

Bergsma, John Sietze, and Scott Walker Hahn. "Noah's Nakedness and the Curse on Canaan (Genesis 9:20–27)." *Journal of Biblical Literature* 121, no. 1 (2005): 25–40.

Best, Ernest. *A Critical and Exegetical Commentary on Ephesians*. London: T&T Clark, 1988.

Biberman, Matthew. *Masculinity, Anti-Semitism and Early Modern English Literature: From the Satanic to the Effeminate Jew*. Aldershot, U.K.: Ashgate, 2004.

Bishop, T. G. *Shakespeare and the Theatre of Wonder*. Cambridge: Cambridge University Press, 1996.

Boesky, Amy. "Nation, Miscegenation: Membering Utopia in Henry Neville's *Isle of Pines*." *Texas Studies in Literature and Language* 37, no. 2 (1995): 165–84.

Boose, Lynda E. "'Let it be hid': The Pornographic Aesthetic of Shakespeare's *Othello*." In Othello*: Contemporary Critical Essays*, edited by Lena Cowen Orlin, 21–48. New York: Palgrave Macmillan, 2003.

Booty, John, ed. *The Book of Common Prayer: 1559*. Charlottesville: University of Virginia Press, 1976.

Boswell, John. *Same-Sex Unions in Premodern Europe*. Chicago: University of Chicago Press, 1995.

Bovilsky, Lara. *Barbarous Play: Race on the Renaissance Stage*. Minneapolis: University of Minnesota Press, 2008.

Boyarin, Daniel. "Othello's Penis: Or, Islam in the Closet." In *Shakesqueer*, edited by Menon, 254–62.

———. *A Radical Jew: Paul and the Politics of Identity*. Berkeley: University of California Press, 1994.

Bradley, A. C. *Shakespearean Tragedy: Lectures on* Hamlet, Othello, King Lear, *and* Macbeth. 2nd ed. London: Macmillan, 1905.

Bray, Alan. *The Friend*. Chicago: University of Chicago Press, 2006.

Brinthall, Kent L. *Ecce Homo: The Male-Body-in-Pain as Redemptive Figure*. Chicago: University of Chicago Press, 2011.

Bristol, Michael D. "Spatiotemporal Form and the Heterogeneity of Economies in *The Winter's Tale*." *Shakespeare Quarterly* 42, no. 2 (1991): 145–67.

———. "Charivari and the Comedy of Abjection in *Othello*," *Renaissance Drama* 21 (1990): 3–21.

Britton, Dennis Austin. *Becoming Christian: Race, Reformation, and Early Modern English Romance*. New York: Fordham University Press, 2014.

Bromley, James, and Will Stockton, eds. *Sex before Sex: Figuring the Act in Early Modern England*. Minneapolis: University of Minnesota Press, 2013.

Brooten, Bernadette J. *Love between Women: Early Christian Responses to Female Homoeroticism*. Chicago: University of Chicago Press, 1996.

Brown, Peter. *The Body and Society: Men, Women, and Sexual Renunciation in Early Christianity*. 2nd ed. New York: Columbia University Press, 2008.

Bruster, Douglas. *Drama and the Market in the Age of Shakespeare*. Cambridge: Cambridge University Press, 2005.

Burkhardt, Jacob. *The Civilization of the Renaissance in Italy*. Translated by S. G. C. Middlemore. 1980. New York: Penguin, 1990.

Bushnell, Rebecca. *Green Desire: Imagining Early Modern English Gardens*. Ithaca, N.Y.: Cornell University Press, 2003.

Butler, Judith. "Is Kinship Always Already Heterosexual?" *differences: A Journal of Feminist Cultural Studies* 13, no. 1 (2002). 14–44.

Bynum, Carolyn Walker. *Holy Fear and Holy Fast: The Religious Significance of Food to Medieval Women*. Berkeley: University of California Press, 1988.

———. *Jesus as Mother: Studies in the Spirituality of the High Middle Ages*. Berkeley: University of California Press, 1984.

Callaghan, Dympna. "Re-reading Elizabeth Carey's *The Tragedie of Mariam, Faire Queene of Jewry*." In *Women, 'Race,' and Writing in the Early Modern Period*, edited by Margo Hendricks and Patricia Parker, 163–77. New York: Routledge, 1994.

Callaghan, Dympna, ed. *A Feminist Companion to Shakespeare*. Malden, Mass.: Blackwell, 2000.

Calvin, John. *Commentary on the Epistles of Paul the Apostle to the Corinthians*. Translated by Rev. John Pringle. Vol. 1. Grand Rapids, Mich.: Baker Book House, 1998.

———. *Commentaries on the First Book of Moses Called Genesis*. Trans John King. *Calvin's Commentaries*. Vol. 1. Grand Rapids, Mich.: Baker Book House, 1984.

Canons and Decrees of the Council of Trent. Translated by Henry Joseph Schroeder, o.p. 1941. Rockford, Ill.: Tan Books and Publishers, 1978.

Carey, Elizabeth. *The Tragedy of Mariam*. Edited by Karen Britland. London: Methuen, 2010.

Carlson, Eric Joseph. *Marriage and the English Reformation*. Oxford, U.K.: Blackwell, 1994.

Cavell, Stanley. *Disowning Knowledge in Six Plays of Shakespeare*. Cambridge: Cambridge University Press, 1987.

———. "Epistemology and Tragedy: A Reading of *Othello*." *Daedalus* 108, no. 3 (1979): 27–43.

Chaplin, Gregory. "'One Flesh, One Heart, One Soul': Renaissance Friendship and Miltonic Marriage," *Modern Philology* 99 (2001): 266–92.

Charnes, Linda. "Anticipating Nostalgia: Finding Temporal Logic in a Textual Anomaly." *Textual Cultures: Texts, Contexts, Interpretation* 4, no. 1 (2009): 72–83.

———. "Uncivil Unions." In *Presentism, Gender, and Sexuality in Shakespeare*, edited by Gajowski, 195–206.

Christensen, Ann C. "'Because their business still lies out a' door': Resisting the Separation of the Spheres in Shakespeare's *The Comedy of Errors*." *Literature and History* 5 (1996): 19–37.

Chrysostom, John. "Homily IV: Romans 1: 26, 27." In *The Nicene and Post-Nicene Fathers*, edited by Schaff, 11:355–59.

Cleaver, Robert. *A Godlie Forme of Householde Government*. London: n.p., 1598.

Cobb, Michael. *Single: Arguments for the Uncoupled*. New York: Routledge, 2012.

Cohen, Jeffrey Jerome. *Stone: An Ecology of the Inhuman*. Minneapolis: University of Minnesota Press, 2015.

Collins, Raymond F. *First Corinthians*. *Sacra Pagina* Series. Vol. 7. Edited by Daniel H. Harrington. Collegeville, Minn.: The Liturgical Press, 1999.

Colón, Cristobal. "Carta a Luis Santángel." In *Textos ys Documentos Completos*. 3rd ed., edited by Consuelo Varela, 219–26. Madrid: Alianza, 2003.

Conrad, Ryan, ed. *Against Equality: Queer Critiques of Gay Marriage*. Lewiston, Maine: Against Equality Press, 2010.

Cook, Ann Jennalie. "The Design of Desdemona: Doubts Raised and Resolved." *Shakespeare Studies* 13 (1980): 187–96.

Cooper, Helen. *Shakespeare and the Medieval World*. New York: Bloomsbury, 2014.

Crawford, Julie "The Homoerotics of Shakespeare's Elizabethan Comedies." In *A Companion to Shakespeare's Works, Vol. 3: The Comedies*, edited by Richard Dutton and Jean E. Howard, 137–58. Malden, Mass.: Blackwell, 2003.

———. "Shakespeare. Same Sex. Marriage." In *The Oxford Handbook of Shakespeare and Embodiment: Gender, Sexuality, and Race*, edited by Valerie Traub, 287–301. Oxford: Oxford University Press, 2016.

Cressy, David. *Birth, Marriage and Death: Ritual, Religion, and the Life-Cycle in Tudor and Stuart England*. Oxford: Oxford University Press, 1997.

Daileader, Celia R. "Back-Door Sex: Renaissance Gynosodomy, Aretino, and the Exotic." *ELH* 69, no. 2 (2002): 303–34.

Dailey, Timothy J. *The Slippery Slope of Same-Sex Marriage*. Washington, DC: The Family Research Council, 2004.

Daniel, Drew. *The Melancholy Assemblage: Affect and Epistemology in the English Renaissance*. New York: Fordham University Press, 2013.

Dawson, Anthony B. "The Secular Theater." In *Shakespeare and Religious Change*, edited by Kenneth J. E. Graham and Philip Collington, 238–60. New York: Palgrave Macmillan, 2009.

DeCook, Travis. "Francis Bacon's 'Jewish Dreams': The Spectre of the Millennium in *New Atlantis*." *Studies in Philology* 110, no. 1 (2013): 115–31.

DeCook, Travis, and Alan Galey. Introduction: Scriptural Negotiations and Textual Afterlives. In *Shakespeare, the Bible, and the Form of the Book: Contested Scriptures*, edited by De Cook and Galey, 1–24. New York: Routledge, 2012.

Degenhardt, Jane Hwang. *Islamic Conversion and Christian Resistance on the Early Modern Stage*. Edinburgh: Edinburgh University Press, 2010.

Diehl, Huston. "'Does not the stone rebuke me?': The Pauline Rebuke and Paulina's Lawful Magic in *The Winter's Tale*." In *Shakespeare and the Cultures of Performance*, edited by Paul Yachnin and Patricia Badir, 69–82. Aldershot, U.K.: Ashgate, 2008.

———. *Staging Reform, Reforming the Stage: Protestantism and the Popular Theater in Early Modern England*. Ithaca, N.Y.: Cornell University Press, 1997.

DiGangi, Mario. *The Homoerotics of Early Modern Drama*. Cambridge: Cambridge University Press, 1996.

———. "Queering the Shakespearean Family." *Shakespeare Quarterly* 47, no. 3 (1996): 269–90.

———. *Sexual Types: Embodiment, Agency, and Dramatic Character from Shakespeare to Shirley*. Philadelphia: University of Pennsylvania Press, 2011.

Dobson, Dr. James, and Shirley Dobson. *Night Light: A Devotional For Couples*. Sisters, Oreg.: Multnomah, 2000.

Dolan, Frances E. "Hermione's Ghost: Catholicism, the Feminine, and the Undead," In *The Impact of Feminism*, edited by Dympna Callaghan, 213–37. New York: Palgrave Macmillan, 2007.

———. *Marriage and Violence: The Early Modern Legacy*. Philadelphia: University of Pennsylvania Press, 2008.

Dollimore, Jonathan. *Sexual Dissidence: Augustine to Wilde, Freud to Foucault*. Oxford: Oxford University Press, 1991.

Dubrow, Heather. *A Happier Eden: The Politics of Marriage in the Stuart Epithalamium*. Ithaca, N.Y.: Cornell University Press, 1990.

Dugan, Holly. "Aping Rape: Animal Ravishment and Sexual Knowledge in Early Modern England," in *Sex before Sex*, edited by Bromley and Stockton, 213–32.

Duggan, Lisa. "Beyond Marriage: Democracy, Equality, and Kinship for a New Century." *S&F Online* 10, no. 1–2 (Fall 2011/Spring 2012).

———. *The Twilight of Equality: Neoliberalism, Cultural Politics, and the Attack on Democracy*. Boston: Beacon Press, 2003.

Duffy, Eamon. *The Stripping of the Altars: Traditional Religion in England*. New Haven, Conn.: Yale University Press, 1992.

Dunning, Benjamin. *Christ without Adam: Subjectivity and Sexual Difference in the Philosopher's Paul*. New York: Columbia University Press, 2014.

———. *Specters of Paul: Sexual Difference in Early Christian Thought*. Philadelphia: University of Pennsylvania Press, 2011.

Duns Scotus, John. *Quaestiones in IV libros Senteniarum. Opera omnia*. Vol. 19. Farnbough, U.K.: Gregg, 1969.

Egan, Gabriel. *Green Shakespeare: From Ecopolitics to Ecocriticism*. New York: Routledge, 2006.

Engle, Lars. *Shakespearean Pragmatism: Market of His Time*. Chicago: University of Chicago Press, 1993.

Enterline, Lynne. *The Tears of Narcissus: Melancholia and Masculinity in Early Modern Writing*. Stanford, Calif.: Stanford University Press, 1995.

Ephraim, Michelle. "Hermione's Suspicious Body: Adultery and Superfetation in *The Winter's Tale*." In *Performing Maternity in Early Modern England*, edited by Kathryn M. Moncrief and Kathryn Read McPherson, 45–58. Burlington, Vt.: Ashgate, 2007.

Erasmus, Desiderius. *Paraphrases on the Epistles to the Corinthians, Ephesians, Philippians, Colossians, and Thessalonians*. Collected Works of Erasmus 43. Edited by Robert D. Sider. Toronto: University of Toronto Press, 2009.

The Familie of Love. London: n.p., 1608.

"Families and Living Arrangements." The United States Census Bureau. Online.

Fatum, Lone. "Images of God and the Glory of Man: Women in the Pauline Congregation." In *The Image of God: Gender Models in Judeo-Christian Tradition*, edited by Kari Elisabeth Børresen, 50–133. Minneapolis, Minn.: Fortress Press, 1995.

Feerick, Jean E., and Vin Nardizzi, eds. *The Indistinct Human in Renaissance Literature*. New York: Palgrave Macmillan, 2012.

Felix, Minucius. *Octavius*. Translated by R. E. Wallis. *The Ante-Nicene Fathers: Translations of the Writings of the Fathers down to A.D. 325*. Edited by Alexander Roberts and James Donaldson. Vol. 4. Grand Rapids, Mich.: W. B. Eerdmans, 1965. 173–98.

Felperin, Howard. "'Tongue-tied our queen?': The Deconstruction of Presence in *The Winter's Tale*." In *Shakespeare and the Question of Theory*, edited by Geoffrey H. Hartmann and Patricia Parker, 3–18. New York: Routledge, 1985.

Fernie, Ewan. "Shakespeare and the Prospect of Presentism." *Shakespeare Survey* 58 (2005): 169–84.

Fiorenza, Elisabeth Schüssler. *But She Said: Feminist Practices of Biblical Criticism*. Boston: Beacon Press, 1993.

Fiorenza, Francis Schuüssler. *Systematic Theology: Roman Catholic Perspectives*. Vol. 2 Minneapolis, Minn.: Fortress Press, 1991.

Fisher, Will. "The Renaissance Beard: Masculinity in Early Modern England and Europe." *Renaissance Quarterly* 54, no. 1 (2001): 155–87.

———. "Queer Money." *ELH* 66, no. 1 (1999): 1–23.

Flaherty, Jennifer. "How Desdemona Learned to Die: Resistance in Paula Vogel's *Desdemona*." *Gender Forum: An Internet Journal for Gender Studies* 49 (2014).

Floyd-Wilson, Mary. *English Ethnicity and Race in Early Modern Drama*. Cambridge: Cambridge University Press, 2003.

Foster, Lawrence. "Free Love and Community: John Humphrey Noyes and the Oneida Perfectionists." In *American Communal Utopias*, edited by Donald E. Pitzer, 253–78. Chapel Hill: University of North Carolina Press, 2010.

Foucault, Michel. *The History of Sexuality, Volume I: An Introduction*. Translated by Robert Hurley. New York: Vintage, 1990.

———. "Of Other Spaces." *Diacritics* 16, no. 1 (1986): 22–27.

Ford, John. *'Tis Pity She's a Whore*. Edited by Martin Wiggins. London: Bloomsbury, 2003.

Fowl, Stephen. *Ephesians: Being a Christian at Home and in the Cosmos*. Sheffield, U.K.: Phoenix Sheffield Press, 2014.

Freedman, Barbara. *Staging the Gaze: Postmodernism, Psychoanalysis, and Shakespearean Comedy*. Ithaca, N.Y.: Cornell University Press, 1991.

Freud, Sigmund. *Civilization and Its Discontents*. In *The Complete Psychological Works of Sigmund Freud*, edited by James Strachey, 21:57–146. London: Hogarth Press, 1961.

Frienkel, Lisa. "*The Merchant of Venice*: Modern Anti-Semitism and the Veil of Allegory." In *Shakespeare and Modernity*, edited by Hugh Grady, 122–41. New York: Routledge, 2000.

Froide, Amy M. *Never Married: Singlewomen in Early Modern England*. Oxford: Oxford University Press, 2007.

Fuss, Diane. *Dying Modern: A Meditation on Elegy*. Durham, N.C.: Duke University Press, 2013.

Gajowski, Evelyn, ed. *Presentism, Gender, and Sexuality in Shakespeare*. New York: Palgrave Macmillan, 2009.

Garner, S. N. "Shakespeare's Desdemona." *Shakespeare Studies* 9 (1976): 233–52.

Garrison, John. *Friendship and Queer Theory in the Renaissance: Gender and Sexuality in Early Modern England*. New York: Routledge, 2014.

Geiseidt, Edward J. "Antonio's Claim: Triangulated Desire and Queer Kinship in Shakespeare's *The Merchant of Venice*." *Shakespeare* 5, no. 4 (2009): 338–54.

Gil, Daniel Juan. *Shakespeare's Anti-Politics: Sovereign Power and the Life of the Flesh*. New York: Palgrave Macmillan, 2013.

Goldberg, Jonathan. "*Romeo and Juliet*'s Open Rs." In *Queering the Renaissance*, edited by Jonathan Goldberg, 218–35. Durham, N.C.: Duke University Press, 1994.

Gordon, Sarah Barringer. *The Mormon Question: Polygamy and Constitutional Conflict in Nineteenth-Century America*. Chapel Hill: University of North Carolina Press, 2002.

Gouge, William. *Of Domesticall Duties*. London: n.p., 1622.

Gowing, Laura. *Common Bodies: Women, Touch, and Power in Seventeenth-Century England*. New Haven, Conn.: Yale University Press, 2003.

Gratian. *Corpus iuris canonici*. Vol. 1. Edited by Aemilius Friedberg. Union, N.J.: The Lawbook Exchange, 2000.

Greene, Roland. "Recent Studies in Tudor and Stuart Drama." *Studies in English Literature, 1500–1900* 55, no. 2 (2015): 465–96.

Greenblatt, Stephen. "Fiction and Friction." In *Shakespearean Negotiations: The Circulation of Social Energy in Renaissance England*, 66–93. Berkeley: University of California Press, 1996.

———. *Renaissance Self-Fashioning: From More to Shakespeare*. Chicago: University of Chicago Press, 1980.

Greenstadt, Amy. "The Kindest Cut: Circumcision and Queer Kinship in *The Merchant of Venice*." *ELH* 80, no. 4 (2013): 845–80.

Gregory, Brad S. *The Unintended Reformation: How a Religious Revolution Secularized Society*. Cambridge, Mass.: Belknap Press of Harvard University Press, 2012.

Grennan, Eamon "The Women's Voices in 'Othello': Speech, Song, Silence." *Shakespeare Quarterly* 38, no. 3 (1987): 275–920.

Gross, Kenneth. *Dream of a Moving Statue*. 1992. University Park: Pennsylvania State University Press, 2006.

Gundry-Volf, Judith. "Male and Female in Creation and New Creation: Interpretations of Galatians 3:28c in 1 Corinthians 7." In *To Tell the Mystery: Essays on New Testament Eschatology in Honor of Robert H. Gundry*, edited by Thomas E. Schmidt and Moises Silva, 95–121. Sheffield, U.K.: Sheffield Academic Press, 1994.

Gurr, Andrew. "The Bear, the Statue, and Hysteria in *The Winter's Tale*." *Shakespeare Quarterly* 34, no. 4 (1983): 420–25.

Guy-Bray, Stephen. "Animal, Vegetable, Sexual: Metaphor in John Donne's 'Sappho to Philaenis' and Andrew Marvell's 'The Garden.'" In *Sex before Sex*, edited by Bromley and Stockton, 195–212.

Halpern, Richard. *Shakespeare's Perfume: Sodomy and Sublimity in the Sonnets, Wilde, Freud, and Lacan*. Philadelphia: University of Pennsylvania Press, 2002.

Hamlin, Hannibal. *The Bible in Shakespeare*. Oxford: Oxford University Press, 2013.

Hammill, Graham, and Julia Reinhard Lupton, eds. *Political Theology and Early Modernity*. Chicago: University of Chicago Press, 2012.

Hanson, Elizabeth. *Discovering the Subject in Renaissance England*. Cambridge: Cambridge University Press, 1998.

Harper, Kyle. *From Shame to Sin: The Christian Transformation of Sexual Morality in Late Antiquity*. Cambridge, Mass.: Harvard University Press, 2013.

Harris, Jonathan Gil. *Untimely Matter in the Time of Shakespeare*. Philadelphia: University of Pennsylvania Press, 2011.

Hawkes, David. "Sodomy, Usury, and the Narrative of Shakespeare's Sonnets." *Renaissance Studies* 14, no. 3 (2000): 344–61.

Heacock, Anthony. *Jonathan Loved David: Manly Love in the Bible and the Hermeneutics of Sex*. Sheffield, U.K.: Sheffield Phoenix Press, 2011.

Heath, Melanie. *One Nation under God: The Campaign to Promote Marriage in America*. New York: New York University Press, 2012.

Heilman, Robert B. *Magic in the Web: Action and Language in* Othello. Lexington: University of Kentucky Press, 1953.

Hieber, Theodore. *The Yahwist's Landscape: Nature and Religion in Early Israel*. Oxford: Oxford University Press, 1996.

Hillman, David. "Freud's Shylock." *American Imago* 70, no. 1 (2013): 1–50.

———. *Shakespeare's Entrails: Belief, Skepticism, and the Interior of the Body*. New York: Palgrave Macmillan, 2007.

Hiltner, Ken. *Milton and Ecology*. Cambridge: Cambridge University Press, 2010.

Hirschfield, Heather Anne. "'We all expect a gentle answer, Jew': *The Merchant of Venice* and the Psychotheology of Conversion." *ELH* 73, no. 1 (2006): 61–81.

Holmes, Wayne. "Othello: Is't Possible?" *The Upstart Crow* 1 (1978): 1–23.

Honigmann, A. J. Introduction to *Othello* by William Shakespeare, 1–111. Walton-on-Thames, U.K.: Thomas Nelson, 1997.

Horsley, Richard A. *I Corinthians*. Nashville, Tenn.: Abington Press, 1998.

Howard, Jean E. *The Stage and Social Struggle in Early Modern England*. New York: Routledge, 1993.

Huffer, Lynne. "In Praise of Error." In *Shakesqueer*, edited by Menon, 72–80.

Hughes, Paul H., and James F. Larkin, eds. *Tudor Royal Proclamations, Volume II: The Later Tudors (1553–1587)*. New Haven, Conn.: Yale University Press, 1969.

Hull, Kathleen E. *Same-Sex Marriage: The Cultural Politics of Love and Law*. Cambridge: Cambridge University Press, 2006.

Hunt, Maurice. "Predestination and the Heresy of Merit in *Othello*." *Comparative Drama* 30, no. 3 (1996): 346–76.

Hunter, Robert G. *Shakespeare and the Mystery of God's Judgment*. Athens, Ga.: University of Georgia Press, 1976.

Ingram, Martin. *Church Courts, Sex and Marriage in England, 1571–1640*. Cambridge: Cambridge University Press, 1987.

Instone-Brewer, David. *Divorce and Remarriage in the Bible: The Social and Literary Context*. Grand Rapids, Mich.: William B. Eerdmans Publishing Company, 2002.

Jacobson, Cardell, and Lara Burton, eds. *Modern Polygamy in the United States: Historical, Cultural, and Legal Issues*. Oxford: Oxford University Press, 2011.

Jackson, Ken, and Arthur F. Marotti. "The Turn to Religion in Early Modern English Studies." *Criticism* 46, no. 1 (2004): 167–90.

Jackson, Ken, and Arthur F. Marotti, eds. *Shakespeare and Religion: Early Modern and Postmodern Perspectives*. South Bend, Ind.: University of Notre Dame Press, 2011.

Jankowski, Theodora A. " . . . in the Lesbian Void: Female Same-Sex Eroticism in Shakespeare's Plays." In *A Feminist Companion to Shakespeare*, edited by Callaghan. 299–319.

———. *Pure Resistance: Queer Virginity in Early Modern Drama*. Philadelphia: University of Pennsylvania Press, 2000.

Jardine, Lisa. *Reading Shakespeare Historically*. New York: Routledge, 1996.

Jensen, Phebe. "Singing Psalms to Horn-Pipes: Festivity, Iconoclasm, and Catholicism in *The Winter's Tale*." *Shakespeare Quarterly* 55, no. 3 (2004): 279–304.

[Jewel, John.] *The Seconde Tome of Homilies*. London: n.p., 1563.

Jones, Ann Rosalind, and Peter Stallybrass. *Renaissance Clothing and the Materials of Memory*. Cambridge: Cambridge University Press, 2001.

Jordan, Mark. *The Invention of Sodomy in Christian Theology*. Chicago: Chicago University Press, 1997.

Jordan, Mark D., ed. *Blessing Same-Sex Unions: The Perils of Queer Romance and the Confusions of Christian Marriage*. Chicago: University of Chicago Press, 2005.

Julian of Norwich. *The Shewings of Julian of Norwich*. Edited by Georgia Ronan Crampton. Kalamazoo, Mich.: Medieval Institute Publications, 1994.

Kahl, Brigitte. "Galatians: On Discomfort about Gender and Other Problems of Otherness," translated by Everett R. Kalin, in *Feminist Biblical Interpretation: A Compendium of Critical Commentary on the Books of the Bible and Related Literature*, edited by Luise Schottroff and Marie-Theres Wacker, 755–66. Grand Rapids, Mich.: William B, Eerdmans, 2012.

Kaplan, M. Lindsay. "Jessica's Mother: Medieval Constructions of Jewish Race and Gender in *The Merchant of Venice*." *Shakespeare Quarterly* 58, no. 1 (2007): 1–30.

Kearney, James. *The Incarnate Text: Imagining the Book in Reformation England*. Philadelphia: University of Pennsylvania Press, 2009.

Keener, Craig S. *1–2 Corinthians*. Cambridge: Cambridge University Press, 2005.

Kelly, Kathleen Coyne. *Performing Virginity and Testing Chastity in the Middle Ages*. New York: Routledge, 2000.

Kneidel, Gregory. *Rethinking the Turn to Religion in Early Modern English Literature: The Poetics of All Believers*. New York: Palgrave Macmillan, 2008.

Knust, Jennifer Wright. *Abandoned to Lust: Sexual Slander and Ancient Christianity*. New York: Columbia University Press, 2005.

———. *Unprotected Texts: The Bible's Surprising Contradictions about Sex and Desire*. New York: HarperOne, 2011.

Kolin, Philip C. "Blackness Made Visible: A Survey of *Othello* in Criticism, on Stage, and on Screen." In Othello*: New Critical Essays*, edited by Philip C. Kolin, 1–88. New York: Routledge, 2002.

Korda, Natasha. "Dame Usury: Gender, Credit, and (Ac)counting in the Sonnets and *The Merchant of Venice*." *Shakespeare Quarterly* 60, no. 2 (2009): 129–53.

Kott, Jan. *Shakespeare Our Contemporary*. New York: Norton, 1974.

Krier, Theresa. "Generations of Blazons: Psychoanalysis and the Song of Songs in the *Amoretti*." *Texas Studies in Literature and Language* 40, no. 3 (1998): 292–327.

Kruger, Stephen F. *The Spectral Jew: Conversion and Embodiment in Medieval Europe*. Minneapolis: University of Minnesota Press, 2006.

Kueffler, Matthew. *The Manly Eunuch: Masculinity, Gender Ambiguity, and Christian Ideology in Late Antiquity*. Chicago: University of Chicago Press, 2001.

Kuzner, James. "*The Winter's Tale*: Faith in Law and the Law of Faith." *Exemplaria* 24, no. 3 (2012): 260–81.

Lacan, Jacques. *The Ethics of Psychoanalysis, 1959–1960: The Seminar of Jacques Lacan, Book VII*. Edited by Jacques-Alain Miller. Translated by Dennis Porter. New York: Norton, 1992.

Lampert, Lisa. *Gender and Jewish Difference from Paul to Shakespeare*. Philadelphia: University of Pennsylvania Press, 2004.

Landis, Joan Hutton, "'By two-headed Janus': Double Discourse in *The Merchant of Venice*." *Upstart Crow* 16 (1996): 13–30.

Lanier, Douglas. "'Stigmatical in Making': The Material Culture of *The Comedy of Errors*." *English Literary History* 23 (1993): 81–112.

Laqueur, Thomas. *Making Sex: Body and Gender from the Greeks to Freud*. Cambridge, Mass.: Harvard University Press, 1992.

Lehnhof, Kent R. "'Nor turnd I weene': *Paradise Lost* and Prelapsarian Sexuality." *Milton Quarterly* 34, no. 3 (2007): 67–83.

———. "Relation and Responsibility: A Levinasian Reading of *King Lear*." *Modern Philology* 111, no. 3 (2014): 485–509.

Levin, Richard. *Love and Society in Shakespearean Comedy*. Newark: University of Delaware Press, 1995.

Levine, Laura. *Men in Women's Clothing: Anti-theatricality and Effeminization, 1579–1642*. Cambridge: Cambridge University Press, 1994.

Lewalski, Barbara K. "Biblical Allusion and Allegory in *The Merchant of Venice*." *Shakespeare Quarterly* 13, no. 3 (1962): 327–43.

Lim, Walter S. H. "Knowledge and Belief in *The Winter's Tale*," *SEL: Studies in English Literature, 1500–1900* 41, no. 2 (2001): 317–34.

Little, Arthur L, Jr. "'An essence that's not seen': The Primal Scene of Racism in *Othello*." *Shakespeare Quarterly* 44, no. 3 (1993): 304–24.

———. "'A Local Habitation and a Name': Presence, Witnessing, and Queer Marriage in Shakespeare's Romantic Comedies." In *Presentism, Gender, and Sexuality in Shakespeare*, edited by Gajowski, 207–36.

———. "The Rites of Queer Marriage in *The Merchant of Venice*." In *Shakesqueer*, edited by Menon, 216–24.

Loomba, Ania. *Shakespeare, Race, and Colonialism*. Oxford: Oxford University Press, 2002.

Loughlin, Marie H. *Hymeneutics: Interpreting Virginity on the Early Modern Stage*. Lewisburg, Pa.: Bucknell University Press, 1997.

Lupton, Julia Reinhard. *Afterlives of the Saints: Hagiography, Topology, and Renaissance Literature*. Stanford, Calif.: Stanford University Press, 1996.

———. *Citizen-Saints: Shakespeare and Political Theory*. Chicago: University of Chicago Press, 2005.

———. *Thinking with Shakespeare: Essays on Politics and Life*. Chicago: University of Chicago Press, 2011.

Luther, Martin. *The Babylonian Captivity of the Church*. Translated by A. T. W. Steinhäuser. Edited by Abdel Ross Wentz. In *Luther's Works*, edited by Helmut T. Lehmann, 36:3–126. Philadelphia: Fortress Press, 1959.

———. *Lectures on Romans*. In *Luther's Works*, edited by Hilton C. Oswald, vol. 25. E. St. Louis, Mo.: Concordia Publishing House, 1972.

———. *The Misuse of the Mass*. Translated by Frederick C. Ahrens. Edited by Abdel Ross Wentz. In *Luther's Works*, edited by Helmut T. Lehmann, 36:127–230. Philadelphia: Fortress Press, 1959.

Luxon, Thomas. "A Second Daniel: The Jew and the 'True Jew' in *The Merchant of Venice*." *Early Modern Literary Studies* 4, no. 3 (1999).

———. *Single Imperfection: Milton, Marriage, and Friendship*. Duquesne, Pa.: Duquesne University Press, 2005.

MacDonald, Dennis Ronald. "Corinthian Veils and Gnostic Androgynes." In *Images of the Feminine in Gnosticism*, edited by Karen L. King. Philadelphia: Fortress Press, 1988. 276–92.

MacDonald, Joyce Green. "Black Ram, White Ewe: Shakespeare, Race, and Women." In *A Feminist Companion to Shakespeare*, edited by Callaghan, 188–207.

MacDonald, Margaret. "Women Holy in Body and Spirit: The Social Setting of 1 Corinthians 7." *New Testament Studies* 36, no. 2 (1990): 161–81.

MacFoul, Thomas. *Male Friendship in Shakespeare and His Contemporaries*. Cambridge: Cambridge University Press, 2002.

Maguire, Laurie. "The Girls from Ephesus." In *The Comedy of Errors: Critical Essays*, edited by Robert S. Miola, 355–91. New York: Routledge, 1997.

Mallin, Eric S. *Godless Shakespeare*. London: Continuum, 2007.

Marchal, Joseph A. "Who's Getting (Some) Biblical Marriage." *Feminist Studies in Religion* 11 (May 2012). http://www.fsrinc.org/blog/whos-getting-some-biblical-marriage.

Marsh, Christopher. *The Family of Love in English Society, 1550–1630*. Oxford: Oxford University Press, 1994.

Martin, Dale. *The Corinthian Body*. New Haven, Conn.: Yale University Press, 1995.

———. *Sex and the Single Savior: Gender and Sexuality in Biblical Interpretation*. Louisville, Ky.: Westminster John Knox Press, 1996.

Martin, John Jeffries. *Myths of Renaissance Individualism*. New York: Palgrave Macmillan, 2006.

Martin, Randall. "Revisioning Pauline Ideology in *The Winter's Tale*." In *Shakespeare, the Bible, and the Form of the Book: Contested Scriptures*, edited by DeCook and Galey, 57–76.

Marvell, Andrew. *The Complete Poems*. Edited by George de Forest Lord. New York: Knopf, 1984.

Marx, Stephen. *Shakespeare and the Bible*. Oxford: Oxford University Press, 2000.

Maus, Katharine Eisaman. *Being and Having in Shakespeare*. Oxford: Oxford University Press, 2013.

———. "Horns of Dilemma: Jealousy, Gender and Spectatorship in English Renaissance Drama." *ELH* 54, no. 3 (1987): 561–83.

———. *Inwardness and Theater in the English Renaissance*. Chicago: University of Chicago, 1995.

McColley, Diane Kelsey. "Beneficent Hierarchies: Reading Milton Greenly." In *Spokesperson Milton*, edited by Charles W. Durham and Kristin Pruitt, 231–48. Selinsgrove, Pa.: Susquehanna University Press, 1994.

McCoy, Richard C. *Faith in Shakespeare*. Oxford: Oxford University Press, 2013.

———. *Milton's Eve*. Urbana: University of Illinois Press, 1983.

Meeks, Wayne. "The Image of the Androgyne: Some Uses of a Symbol in Earliest Christianity." *History of Religions* 13, no. 3 (1974): 165–208.

Menon, Madhavi, ed. *Shakesqueer: A Queer Companion to the Complete Works of Shakespeare*. Durham, N.C.: Duke University Press, 2011.

Mentz, Steve. *At the Bottom of Shakespeare's Ocean*. New York: Continuum, 2009.

Middleton, Thomas, and William Rowley. *The Changeling*. Ed. Michael Neill. London: Methuen, 2006.

Miller, Stephen P. *The Age of Evangelicals: America's Born-Again Years*. Oxford: Oxford University Press, 2014.

Milton, John. *The Riverside Milton*. Edited by Roy Flannagan. New York: Houghton Mifflin, 1998.

Moore, Stephen D. *God's Beauty Parlor: And Other Queer Spaces in and around the Bible*. Stanford, Calif.: Stanford University Press, 2001.

More, Thomas. *The Confutation of Tyndale's Answer*. Edited by Louis A Schuster, Richard C. Marius, James P. Lusardi, and Richard J. Schoeck. In *The Complete Works of St. Thomas More*. vol. 8, part 1. New Haven, Conn.: Yale University Press, 1973.

———. *Responsio ad Luthrum*. Edited by John M. Headley. Translated by Sister Scholastica Mandeville. In *The Complete Works of St. Thomas More*, vol. 5, part 1. New Haven, Conn.: Yale University Press, 1969.

More, Thomas, Francis Bacon, and Henry Neville. *Three Early Modern Utopias*. Edited by Susan Bruce. Oxford: Oxford University Press, 1999.

Morse, Ruth, Helen Cooper, and Peter Holland, eds. *Medieval Shakespeare: Past and Presents*. Cambridge: Cambridge University Press, 2013.

Moslener, Sara. *Virgin Nation: Sexual Purity and American Adolescence*. Oxford: Oxford University Press, 2015.

Mueller, Janel. "'The Whole Island Like a Single Family': Positioning Women in Utopian Patriarchy." In *Rethinking the Henrican Era: Essays on Early Tudor Texts and Contexts*, edited by Peter C. Herman, 93–122. Urbana: University of Illinois Press, 1994.

Munroe, Jennifer. "It's All about the Gillyvors: Engendering Art and Nature in *The Winter's Tale*." In *Ecocritical Shakespeare*, edited by Lynne Bruckner and Dan Brayton, 139–54. Farnham, U.K.: Ashgate, 2011.

Murray, Timothy. Review of Stanley Cavell, *Disowning Knowledge in Six Plays of Shakespeare*. *MLN* 105, no. 5 (1990): 1080–85.

Myers, David G., and Letha Dawson Scanzoni. *What God Has Joined Together: The Christian Case for Gay Marriage*. New York: HarperOne, 2006.

Neely, Carol Thomas. *Broken Nuptials in Shakespeare's Plays*. New Haven, Conn.: Yale University Press, 1985.

Neill, Michael. Introduction to *Othello*, by William Shakespeare, 1–179. Oxford: Oxford University Press, 2006.

———. "Unproper Beds: Race, Adultery, and the Hideous in *Othello*." *Shakespeare Quarterly* 40, no. 1 (1989): 383–412.

Newman, Karen. "'And wash the Ethiop white': Femininity and the Monstrous in *Othello*." In *Shakespeare Reproduced: The Text in History and Ideology*, edited by Jean E. Howard and Marion F. O'Connor, 143–62. New York: Methuen, 1987.

———. *Fashioning Femininity and English Renaissance Drama*. Chicago: University of Chicago Press, 1991.

Niccholes, Alexander. *A Discourse, of Marriage and Wiving*. London: n.p., 1615.

Nissinen, Martti. *Homoeroticism in the Biblical World: A Historical Perspective*. Minneapolis, Minn.: Fortress Press, 1998.

Novy, Marianne. *Shakespeare and Outsiders*. Oxford: Oxford University Press, 2013.

Nyquist, Mary. "The Genesis of Gendered Subjectivity in the Divorce Tracts and *Paradise Lost*." In *Critical Essays on John Milton*, edited by Christopher Kendrick, 165–93. New York: G. K. Hall, 1995.

O'Brien, Peter T. *The Letter to the Ephesians*. Grand Rapids, Mich.: William B. Eerdmans Publishing, 1999.

O'Connell, Michael. *The Idolatrous Eye: Theater and Iconoclasm in Early-Modern England*. Oxford: Oxford University Press, 2000.

O'Rourke, James. *Retheorizing Shakespeare through Presentist Readings*. New York: Routledge, 2011.

Obergefell v. Hodges. 135 S. Ct. 2584.

Orgel, Stephen. *Impersonations: The Performance of Gender in Shakespeare's England*. Cambridge: Cambridge University Press, 1996.

Orlin, Lena Cowen. "Desdemona's Disposition." *Shakespearean Tragedy and Gender*. Edited by Shirley Nelson Garner and Madelon Sprengnether. Bloomington: Indiana University Press, 1996. 171–92.

Orvis, David L. "Figuring Marital Queerness in Shakespeare's Sonnets." In *Magic, Marriage, and Midwifery: Eroticism in the Middle Ages and the Renaissance*, edited by Ian Frederick Moulton, 131–50. Amsterdam: Rodopi, 2015.

Oxford English Dictionary (OED Online). 3rd ed. 2014. S.v. "art." Accessed 5 August 2016. http://www.oed.com.libproxy.clemson.edu/view/Entry/11125?rskey=FvPYsp&result=1&isAdvanced=false#eid.

———. S.v. "individual." Accessed 7 September 2015. http://www.oed.com.libproxy.clemson.edu/view/Entry/94633?redirectedFrom=individual#eid.

Park, Katharine. "The Rediscovery of the Clitoris: French Medicine and the Tribade, 1570–1620." In *The Body in Parts: Fantasies of Corporeality in Early Modern Europe*, edited by Carla Mazzio and David Hillman, 171–93. New York: Routledge, 1997.

Parker, Patricia. *Literary Fat Ladies: Rhetoric, Gender, Property*. Ithaca, N.Y.: Cornell University Press, 1987.

———. *Shakespeare from the Margins: Language, Culture, Context*. Chicago: University of Chicago Press, 1996.

Paster, Gail Kern. *The Body Embarrassed: Drama and the Disciplines of Shame in Early Modern England*. Ithaca, N.Y.: Cornell University Press, 1993.

———. *Humoring the Body: Emotions and the Shakespearean Stage*. Chicago: University of Chicago Press, 2004.

Patterson, Steve. "The Bankruptcy of Homoerotic Amity in Shakespeare's *Merchant of Venice*." *Shakespeare Quarterly* 50, no. 1 (1999): 9–32.

Pechter, Edward. Othello *and Interpretive Traditions*. Iowa City: University of Iowa Press, 1999.

———. "Why Should We Call Her a Whore?: Bianca in *Othello*." In *Shakespeare and the Twentieth Century*, edited by Jonathan Bate, Jill Levenson, and Dieter Mehl. Newark: University of Delaware Press, 1998, 364–77.

Pequigney, Joseph. "The Two Antonios and Same-Sex Love in *Twelfth Night* and *The Merchant of Venice*." *English Literary Renaissance* 22, no. 2 (1992): 201–22.

Perry, Curtis. "Commerce, Community and Nostalgia in *The Comedy of Errors*." *Money and the Age of Shakespeare*. Edited by Linda Woodbridge. New York: Palgrave Macmillan, 2003.

Perry, Curtis, and John Watkins, eds. *Shakespeare and the Middle Ages*. Oxford: Oxford University Press, 2009.

Peterson, Kaara. "Shakespeare Revivifications." *Shakespeare Studies* 32 (2004): 40–66.

Pie, Thomas. *Usuries Spright Conjured: Or a Scholasticall Determination of Usury*. London: n.p., 1604.

Plato. *The Republic of Plato*. 2nd ed. Ed. Allan Bloom. New York: Basic Books, 1991.

Plautus. The Rope *and Other Plays*. Translated by E. F. Watling. London: Penguin, 1964.

Poitevin, Kimberly Woosley. "'Counterfeit Colour': Making Up Race in Elizabeth Carey's 'The Tragedy of Mariam.'" *Tulsa Studies in Women's Literature* 24, no. 1 (2005): 13–34.

Pye, Christopher. *The Vanishing: Shakespeare, the Subject, and Early Modern Culture*. Durham, N.C.: Duke University Press, 2000.

Raman, Shankar. "Marking Time: Memory and Market in *The Comedy of Errors*." *Shakespeare Quarterly*. 56.2 (2005): 176–205.

Rambuss, Richard. *Closet Devotions*. Durham, N.C.: Duke University Press, 1998.

———. "The Straightest Story Ever Told." *GLQ: A Journal of Lesbian and Gay Studies* 17, no. 4 (2011): 243–73.

Reinhard, Kenneth. "Paul and the Political Theology of the Neighbor." In *Paul among the Philosophers*, edited by Ward Blanton and Hent de Vries, 449–65. New York: Fordham University Press, 2013.

Ridley, M. R., ed. *Othello*, by William Shakespeare. London: Methuen, 1958.

Ringrose, Kathryn M. *Perfect Servant: Eunuchs and the Social Construction of Gender in Byzantium*. Chicago: University of Chicago Press, 2003.

Rivlin, Elizabeth. *The Aesthetics of Service in Early Modern England*. Evanston, Ill.: Northwestern University Press, 2012.

Robinson, Gene. *God Believes in Love: Straight Talk on Gay Marriage*. New York: Vintage, 2013.

R[ogers], D[aniel]. *Matrimoniall Honour: or, The Mutuall Crowne and Comforte of Godly, Loyall, and Chaste Marriage*. London: n.p., 1642.

Rubin, Gayle. "Thinking Sex: Notes for a Radical Theory of the Politics of Sexuality." In *Deviations: A Gayle Rubin Reader*. Durham, N.C.: Duke University Press, 2011. 137–81.

Rust, Jennifer R. *The Body in Mystery: The Political Theology of the* Corpus Mysticum *in the Literature of Reformation England*. Evanston, Ill.: Northwestern University Press, 2014.

Rymer, Thomas. *A Short View of Tragedy*. London: n.p., 1693.

Sampley, J. P. *'And the Two Shall Become One Flesh': A Study of Traditions in Ephesians 5:21–33*. Cambridge: Cambridge University Press, 1971.

Satlow, Michael L. *Jewish Marriage in Antiquity*. Princeton, N.J.: Princeton University Press, 2001.

Saunders, Ben. "Iago's Clyster: Purgation, Anality, and the Civilizing Process." *Shakespeare Quarterly* 55, no. 2 (2004): 148–76.

Schaff, Philip, ed. *A Select Library of the Nicene and Post-Nicene Fathers of the Christian Church: First Series*. 14 vols. New York: The Christian Literature Company, 1886–1900.

Schwarz, Kathryn. *What You Will: Gender, Contract, and Shakespearean Social Space*. Philadelphia: University of Pennsylvania Press, 2011.

Shannon, Laurie. *The Accommodated Animal: Cosmopolity in Shakespearean Locales*. Chicago: University of Chicago Press, 2013.

———. "Likenings: Rhetorical Husbandries and Portia's 'True Conceit of Friendship.'" *Renaissance Drama* 31 (2002): 3–26.

———. *Sovereign Amity: Figures of Friendship in Shakespearean Contexts*. Chicago: University of Chicago Press, 2002.

Shapiro, Michael. *Gender in Play on the Shakespearean Stage: Boy Heroines and Female Pages*. Ann Arbor, Mich.: University of Michigan Press, 1996.

Shell, Marc. *The End of Kinship: "Measure for Measure," Incest, and the Ideal of Universal Siblinghood*. Stanford, Calif.: Stanford University Press, 1988.

Sherman, Anita Gilman. *Skepticism and Memory in Shakespeare and Donne*. New York: Palgrave, 2007.

Schwarz, Kathryn. "Death and Theory: Or, the Problem of Counterfactual Sex." *Sex before Sex*, edited by Bromley and Stockton, 53–88.

Shuger, Debora Keller *The Renaissance Bible: Scholarship, Sacrifice, and Subjectivity*. Berkeley: University of California Press, 1994.

Sinfield, Alan. *Shakespeare, Authority, Sexuality: Unfinished Business in Cultural Materialism*. New York: Routledge, 2006.

Slattery, Juli. "Five Lies That Make Sexual Purity More Difficult." *Boundless*. 14 May 2014.

Smith, Bruce R. *Homosexual Desire in Shakespeare's England: A Cultural Poetics*. Chicago: University of Chicago Press, 1994.

Smith, Henrie. *A Preparative to Marriage*. London: n.p., 1951.

Snow, Edward. "Sexual Anxiety and the Male Order of Things in *Othello*." *English Literary Renaissance* 10 (1980): 384–412.

Sokol, B. J. and Mary Sokol. *Shakespeare, Law, and Marriage*. Cambridge: Cambridge University Press, 2003.

Spenser, Edmund. *Edmund Spenser's Poetry*. 4th ed. Edited by Anne Lake Prescott and Andrew D. Hadfield. New York: Norton, 2014.

Stockton, Will. "An Introduction Justifying Queer Ways." *Early Modern Culture* 10 (2014).

———. *Playing Dirty: Sexuality and Waste in Early Modern Comedy*. Minneapolis: University of Minnesota, 2011.

———. "The Seduction of Milton's Lady: Rape, Psychoanalysis, and the Erotics of Consumption in *Comus*." In *Sex before Sex*, edited by Bromley and Stockton, 233–62.

Strier, Richard. *Resistant Structures: Particularity, Radicalism, and Renaissance Texts*. Berkeley: University of California Press, 1997.

———. *The Unrepentant Renaissance: From Petrarch to Shakespeare to Milton*. Chicago: University of Chicago Press, 2011.

Streete, Adrian. *Protestantism and Drama in Early Modern England*. Cambridge: Cambridge University Press, 2009.

Swancutt, Diana M. "'The Disease of Effemination': The Charge of Effeminacy and the Verdict of God (Romans 1:18–2:16)." In *New Testament Masculinities*, edited by Stephen D. Moore and Janice Capel Anderson, 193–233. Atlanta, Ga.: Society of Biblical Literature, 2003.

Taubes, Jacob. *The Political Theology of Paul*. Translated by Donna Hollander. Stanford, Calif.: Stanford University Press, 2003.

Talvacchia, Kathleen T., Michael F. Pettinger, and Mark Larrimore, eds. *Queer Christianities: Lived Religion in Transgressive Forms*. New York: New York University Press, 2014.

Tigner, Amy L. "*The Winter's Tale*: Gardens and the Marvels of Transformation," *English Literary Renaissance* 36, no. 1 (2006): 114–34.

Todd, Margo. "Humanists, Puritans, and the Spiritualized Household." *Church History* 49, no. 1 (1980): 18–34.

Tompkins, Joanne. *Theater's Heterotopias: Performance and the Cultural Politics of Space*. New York: Palgrave Macmillan, 2014.

Traub, Valerie. *Desire and Anxiety: Circulations of Sexuality in Shakespearean Drama*. New York: Routledge, 1992.

———. *The Renaissance of Lesbianism in Early Modern England*. Cambridge: Cambridge University Press, 2002.

———. *Thinking Sex with the Early Moderns*. Philadelphia: University of Pennsylvania Press, 2015.

Turner, James Grantham. *One Flesh: Paradisal Relations in the Age of Milton*. Oxford: Oxford University Press, 1993.

Vanita, Ruth. "Mariological Memory in *The Winter's Tale* and *Henry VIII*." *Studies in English Literature, 1500–1900* 40, no. 2 (2000): 311–37.

Viefhues-Bailey, Ludger H. *Between a Man and a Woman?: Why Conservatives Oppose Same-Sex Marriage*. New York: Columbia University Press, 2010.

Vitkus, Daniel. *Turning Turk: The English Theater and the Multicultural Mediterranean*. New York: Palgrave Macmillan, 2002.

Vives, Juan Luis. *The Education of a Christian Woman: A Sixteenth-Century Manual*. Edited by and translated by Charles Fantazzi. Chicago: University of Chicago Press, 2000.

Vogel, Paula. *Desdemona: A Play about a Handkerchief*. New York: Dramatists Play Service, 1994.

Waldron, Jennifer. "Of Stones and Stony Hearts: Desdemona, Hermione, and Post-Reformation Theater." In *The Indistinct Human in Renaissance Literature*, edited by Feerick and Nardizzi, 205–28.

———. *Reforming the Body: Idolatry, Sacrifice, and Early Modern Theater*. New York: Palgrave Macmillan, 2013.

Waller, Marguerite. "Academic Tootsie: The Denial of Difference and the Difference it Makes." *Diacritics* 17, no. 1 (1987): 2–20.

Walsham, Alexandra. *The Reformation of the Landscape: Religion, Identity, and Memory in Early Modern Britain and Ireland*. Cambridge: Cambridge University Press, 2012.

Walters, Jonathan. "'No More Than a Boy': The Shifting Construction of Masculinity from Ancient Greece to the Middle Ages." *Gender & History* 5 (1991): 20–33.

Warner, Michael. *The Trouble with Normal: Sex, Politics, and the Ethics of Queer Life*. Cambridge, Mass.: Harvard University Press, 2000.

Watson, Robert N. "*Othello* as Protestant Propaganda," in *Religion and Culture in Early Modern England*, edited by Claire McEachern and Debora Shuger. Cambridge: Cambridge University Press, 1997. 234–57.

Wayne, Valerie. "Historical Differences: Misogyny and *Othello*." In *The Matter of Difference: Materialist Feminist Criticism of Shakespeare*, edited by Valerie Wayne, 153–80. Ithaca, N.Y.: Cornell University Press, 1991.

Werth, Tiffany Jo. "A Heart of Stone: The Ungodly in Early Modern England." In *The Indistinct Human in Renaissance Literature*, edited by Feerick and Nardizzi, 181–204.

Wilken, Robert Luis. *Christians as the Romans Saw Them*. 1984. New Haven, Conn.: Yale University Press, 2003.

Willet, Andrew. *Hexapla: That Is, a Six-fold Commentarie upon the Most Divine Epistle of the Holy Apostle S. Paul to the Romanes*. Cambridge: n.p., 1611.

Wilson, Thomas. *A Commentary upon the Most Divine Epistle of S. Paul to the Romans*. London: n.p., 1614.

Witmore, Michael. *Culture of Accidents: Unexpected Knowledges in Early Modern England*. Stanford, Calif.: Stanford University Press, 2001.

Witte, John, Jr. *From Sacrament to Contract: Marriage, Religion, and Law in the Western Tradition*. 2nd ed. Louisville, Ky.: Westminster John Knox Press, 2012.

Yachnin, Paul. "Sheepishness in *The Winter's Tale*." In *How to Do Things with Shakespeare: New Approaches, New Essays*, edited by Laurie Maguire, 210–30. New York: Bloomsbury, 2008.

Žižek, Slavoj. *In Defense of Lost Causes*. New York: Verso, 2008.

———. *The Puppet and the Dwarf: The Perverse Core of Christianity*. Cambridge, Mass.: The MIT Press, 2003.

Žižek, Slavoj, Eric L. Santner, and Kenneth Reinhard. *The Neighbor: Three Inquiries in Political Theology*. Chicago: University of Chicago Press, 2006.

INDEX